Penguin Books
The New Penguin Freud
General Editor: Adam Pl

On Murder, Mourning a

Sigmund Freud was born in 1856 in Moravia; between the ages of four and eighty-two his home was in Vienna: in 1938 Hitler's invasion of Austria forced him to seek asylum in London, where he died in the following year. His career began with several years of brilliant work on the anatomy and physiology of the nervous system. He was almost thirty when, after a period of study under Charcot in Paris, his interests first turned to psychology; and after ten years of clinical work in Vienna (at first in collaboration with Breuer, an older colleague) he invented what was to become psychoanalysis. This began simply as a method of treating neurotic patients through talking, but it quickly grew into an accumulation of knowledge about the workings of the mind in general. Freud was thus able to demonstrate the development of the sexual instinct in childhood and, largely on the basis of an examination of dreams, arrived at his fundamental discovery of the unconscious forces that influence our everyday thoughts and actions. Freud's life was uneventful, but his ideas have shaped not only many specialist disciplines, but also the whole intellectual climate of the twentieth century.

Shaun Whiteside was educated at the Royal School, Dungannon and King's College, Cambridge, where he graduated with a First in Modern Languages. He has translated many works of fiction and non-fiction from French, German, Italian and Dutch, and his translation of Lilian Faschinger's novel *Magdalena the Sinner* won the Schlegel-Tieck Prize in 1997. His translations of Nietzsche, Schnitzler and Musil have been published by Penguin.

Maud Ellmann is currently Donald and Marilyn Keough Professor of Irish Studies at the University of Notre Dame, and formerly Reader in Modern Literature at the University of Cambridge, where she was also Fellow in English at King's College. Her books include *The Poetics of Impersonality: T. S. Eliot and Ezra Pound*, *The Hunger Artists: Starving, Writing, and Imprisonment*, and a Longman Reader in *Psychoanalytic Literary Criticism*. Her most recent book, *Elizabeth Bowen: The Shadow Across the Page*, won the British Academy's Rose Mary Crawshay Prize in 2004.

Adam Phillips was formerly Principal Child Psychotherapist at Charing Cross Hospital in London. He is the author of several books on psychoanalysis including *On Kissing, Tickling and Being Bored*, *Darwin's Worms*, *Promises* and *Houdini's Box*.

SIGMUND FREUD

On Murder, Mourning and Melancholia

Translated by Shaun Whiteside
with an Introduction by Maud Ellmann

PENGUIN BOOKS

PENGUIN BOOKS

Published by the Penguin Group
Penguin Books Ltd, 80 Strand, London WC2R ORL, England
Penguin Group (USA) Inc., 375 Hudson Street, New York, New York 10014, USA
Penguin Group (Australia), 250 Camberwell Road, Camberwell, Victoria 3124, Australia
Penguin Group Canada, 90 Eglinton Avenue East, Suite 700, Toronto, Ontario, Canada M4P 2Y3
Penguin Ireland, 25 St Stephen's Green, Dublin 2, Ireland (a division of Penguin Books Ltd)
Penguin Books India (Pvt) Ltd, 11 Community Centre, Panchsheel Park, New Delhi – 110 017, India
Penguin Group (NZ), cnr Airborne and Rosedale Roads, Albany, Auckland 1310, New Zealand
Penguin Books (South Africa) (Pty) Ltd, 24 Sturdee Avenue, Rosebank, Johannesburg, 2196, South
Africa

Penguin Books Ltd, Registered Offices: 80 Strand, London WC2R ORL, England

www.penguin.com

Totem und Tabu, Parts I – II first published in 1913 in *Imago*, 1 (I), 17–33; (3), 213–27; (4), 301–33.
Parts III–IV first published in 1913 in *Imago*, 2 (I), 1–21; (4), 357–408. (First published under the
title 'Über einige Übereinstimmungen im Seelenleben der Wilden und der Neurotiker'.)
Zeitgemässes Über Krieg und Tod first published in 1915 in *Imago*, 4 (I), 1–21
Trauer und Melancholie first published in 1917 in *Int. Z. ärztl. Psychoanal.* 4 (6), 288–301
Warum Krieg? first published in 1933 (Paris: Internationales Institut für Geistige Zusammenarbeit
(Volkerbund))

This translation published in Penguin Classics 2005

6

Sigmund Freud's German texts collected in *Gesammelte Werke* (1940–52) copyright © Imago
Publishing Co., Ltd, London, 1940, 1946, 1950
Translation and editorial matter copyright © Shaun Whiteside, 2005
Introduction copyright © Maud Ellmann, 2005

Set in 10/12.5pt PostScript Adobe New Caledonia
Typeset by Palimpsest Book Production, Polmont, Stirlingshire
Printed in England by Clays Ltd, St Ives plc

ISBN-13: 978–0–14–118379–4

Contents

Introduction by Maud Ellmann vii
Translator's Preface xxix

Totem and Taboo. Some correspondences between the psychical lives of savages and neurotics 1

Timely Reflections on War and Death 167

Transience 195

Mourning and Melancholia 201

Why War? 219

Letter to Romain Rolland (A Disturbance of Memory on the Acropolis) 233

Introduction
Bad Timing

Murder, mourning, melancholia: this alliterative trio encapsulates Freud's story of the human race, from the murder of the primal father to the penitential melancholy of modernity. Missing, however, from this murmurous miscellany of Ms is the word 'mother' – a symptomatic omission, for the mother is conspicuously missing from Freud's reconstruction of prehistory. Another three Ms – the Marx Brothers – try to guess a missing M-word in the movie *Love Happy* (1950). Harpo outlines hourglasses in the air, and Chico guesses 'mother', but Harpo makes vigorous gestures of negation. After several failed attempts to mime the word, Harpo grabs Chico by the cheeks, squeezing his mouth into a figure-eight so that the word 'mother' comes out as 'murder'. Freud, on the other hand, finds 'mother' harder to pronounce than 'murder', judging by the mother's absence from his works. Symbolically, he murders her with silence.

Better to murder than to marry the mother, if the prohibition of incest is the fundamental law of human culture, as Freud affirms in 'Totem and Taboo'. It has often been remarked that Sophocles's Oedipus finds the crime of incest with his mother much more horrifying than the murder of his father. In Freud, a similar aversion to his own incestuous desires may have caused him to suppress the mother and exaggerate the father's importance to psychic development. Amalia Freud, his beautiful young mother, much closer to his age than Jacob Freud, his all too conquerable father, mysteriously disappears from Freud's mythologies of self and world.

In *Beyond the Pleasure Principle* (1920), Freud observes a little boy (his grandson Ernst) miming his mother's comings-and-goings by hurling a spool into his curtained crib, crowing 'o-o-o-o' with sadistic satisfaction, and then retrieving it with a joyful *'da'*. *'Da'* means 'there' in German; Freud interprets the contrasting syllable as *'fort'*, meaning 'gone', and argues that the child plays the *fort/da* game to gain illusory control over his mother's presences and absences. Freud should know, since he himself plays *fort/da* with the figure of the mother in his works, throwing her away to pull her back in new disguises, a process that resembles the return of the repressed in dreams. By missing *out* the mother, Freud assumes control of *missing* her, making his own erasure the cause of her defection.

In Elizabeth Bowen's novel *The House in Paris*, the child Leopold begins to love his long-lost mother when she misses her reunion with him, for this is how he learns that she is something other than the creature of his thought. 'So she lived outside himself; she was alive truly. She set up that opposition that is love.'[1] In Freudian theory, likewise, every child has to miss the mother; the father has a prior claim on the maternal body, that first home to which no exile returns. This loss is the origin of love, with all its martial music of murder, mourning and melancholia.

Freud's essays in the present volume investigate how humankind responds to loss, particularly through disturbances of memory – amnesia, déjà vu, compulsive repetition – disturbances in which the losses of the past irrupt into the present, mining consciousness with gaps and intermittencies. In 'Totem and Taboo' (1913), Freud argues that the totem arises in the place of the primal father, doubly lost through parricide and subsequent amnesia, while the taboo against incest ensures that the mother remains lost to the child. 'Mourning and Melancholia' (1917) examines the refusal of loss, in which the lost love-object is 'incorporated' in the ego in defiance of its death or disappearance. The late essay 'A Disturbance of Memory on the Acropolis' analyses Freud's momentary loss of presence to himself, when unconscious piety for his lost father – who never got so far as the Acropolis – 'de-realizes' the monument before his eyes. Finally, Freud's essays on war ask the question why the human race inflicts loss on itself, specifically the incalculable losses of world war – a question that finally leaves Freud lost for words.

But it is love, rather than loss, which is customarily regarded as the dominant theme, not to say obsession, of psychoanalysis – love in its most luridly erotic form. Freud's wife Martha regarded her husband's newfound science as 'pornography', and many commentators have endorsed her verdict.[2] In the 'Circe' episode of *Ulysses*, Joyce depicts the unconscious as a red-light district, and Freud's analyses suggest a similar conception of the netherworld of dreams. Time and again Freud strips dreams of their ingenious disguises to reveal their lascivious intents. By reminding us of the monotony of our desires, even more than their obscenity, Freud continues to be irksome in an age when sex is on show everywhere; we don't like to be told that we have feet of clay, much less that we have one-track minds.

Nor do we like to be reminded that sexual repression persists in modern life, long after Victorian hang-ups have supposedly dissolved. If sexual intercourse began in 1963, as Philip Larkin has it, sexual repression was never far behind. In spite of the vaunted openness towards sexuality today, the taboo against incest has recently intensified, especially in Britain and the United States, where the embargo now encompasses all intergenerational sex. Current hysteria about child abuse might have altered Freud's view in 'Totem and Taboo' that the fear of incest is stronger among 'savages' than moderns, although it would confirm his view that the desire to transgress increases in proportion to the strictness of the ban. Thus the media today eroticizes adolescent bodies on the one hand, while ranting against paedophiles on the other, demonstrating that such impulses go hand in hand, the prohibition merely whetting the appetite for the prohibited. This is why Freud disapproves of disapproval.

Psychoanalysis contends that sexual impulses, debarred from direct expression, resurface wherever they can find an opening; by the same token, sexual repression reasserts itself wherever it can find a lid. What is remarkable about Freud's work is the insight that impulse and repression are complicit rather than opposed. Law is not the antithesis of violence, Freud argues in 'Why War?' – on the contrary, law *is* violence. At the level of the state, it is the presidents, the armies, the police who are the terrorists: legal violence is deadlier, if sometimes less spectacular, than lawless violence. At the level of the psyche, the superego is the stern face of the id, disguising its sadistic *jouissance* as moral rectitude.

This analogy between the superego and the superstructure of the state persists throughout Freud's thought, and belongs to his conviction that ontogeny recapitulates phylogeny. In other words, the evolution of the species repeats itself in the development of every mind; a proposition previously urged by Darwin, who claimed that 'every human brain passes in the course of its development through the same stages as those occurring in the lower vertebrate animals'.[3] In Freud's account of psychic evolution, each individual struggles with the impulse to possess the mother and destroy all rivals for her love; each renounces those desires under threat of punishment, gambling on secondary satisfactions, much as the bourgeois sacrifices short-term gain for long-term profit. At the world-historical level, Freud conceives of the social order as the psyche inside out, an external version of the inner workings of the mind. The cycle of incest, murder and mourning, which takes place in the unconscious fantasies of every infant, literally took place in the infancy of humankind.

But the word 'murder' must be taken in the widest sense, for every death is treated as suspicious in the unconscious: a superstitious world where no one dies by accident, but only by malevolent design. When our loved ones die, it is because we wanted them to disappear – a wish can kill. According to Freud, this fear of the omnipotence of wishes represents a reversion to a primitive belief in magic.[4] But Freud himself indulges in a form of magical thinking in 'Totem and Taboo', when he argues that the wish to kill the father actually came true in the prehistory of the human species. 'In the beginning was the deed,' he concludes resoundingly. This is what Nietzsche might have called the error of mistaking the last for the first: Freud posits a beginning on the basis of the end, inferring the initial murder from its melancholy aftermath.

Such logical inversions typify Freud's thought, particularly in his speculations about murder. D. H. Lawrence once remarked that it takes two people to make a murder, a murderer and a murderee, but Freud insists that these agents are reversible. In his reflections on war, he interprets global slaughter as the outer image of the war of faculties within the mind. In 'Mourning and Melancholia' he argues that the self-destructive feelings of the melancholic are disguised attacks against a lost love-object, so that suicide is murder by proxy. These works therefore depend upon a logical somersault, arguably a logical mistake, yet also demonstrate the creativity of such inversions. As Joyce says of Shakespeare, 'A man of genius makes no mistakes. His errors are volitional and are the portals of discovery.'[5]

Freud's works are also meditations on untimeliness. To borrow the words of Hamlet – probably the most famous melancholic in the West – 'the time is out of joint' in psychic life. Trauma, for example, arises from the time lag between experience and understanding; the psyche is permanently scarred when the event arrives too soon, the sense too late. 'We had the experience but missed the meaning,' T. S. Eliot writes in *Four Quartets*: in trauma, this missing meaning functions like a scratch on a broken record, forcing the psyche to repeat the shattering experience ad infinitum. This preoccupation with disturbances of memory attracted Freud to evolutionary anthropology, which investigated the persistence of the past in human cultures. Edwin R. Wallace has pointed out that Freud was never far from anthropology, literally in the sense that he surrounded himself with his collection of antiquities, culled from ancient Egypt, Greece, and Rome.[6] In his consulting room, preserved in the Freud Museum in Hampstead, every surface bristles with figurines – even his writing desk, where these incurious dolls must have watched over the birth-pangs of psychoanalysis. In 1938, when the ailing Freud left Vienna for London 'to die in freedom', his collection amounted to two thousand artefacts, and he felt almost as anxious for their safety as his own.[7] Much to his relief, the Nazis permitted the antiquities to leave with Freud, possibly because there were no Jewish artefacts in the collection, but probably because they lacked much retail value. Although Freud claimed to have made sacrifices for his collection, a modest income and six children kept his passion for acquisition within bounds.[8]

Throughout his writings, Freud makes a point of likening psychoanalysis to archaeology, comparing the psyche to a buried city and his own procedures to the excavation of a ruined site, though it is striking that he never mentions his antiquities in this connection. If Freud's unconscious is a red-light district, it bears more resemblance to the erotica of Pompeii than to Joyce's 'Nighttown'. Indeed, one of Freud's rare excursions into literary criticism considers Wilhelm Jensen's archaeological novel *Gradiva* (1903), subtitled 'A Pompeian Fantasy', in which the excavation of Pompeian relics corresponds to the revival of childhood love.[9] But Pompeii is a dead city, wiped out at a single stroke, which therefore lacks the anachronistic character of the unconscious. To convey the sense of past and present crushed together, Freud had to change the metaphor to Rome, a living city where 'the earlier phases of development continue to exist alongside the latest one'.[10] The same applies to the unconscious, where relics of the past sabotage the innovations of the present, like lead pipes in a hasty DIY conversion.

In a letter to Stefan Zweig of 1931, Freud claims to have read more anthropology than psychology, an exaggeration true to his enthusiasm, the intensity of which suggests nostalgia for a missed vocation.[11] He told Sandor Ferenczi in 1922 that fondling his dolls aroused 'strange secret yearnings . . . for a life of quite another kind: wishes from childhood never to be fulfilled and not adapted to reality'.[12] These strange secret yearnings may have contributed to Freud's disturbance of memory on the Acropolis, his sense of being split into observer and observed, the psychoanalyst 'amazed' by the amazement of the archaeologist. In his library in London, which consists only of the books the Nazis permitted him to take, works of anthropology comprise one fifth of the collection. Included are the evolutionary anthropologists, discovered by Freud in his student years, who anticipated his concern with the persistence of 'survivals'. Itself a survival from biology, the term 'survival' had been previously coined by Darwin, a figure idolized by Freud for his fearless iconoclasm in the name of science. Darwin employed the term to describe the resurgence of primeval traits within the present. Species do not progress in a straight line from the primitive to the sophisticated; instead, survivals of earlier forms of life persist in later periods of evolution, such as the vestigial wings of flightless birds, or the human appendix, which causes as much trouble in the body as encysted memories in the neurotic mind.

Freud also would have come across the term 'survivals' in the works of Edward Burnett Tylor, the famous evolutionary anthropologist who used it to refer to archaic practices in human culture. 'An idea, the meaning of which has perished . . . may continue to exist, simply because it has existed,' Tylor wrote.[13] Such ideas, emptied of meaning, whose preservation cannot be explained, obtrude in advanced stages of civilization, testifying to the survival of the unfit – the inappropriate, impractical, impertinent – in the midst of the survival of the fittest. In the same way, Freud argues, shards of the forgotten past resurface in neurotic symptoms like fragments of necrotic bone. Incidentally, another evolutionary thinker, Karl Marx, adopted the doctrine of survivals in his theory that ideologies necessarily outlive their economic usefulness, creating faultlines of anachronism that precipitate the seismic convulsions of society.

In Freud's account of mental development, sex and death are the anachronisms that disrupt the psyche's linear progression to maturity, necessitating the compulsive repetition of the past. For humankind cannot bear very much reality, especially when reality takes them by storm. In Freud, realities that matter always strike too early: sex before the infant understands the language of desire, death before the ego is ready to let go of the beloved. Survivals of these premature events lodge themselves in the unconscious, demanding re-enactment in the form of symptoms and phantasmagoria. Because of these precocious shocks, the psyche is condemned to be forever out of synch with daily life, absorbed in the unfinished business of the past.

In this sense it is Hamlet's inability to act on time, even more than any putative incestuous and parricidal fantasies, that makes him the archetypal psychoanalytic subject. Freud saw Hamlet as a modern Oedipus, whose inhibitions demonstrate the 'secular advance of repression in the emotional life of mankind'; for Hamlet's desires have gone underground, emerging only in the things he cannot do, rather than the things he does.[14] But these inhibitions also put his timing out of joint. While King Hamlet was murdered too soon, cut off in the blossoms of his sin before he was prepared for death, Prince Hamlet is condemned to act too rashly or too late, as if action were inherently unpunctual. Gertrude attributes Hamlet's melancholia not only to his father's premature death, but also to her own 'o'erhasty marriage'. It seems that Hamlet's weapon against haste is tardiness; if the time was underripe for murder and marriage, the time is overripe for his revenge.

In *Hamlet*, the murder of the father occurs in the prehistory of the play, unwitnessed and unverifiable. Yet this event, which never literally takes place or time, is re-enacted time and again: in the dumbshow and the mousetrap, in Hamlet's accidental slaying of Polonius, and in the carnage that completes the tragedy. Similarly, Freud argues that the primal parricide took place long before the origins of history, but this forgotten crime continues to disturb the collective memory of humankind, demanding re-enactment in the form of religious and obsessive ceremonials. A murder, he writes in 'Moses and Monotheism', is easy to commit, but hard to hide: 'the difficulty is not in perpetrating the deed, but in getting rid of its traces'.[15] In 'Totem and Taboo', Freud pursues these traces back to their origins in shame and gore. Once upon a time, he speculates, a band of brothers murdered the father and devoured him, taking possession of his wives. But each brother wanted all the women to himself, so they soon started killing one another, and their new regime degenerated into chaos. Realizing that nobody could win this battle of all against all, the brothers ultimately renounced the women they desired, instituting the law against incest. At the same time, they installed a totem in the father's place, a sacred animal, which signified the prohibition of sexual relations among members of the totem clan. The totem feast, in which the sacred animal is sacrificed and eaten, represents a repetition of the founding parricide.

But Freud would not be Freud if he attributed the social contract merely to political expediency. Instead, he argues that civilization and its discontents externalize the struggle between psychic agencies, resulting in a kind of mystery play in which the forces of temptation and chastisement materialize in flesh and stone. At the root of the vicissitudes of history is ambivalence: 'the tumultuous band of brothers was governed by the same contradictory emotions towards their father which we can show to be the content of the ambivalence of the father-complex in all present-day children and neurotics,' Freud declares. The brothers loved their father, even though they also hated him, but they could not have their father and eat him too. Once they had devoured him, satisfying their hatred and their desire for identification with him, the affection they had overcome was bound to re-emerge, although too late to undo the murder that occurred too early. As in *Hamlet*, bad timing was the source of the catastrophe, which could have been staved off by the punctual return of filial devotion; instead, the brothers murdered in haste and regretted at leisure. A sense of guilt took possession of the human race: 'the dead man now became stronger than the living man had been,' exacting a 'deferred obedience' – much as Hamlet's father comes back from the grave to impose his dread commandment on his son.

Ever since this original sin, the descendants of the murdered father suffer the remorse without understanding the nature of their crime. Moreover, they find themselves compelled to re-enact both crime and punishment in the form of religious rituals, which Freud perceives as the collective version of obsessive handwashing. Such rituals also represent the traces of the immemorial event, imprinted on the psyche and passed down through the generations – a theory Freud adapts from Lamarck's account of evolution, whereby species inherit the acquired characteristics of their ancestors. For Freud, the most intriguing ritual of re-enactment is the totem feast, which survives in the Communion service of the Christian Church. Here the supplicant devours the dead god in order to identify with him, but also to destroy him through the process of incorporation. As Freud observes in *Mass Psychology and the Analysis of the 'I'*, 'the object that we long for and prize is assimilated by eating and is in that way annihilated as such'. Thus the deity is slain again but also propitiated in the rite, restored to life in the bodies of his own devourers.

Freud is aware that the details of his enthralling myth of origins are scarcely plausible: the 'hypothesis may appear fantastic,' he admits. An early reviewer described it as a 'just-so story', a joke that Freud found witty enough not to resent. 'The man is good, he is only deficient in phantasy,' Freud remarked to Ernest Jones. No one could accuse Freud of this deficiency after reading 'Totem and Taboo'.[16] Although subsequent anthropological research cast doubt on Freud's sources, which included Darwin's notion of the primal horde and W. Robertson Smith's theory of totemism, Freud never recanted his grandiose conclusion: 'In the beginning was the deed.' Yet the fact that this plangent phrase derives from Goethe's *Faust* adds an element of irony to the assertion, for Faust, like Hamlet, makes considerable efforts to avoid the deed, preferring spectacle to action.

○

If Freud's theory of the primal parricide collapses at the level of historical fact, it shows remarkable resilience in the realm of fiction. In Bram Stoker's *Dracula* (1897), for instance, Dracula assumes the role of the father who possesses all the women.[17] A brotherhood of youths is formed to overthrow the father, and the battle for his women actually takes place within the female body: Dracula sucks blood out of a dozing virgin, while her suitors pump their own back in again, in a series of transfusions conducted with fearless disregard to blood-type. Freud speculates that the original band of brothers was united not only by parricidal and incestuous impulses, but also by homosexual desire. The same could be said of Stoker's vampire-hunters, who use the female body as a receptacle for a homoerotic exchange of bodily fluids. Instead of enjoying the father's women, the brothers tacitly consent to celibacy, and heterosexual intercourse takes place only in a gory ritual designed to ward it off, in which each of the young men takes turns to drive a stake through the vampirella's heart. This episode confirms Freud's principle that ritual is ostensibly a protection against the prohibited act, but *actually* a repetition of it. The same principle applies to modern obsessives: 'it is a law that . . . compulsive actions are placed increasingly at the service of the drive, and come ever closer to the originally forbidden acts.' Thus the young men in *Dracula* ostensibly refrain from sexual relations with the father's bride, yet actually perform a gang-rape in the form of an impalement. The happy ending is one in which a boy-child is born, bearing the names of all the brotherhood, and establishing the hero as the patriarch. The threat of unrestrained copulation, embodied in the vampirella, is literally staked down, the stake representing the restored paternal phallus.

The heist movie also exemplifies the logic of 'Totem and Taboo'. Take Jules Dassin's *Rififi chez les hommes* (1955), translated (badly) as *Brawl among the Men*, in which a band of brothers tunnels into the maternal body of the jewellery store Mappin and Webb – a pun for English-speaking viewers on the intricacies of the crime, for Freudians on the ensnaring powers of the mother's body. Penetration is portrayed in loving detail: first the crooks slip into the proprietor's flat above the shop, using a key struck from a mould inserted in his keyhole; then in an extended silent pantomime, they dig a hole through the floor above the jewels. A hymeneal handkerchief, placed over the hole, flutters in a draught, indicating that the diggers have got through. At this point an umbrella, carefully inserted through the aperture, unfurls to create a bowl or diaphragm to catch the chisel-dust. In a comically suggestive shot, four male heads gaze down into the enticing hole before the burglars shimmy through the chute. Just in case the analogy between the treasure and the female body might be missed, one of the crooks proclaims that there is no safe that can resist César the Milanesi, the famous safebreaker, and no woman that César can resist. In fact it is César's weakness for women that precipitates the downfall of the gang, when he gives a stolen ring to the sexy songstress of the theme tune 'Rififi' (slang for sex or 'rough-and-tumble'), thus breaking faith with 'rififi chez les hommes'.

In this movie, the primal father is not killed, but a series of paternal substitutes is overthrown: the absent jeweller is outwitted, the concierge's husband is knocked out, along with a policeman who pops up inopportunely. As for the primal mother, she makes her first appearance armed with a vacuum cleaner, a comic contrast to the male umbrella, but in this movie both organs serve the same purpose – gathering dust. The mother predicts that all the crooks will kill each other for the jewels, just as the brothers in 'Totem and Taboo' kill each other for the women. In *Rififi*, the mother's prophecy comes true, for the gang self-destructs through greed, much as Freud's band of brothers self-destructs through lust. And just as *Dracula* concludes with the birth of a boy-child, so *Rififi* concludes with the survival of the son. The movie ends with a terrifying car-drive, literally a death-drive in which the driver dies at the moment of restoring the heir-apparent to his mother. Thus the band of brothers is vacuumed away, leaving a lone male from the untainted younger generation to accede to the position of the patriarch.

A heist depends for its success on perfect timing: 'we've timed it at least twenty times,' one burglar boasts. In the heist *movie*, on the other hand, the time is always slightly out of joint; the best-laid plots are scrambled by the unexpected. The narcissistic fantasy that reality can be controlled by plots is shattered by the crude intrusion of the actual: the policeman, the accidental passer-by. In 'Totem and Taboo', bad timing also undermines the brothers' plot, preventing them from reaping the rewards of their revenge, because their love resurfaces too late, after the rash and bloody deed is irreversible. Thus the contradiction between love and hate manifests itself as temporal disjunction, producing a stutter between opposite emotions that coincide in space but not in time. This is reminiscent of an anecdote, related to me by Robert Dolan, a forensic psychiatrist, who interviewed a woman who had killed her father. After initial denials she admitted to the murder, but when Dolan asked her why she had committed it, she replied, 'He was beginning to annoy me.' The primal parricide was also a pre-emptive strike, unmindful of the consequences of ambivalence.

For today's readers, what is hardest to take in 'Totem and Taboo' is Freud's blithe confidence in the superiority of Western culture. Like James G. Frazer, whose encyclopaedic study of mythology, *The Golden Bough* (1890–1915), is plundered in 'Totem and Taboo', Freud would have shuddered at the thought of field work; both writers assume that the 'primitive' mind can be investigated at a safe distance in space and time. Both also believe that the current state of the ignoble savage corresponds to an archaic stage of Western evolution; a belief reflected in Joseph Conrad's *Heart of Darkness* (1899), where the barbarity of Kurtz, the ideologue of imperialism, is diagnosed as a regression to the 'primitive'. Yet Conrad's ambiguous title also hints that the heart of darkness resides within the Western soul, implying that the myth of the Dark Continent is a projection of the savagery of modernity. A similar paradox emerges in 'Totem and Taboo': on the one hand, Freud pours scorn on 'savages', casting ridiculous aspersions on their practices, such as the unsubstantiated claim that 'savages eat apart and alone'; yet on the other hand, he undercuts his own chauvinism by insisting on the psychic unity of humankind. In his theory of neurosis, the primitive is implicated in the over-civilized. Like the nerve-specialists of his day, Freud attributed neurosis to the stress of modern urban civilization, but whereas others held that the city, with its haste and bustle, its excessive stimulation of the mind, its democratic politics and emancipated women, was responsible for modern nervousness, Freud imputed the disorder to excessive sexual restriction. Under this pressure, he contended, atavistic practices and superstitions re-emerge, privatized as neurotic symptoms and obsessive rituals.

Melancholia is another malady in which the civilized and atavistic coincide. As Peter Gay has pointed out, the nineteenth century was 'an age of Hamlets', in which the so-called 'English malady' of melancholia spread across the European continent. Not only did young men suffer the sorrows of young Werther, but confessed them with a frankness bordering on exhibitionism.[18] One of the puzzles of this 'disorder of self-esteem', in Freud's view, is the shamelessness with which the melancholic castigates his failings, often with uncanny perspicacity. If anything, the melancholic shows a keener awareness of his character than 'normal' people are capable of exercising on themselves. As Freud observes:

we can only wonder why one must become ill in order to have access to such truth. For there can be no doubt that anyone who has reached such an assessment of himself, and expresses it to others – an assessment like that which Prince Hamlet has ready for himself and everyone else – is sick, whether he is telling the truth or treating himself more or less unjustly. (p. 206)

To loathe yourself is crazy, especially if you do it loudly, no matter how loathsome you really are.

Oscar Wilde remarked that 'Schopenhauer has analysed the pessimism that characterizes modern thought, but Hamlet invented it. The world has become sad because a puppet was once melancholy.'[19] Freud also looks to Hamlet as the archetype of melancholia, treating his patients as sad imitations of Shakespeare's self-lacerating puppet. Just as Hamlet lashes himself with 'words, words, words', so the modern melancholic talks, talks, talks about the futility of talking, with all the vigour mortis of a chatterbox in Beckett. As Freud observes:

the melancholic does not behave just as someone contrite with remorse and self-reproach would normally do. The shame before others that characterizes the latter state is missing, or at least not conspicuously present. In the melancholic one might almost stress the opposite trait of an insistent talkativeness, taking satisfaction from self-exposure – (p. 207)

like a guest on the Oprah Winfrey show. But this exhibitionism betrays the fact that the melancholic isn't really sorry. Not only are his self-inflicted torments 'indubitably pleasurable', but they are meant for someone else, because instead of showing shame or contrition for his worthlessness, the melancholic acts as if he had been wronged. The analyst who listens closely to these plaints '[*Klagen*]' can overhear complaints '[*Anklagen*]' against another person, whom the melancholic loves too much to murder. If 'all men kill the thing they love' (in the words of Wilde's 'Ballad of Reading Gaol'), in melancholia the killing of the thing is carried out upon the self, sometimes to the point of suicide. Thus 'the woman who loudly pities her husband for being bound to such a useless woman is actually seeking to accuse her husband of uselessness'. In every case, Freud argues, attacks against the ego turn out to be attacks against the other, which has usurped the position of the self. In Freud's spine-chilling Gothic formulation, 'the shadow of the object [falls] over the ego'.

This is where atavism comes into the picture. According to Freud, the melancholic regresses from object-love to identification, a primitive relation to the object corresponding to the oral or 'cannibalistic' phase of psychic development. In fantasy, the love-object is eaten in order to imprison it within the self, thus overcoming its propensity to die, defect or disappear. 'It is by taking flight into the ego that love escapes abolition.' Yet the object, once incorporated, preys upon the subject in return until the latter is 'totally impoverished'. Thus the ego, like a healthy savage, gobbles up the object in one gulp, but the object behaves like the stealthy vampires of the *fin de siècle*, substituting nightly sucking for the cannibal's almighty bolt. According to Freud's principle that ontogeny recapitulates phylogeny, these cannibalistic fantasies hark back to a primitive stage of human evolution, when people really ate each other, as 'savages' still do – though it is hard to see how they could eat alone when they have people for dinner.

A fictional version of this melancholy cannibalism may be found in Toni Morrison's *Beloved* (1987). In the prehistory of the novel, Sethe murdered her beloved daughter to save her from a life of slavery, but this nameless child comes back from the grave to batten on her mother's house. As Freud says of the murdered father, the dead girl becomes stronger than the living girl had been, exacting a 'deferred obedience'. A wraith on her arrival, Beloved soon grows fat, feasting on the energies of those who mourn her.

Anything she wanted she got . . . The best chair, the biggest piece, the prettiest plate, the brightest ribbon for her hair, and the more she took, the more Sethe began to talk, explain, describe how much she had suffered, been through, for her children, waving away flies in grape arbours, crawling on her knees to a lean-to.[20]

As Beloved flourishes, her family starves: it is clear that she is eating them alive. She takes over her mother's personality – just as the lost object takes over the ego in 'Mourning and Melancholia' – dressing in her clothes, laughing her laugh, walking her walk. This phase of identification, however, is followed by arguments in which mother and daughter start to separate. Their battles dramatize the internal struggle of melancholia, in which the ego attacks itself as a stand-in for the beloved object. The fact that Sethe begins to talk is also reminiscent of the wordiness of melancholia, a process in which each libidinal investment in the object is gradually talked away. In Freud's words, 'each individual battle of ambivalence loosens the fixation of the libido upon the object by devaluing, disparaging and, so to speak, killing it'. In this 'piecemeal' labour of detachment, 'now this, now that memory is activated, [so] that the identical-sounding laments, tiresome in their monotony, have a different unconscious explanation each time'.

In Morrison's novel, however, Sethe's talking only seems to make Beloved fatter, and eventually the whole community has to unite to exorcize the ghostly cannibal. Once freed from their enslavement to the lost object, they forget the revenant 'like an unpleasant dream', just as they forget the history of slavery that she brought home to them. Like the primal parricide in Freud, 'this is not a story to pass on'; a collective amnesia descends upon the past. 'Disremembered and unaccounted for, she cannot be lost because no one is looking for her, and even if they were, how can they call her if they don't know her name?'[21] In order to be lost the object must be looked for; it is the seeking that establishes its absence. In Graham Greene's *The End of the Affair*, by contrast, the widower feels oppressed by the omnipresence of his wife, because he doesn't know how to begin to look for her. He explains: 'Because she's always away, she's never away. You see, she's never anywhere else. She's not having lunch with anybody, she's not at a cinema with you. There's nowhere for her to be but at home.'[22] To miss the love-object is to hold it in the mind, but also to make it go away. For this reason, the only way that the bereaved can get rid of the beloved is by looking for her, calling her by name.

Art is the means by which we lose the object in order to call it back in a new form: thus in Poe's 'The Oval Portrait', the painting is complete only when the sitter dies, her vital force absorbed into the artefact. As Schiller laments in his poem 'The Greek Gods': 'that which shall live immortal in song/Must perish in life'. The art of architecture is thought to have originated in the funerary monument, which serves the double purpose of preserving the lost object and killing it a second time, with culture rather than with nature. The ghost is a similar 'compromise-formation': Freud proposes that our ancestors invented ghosts when they accepted the reality of death, yet also disavowed its permanence by asserting that the dead return. Today's world may seem ghost-free, but melancholia rejects this vivacentric outlook, for the melancholic is possessed by the lost object, in the same way that the 'savage' is supposedly possessed by demons. Freud belongs to an Enlightenment tradition of ghost-busters, committed to driving the demons from our streets. Toni Morrison, on the contrary, intimates that disbelief in ghosts is tantamount to murder of the past.

❖

In his 'Timely Reflections on War and Death', published in 1915, Freud moves closer to Morrison's position. Should we not admit, he wonders, that we have been 'living psychologically beyond our means with our civilized attitude to death'? Is it time to let the ghosts back in again? Would we kill less if we feared the retribution of the dead? Freud considers the claim that primeval man was forced to start thinking when confronted with the intellectual mystery of death, which became the origin of all speculation. However, Freud rejects this theory as 'too philosophical': it was not death as such, he urges, but the ambivalence of the survivor, loving and hating the dead object, which drove our primeval ancestors to think. And the first things they thought about were ghosts: 'It was by the corpse of the beloved that [primitive people] invented spirits'. Yet because they felt guilty for the satisfaction that was mixed up with their sorrow for the dead, the first spirits they created were 'fearful, evil demons'.

Thus death is the source of invention, as well as the origin of ghosts, yet it is only through the invention of the ghost that the reality of death can be acknowledged. By getting rid of ghosts, 'civilized man' has lost his grasp of the reality they represent. For this reason Freud speculates: 'If the furious struggle of this war is ever resolved, each of the victorious combatants will return cheerfully home to his wife and children, unchecked and undisturbed by thoughts of the enemies whom he has killed either in close combat or with long-distance weapons.' Death has lost its sting because the ghosts have been dispelled, so that the modern soldier has forgotten how to think. Here Freud is wrong – veterans still find themselves condemned to think, and in the case of recent wars like Vietnam, to think for everyone who doesn't want to know.

'Why War?' (1933) – Freud's famous exchange with Einstein on the eve of the Second World War – begins by saying there is nothing more to say. Not only has Einstein already said it all, taking the wind out of his sails, but Freud's reply is laboured and apologetic, as if he were struggling against a will to silence.[23] If death makes people think, death on the scale of the Second World War seems to drive Freud to despair of thought. Both his diagnoses and his remedies are lame and offered with a sense of resignation: he attributes war to instinctual aggression, blaming the death-drive for death, a near tautology which (as he admits) smacks of the 'mythological'. In some ways, Freud's reluctance to speak in this essay is more eloquent than what he manages to say: he seems to be moving towards Wittgenstein's verdict that 'what we cannot speak about we must pass over in silence'.[24] Freud once admitted that the mysteries of art defeated the explanatory powers of psychoanalysis: 'Before the problem of the creative artist analysis must, alas, lay down its arms.'[25] In 'Why War?' Freud's reticence suggests that before the problem of arms analysis must, alas, lay down its words. In the modern age, murder, mourning and melancholia have grown and multiplied so monstrously that theory proves inadequate at best, or barbarous at worst.

Adorno famously remarked that to write poetry after Auschwitz was barbaric, although he later recanted this prescription for despair. Freud, on the other hand, suggests that art can teach us to respect reality, just as ghosts teach us to respect the dead. There are many ghosts in Freud's own writing that he tries to overcome without success, especially the absent mother – although she creeps in the back door in 'Totem and Taboo', when Freud goes to inordinate lengths to dispel the suggestion that a 'savage' could possibly fancy his mother-in-law. Curiously, Freud's biography reveals that he fell in love with his first girlfriend, Gisela Fluss, in an unconscious effort to deepen his intimacy with her mother, who was clearly a stand-in for his own.[26]

Luce Irigaray has argued that 'the whole of our culture in the west depends upon the murder of the mother' – not the father.[27] In Greek mythology, for instance, Orestes murders his (murderous) mother, leading to the triumph of Apollo and the banishment of the earth-goddesses. The mother also disappears in Christianity, although she comes back with a vengeance in the cult of Mariolatry; none the less, the Christian Trinity is thought to be the only Holy Family in mythology without a mother-goddess. In this bizarre all-male family of Father, Son and Holy Ghost, the mother goddess is not exactly murdered but demoted to a mortal woman who merely incubates the father's fecundating breath, so that God, with a little help from the Holy Ghost, can take full credit for the act of procreation. According to Irigaray, Freud also murders the mother by suppressing her in favour of the father, leaving woman in a state of 'dereliction', homeless in mythology. If this is true, then one could argue that Freud's theory of the primal parricide functions as a smokescreen, distracting his and our attention from the murderous obliteration of the mother.

T. S. Eliot famously accuses *Hamlet* of artistic failure because the mother is too insignificant to justify the histrionics of her son. The implication is that Shakespeare should have killed off Hamlet's mother. Ernest Jones, however, sees *Hamlet* as a matricidal rather than a patriarchal tragedy, closer to the *Oresteia* than to *Oedipus*. Gertrude herself takes this view when Hamlet bursts into her closet, speaking daggers, and the father's ghost is forced to show up in his nightshirt to protect her from the prince's misdirected vengeance. 'When a man who has been betrayed is emotionally moved to murder, whom should he kill, the rival lover or the lady? It is a nice question,' Jones comments slyly.[28] It is a question Freud resolved by 'keeping mum', in every sense, protecting the mother's image from his own iconoclasm by embalming it in silence. What looks like murder by omission also represents an act of piety.

In any case, the mother is not dead enough in Freud to prevent her resuscitation by his followers, notably by Melanie Klein, who recasts psychoanalysis with the mother in the central role. Nor is Freud dead enough to appease our culture, which often loudly disavows its debts to psychoanalysis. Freud did himself no favours with social scientists by inventing the fable of the primal murder, and sticking to it in defiance of hard facts. Yet even at his most preposterous, Freud continues to be wiser than we like to recognize; untimely survivals of his insights haunt our movies, literature and dreams, refusing to be buried in forgetfulness or scorn.

Freud is not yet through with us.

Maud Ellmann, 2005

Notes

1. Elizabeth Bowen, *The House in Paris* (1935; Harmondsworth: Penguin, 1976), pp. 193–4.
2. See Peter Gay, *Freud: A Life for Our Time* (London: J. M. Dent, 1988), p. 61.
3. Charles Darwin, *The Expression of the Emotions in Man and Animal* (London: John Murray, 1872), p. 245.
4. The term 'omnipotence of wishes' was first proposed by Freud's patient, the 'Rat Man' (Ernst Lanzer); see Sigmund Freud, *Notes upon a Case of Obsessional Neurosis* (1909), in *The Complete Psychological Works of Sigmund Freud, Standard Edition*, trans. James Strachey (London: Hogarth Press, 1953–74), vol. X, p. 226. Henceforth cited as *SE*.
5. James Joyce, *Ulysses* (1922), Hans Walter Gabler (ed.) (London: Bodley Head, 1986), Ch. 9, p. 156.
6. Edwin R. Wallace, *Freud and Anthropology: A History and Reappraisal* (New York: International Universities Press, 1983), pp. 2–3.
7. Freud, letter to his son Ernst Freud, 12 May 1938; quoted in Gay, *Freud: A Life for Our Time*, p. 626. The phrase is in English in the original.
8. See Freud, letter to Stefan Zweig, 7 February 1931, in Ernst L. Freud

(ed.), *Letters of Sigmund Freud* (New York: Basic Books, 1960), pp. 402–3.

9. Freud, *Delusions and Dreams in Jensen's 'Gradiva'* (1907), SE, vol. IX, pp. 1–94.

10. Freud, *Civilization and Its Discontents* (1930), SE, vol. XXI, p. 70.

11. Ernst L. Freud, *Letters of Sigmund Freud*, pp. 402–3.

12. Quoted in Gay, *Freud: A Life for Our Time*, p. 172.

13. Quoted from E. B. Tylor, *Primitive Culture: Researches into the Development of Mythology, Philosophy, Religion, Language, Art, and Culture* (1924) in Margaret T. Hodgen, 'The Doctrine of Survivals: The History of an Idea', *American Anthropologist*, 33 (1931), p. 307.

14. Freud, *The Interpretation of Dreams* (1900), SE, vol. IV, p. 264.

15. Freud, *Moses and Monotheism* (1939), in SE, vol. XXIII, p. 43.

16. See Gay, *Freud: A Life for Our Time*, p. 327.

17. See James B. Twitchell, *Dreadful Pleasures: An Anatomy of Modern Horror* (New York: Oxford University Press, 1985), pp. 127–39.

18. Gay, *Freud: A Life for Our Time*, p. 129.

19. Oscar Wilde, 'The Decay of Lying', in *The Artist as Critic: Critical Writings of Oscar Wilde*, Richard Ellmann (ed.) (Chicago: University of Chicago Press, 1982), p. 308.

20. Toni Morrison, *Beloved* (New York: New American Library, 1987), pp. 240–41.

21. Ibid., pp. 274–5.

22. Graham Greene, *The End of the Affair* (Harmondsworth: Penguin, 1975), p. 169.

23. By all accounts, 'Freud found the discussion tedious and sterile,' as Jacqueline Rose has pointed out, and the 'dissatisfied, impatient, self-deprecating tone' of his writing bears this out. See Jacqueline Rose, *Why War?–Psychoanalysis, Politics, and the Return to Melanie Klein* (Oxford: Blackwell, 1993), p. 15.

24. Ludwig Wittgenstein, *Tractatus Logico-Philosophicus*, trans. D. F. Pears and B. F. McGuinness (London: Routledge and Kegan Paul, 1961), p. 74.

25. Freud, 'Dostoevsky and Parricide' (1928), SE, vol. XXI, p. 177.

26. See Gay, *Freud: A Life for Our Time*, pp. 22–3.

27. See Margaret Whitford, *Luce Irigaray: Philosophy in The Feminine* (London and New York: Routledge, 1991), p. 75.

28. Ernest Jones, *Hamlet and Oedipus* (1949; New York: Norton, 1976), p. 92.

Translator's Preface

In 1927, the first Linguistic Commission for the Unification of French Psychoanalytic Vocabulary met in Geneva. By the time it reconvened a year later, its members had reached agreement on precisely four pieces of terminology. As well as revealing the enormous scope for dissent about these matters (and the problems involved in translating by committee), this anecdote does emphasize the monumentality of James Strachey's erudite accomplishment in the production of the *Standard Edition* of Freud's work, which was prepared between 1955 and 1967, and lent added authority by the endorsement of Freud's daughter Anna. Translators working today have the advantage of lateness: we have access both to Strachey's impressive legacy and to a century of rumination on vocabulary and meaning in German and English and many other languages besides. Until the present day, it has been through Strachey that most people outside the German-speaking world have approached Freud's work. As Malcolm Pines puts it in his essay 'The Question of Revising the Standard Edition':[1] 'To study Freud is to study Strachey, the medium through whom his message is transmitted.'

To draw a comparison: work on the French *Oeuvres complètes* did not get under way until 1988, seventy-five years after the first translation of one of Freud's papers into French. In an elegantly revealing essay, 'Translating Freud',[2] the project's editors, Jean Laplanche, Pierre Cotet and André Bourguignon, insist that their intention is not one of 'responding to the psychoanalytic vulgate the *Standard Edition* has become – with all the weight and popularization this implies – with a French imitation', and argue compellingly for 'the greatest freedom possible for a multiplicity of readings and critical interpretations'.

It seems to me that the New Penguin Freud has been commissioned in this entirely laudable spirit: our brief as translators was to approach Freud's writings as 'literary' texts, in other words, to bring as few preconceptions as possible to the task at hand. In many cases this might produce in the writing what the French editors refer to as 'alienness'. This is one of the most difficult tasks a translator faces: if the text reads strangely, the translator is most likely to get the blame, when in fact the 'strangeness' may be fully present in the source material. In their essay, Laplanche and his colleagues note Strachey's tendency to 'flatten' the meaning of the German, by which I take them to be saying that he 'smooths it out'. This is entirely understandable, but it means that he does not always capture the sometimes improvisatory, fractured, even *approximate* nature of Freud's style in German. And bearing in mind the shocking freshness of the material that Freud was bringing to the reading public, it seems only natural that his style should reflect the fact.

New translators of Freud, then, stand in Strachey's shadow, but must guard against the Oedipal stirrings that immediately make themselves apparent in such a situation, and treat with circumspection those attacks on the *Standard Edition* that seem too confident, too noisy. Chief among these is Bruno Bettelheim's polemic *Freud and Man's Soul*,[3] which blames the accepted English translations of Freud for a global misunderstanding of his work, and a skewing of psychoanalysis towards the medical profession and away from lay analysis. He sees in the *Standard Edition* a desire to dehumanize, to strip away the essential spirituality that, in his view, originally fired the psychoanalytic project. Yet, beguilingly vigorous though it may be, his own approach is entirely subjective and fails to take into account the fact that words in different languages are inevitably freighted with secondary echoes and undercurrents. He is also quite confident that he knows 'what Freud really meant', although without ever quite explaining how he came by this knowledge.

The chief focus of Bettelheim's diatribe is the German word *Seele*, which Strachey usually renders as 'mind', or, in its adjectival form, 'mental', as in the phrase *'seelische Gesundheit'* or 'mental health'. Bettelheim's contention is that the idea of the 'soul' is thus forfeited. I would argue, with Strachey, that the notion of 'soul' is fully present within 'psyche', and *'seelisch'* is, in German, a direct equivalent of 'mental'. Again we encounter the problem of echoes, and 'mind' is not a direct translation of *'Seele'*. It is true that *'Geist'* and *'geistig'* are closer to Anglophone conceptions of the mind, but emphatically not in the sense that Freud intends. *'Der Geist'* is the intellect, the conscious, reasoning mind, a small part of the vast zone that Freud was attempting to map, with its unconscious drives and agencies. I have accordingly stayed with 'psyche', but opted for 'mental' when the adjective referred to a medical condition. I am pleased to note that in most cases Strachey appears to have done the same.

Bettelheim is even more vociferous in his condemnation of the rigid terms 'ego', 'id' and 'super-ego'. For 'ego' and 'id' Freud himself used capitalized versions of the ordinary German pronouns, *'das Ich'* and *'das Es'* and, for 'super-ego', *'das Über-Ich'*. Were one to go down the Oedipal route and seek to demolish Strachey's terminology, there could be no more obvious way to go about it than to replace these terms. Bettelheim cheerfully suggests 'the I', 'the it' and 'the above-I' or 'upper-I', as preserving the immediacy of words in everyday language: 'To mistranslate *Ich* as "ego" is to transform it into jargon that no longer conveys the personal commitment we make when we say "I" or "me" – not to mention our subconscious memories of the deep emotional experience we had when, in infancy, we discovered ourselves as we learned to say "I".' Leaving aside the use of the word 'mistranslate', a term which the author is particularly fond of, there can be no doubt that Bettelheim is on to something here. Yet he writes as though the very term *'das Ich'* were one of Freud's own invention. In fact it has a very respectable history in idealist philosophy, where it can generally be taken to mean 'the self'. And throughout Freud's work it frequently retains that meaning and can be used to mean both 'the self' and 'the ego' within a single paragraph.

In early drafts of this book, in fact, I experimented with 'the I' and 'the It', as a way of deliberately distancing the translation from the *Standard Edition*, but discovered that all sorts of unexpected problems arose. What, for example, is the plural of 'the It'? 'Its'? Or of 'the I', or 'the above-I'? Finally, and not without some regret, I had to concede that Strachey and his team had reached an ingenious solution to an almost intractable problem – and one recognized as such by Freud himself. The more 'colloquial' versions proved utterly unmanageable, at least to me, and I was able to console myself with the reflection that the terms familiar from the *Standard Edition* had already taken firm root in the English language.

Not all such terms have done so, however, and some continue to provoke a degree of dissent. One such is *Trieb*, which Strachey renders as 'instinct'. In his General Preface to the *Standard Edition* he justifies his choice as follows: 'The term almost invariably proposed by critics as an alternative is "drive". There are several objections to this. First, I should like to remark that "drive", used in this way, is not an English word and, as I have explained in my preface, this translation aims at being a translation into English. [. . .] It requires, I think, a very brave man seriously to argue that rendering Freud's "*Trieb*" by "drive" clears up the situation.' Questions of personal bravery aside, as I have suggested in my preface to another volume in the Penguin Freud series,[4] the word 'drive' in this sense has developed a life of its own, independent of Strachey, and can now safely be considered as an English word. 'Drive', in Freud's conception, does not seem to me to be perfectly coterminous with 'instinct', and I have generally opted for the former, even though it can make for some rather cumbersome prose; as Strachey points out, one pragmatic reason for choosing 'instinct' as a translator is 'the impossibility of finding an adjectival form for "drive"'. He is right, there is no such form, but I cannot in the end agree with his dismissal of my own phrase 'drive-impulse' some forty years before I came up with it.

One further observation: in the many translations of passages from J. G. Frazer that pepper 'Totem and Taboo', Freud himself invariably translates Frazer's 'instinct' as *Trieb*. This immediately seems to support Strachey's position, but I would plead, once again, for a degree of terminological latitude, and suggest that when *Trieb* is used to mean a goal-seeking force, a vector (in Laplanche and Pontalis's version a 'dynamic process consisting in a *pressure* (charge of energy, motricity factor) which directs the organism towards an aim')[5] – as in the *Three Essays on Sexual Theory*,[6] it is best translated as 'drive' – death-drive, sexual drive – but when it is used in a non-technical, colloquial sense, the word 'instinct' should be preserved. Freud does indeed use the word '*Instinkt*', but solely to refer to inherited behaviour in animals. I would argue that when referring to unbridled or uncivilized behaviour in human beings, this is precisely what Freud has in mind, and so would preserve the distinction of the two meanings in English translation.

As to the notorious term 'cathexis' (German '*Besetzung*'), Darius Gray Ornston[7] argues intriguingly that the term barely means anything at all, and that it is 'Strachey's earnest and inadvertent concoction' based on a misreading of semantically related German terms based on a single word-stem. Attractive as this notion is, the idea of *Besetzung* – the attachment of a quantity of psychical energy to an idea, a person, a body part etc. – does appear to have a specific significance within Freud's economic system, and cannot be wished away as lightly as that. But the German word is not itself an obscure one, and I have followed Freud's continental translators in opting for 'investment' and, very occasionally and where the context required it, 'charge'.

All translations are by their nature partial and provisional, and the *Standard Edition* is no exception. Freud's early translators, Ernest Jones and A. A. Brill,[8] as well as Strachey himself, laid claim to special status because they themselves had learned at the feet of the master. But the principle of apostolic succession, questionable as it is in any intellectual tradition, cannot apply in perpetuity. I am hopeful that translations of Freud's work will continue to evolve over time, through dialogue both between translators in English, and with those working in other tongues, and that our contemporary understanding of Freud and his work will be greatly enriched in the process.

❖

Many thanks to Sebastian Gardner, Susan Wiseman, Tim Armstrong and John Stevens for talking me through some of the thornier concepts raised in these essays; to Simon Winder, Adam Phillips and my endlessly patient copy-editor Jane Robertson for their valuable advice on the translation; and finally, as always, to Georgina Morley and Charlie Whiteside, to whom it is dedicated.

A word about the text: footnotes are Freud's own, and any emendations that I have made are shown in square brackets.

Notes

1. In *Freud in Exile*, Edward Timms and Naomi Segal (eds) (New Haven and London, 1988).
2. In *Translating Freud*, Darius Gray Ornston Jr. (ed.) (New Haven and London, 1992).
3. (Harmondsworth, 1982).
4. *The Psychology of Love*.
5. Jean Laplanche and Jean-Bertrand Pontalis, *The Language of Psychoanalysis*, trans. Donald Nicholson-Smith, (London, 1973).
6. These essays are included in *The Psychology of Love*.
7. *Translating Freud*, p. 14.
8. I discovered, while preparing the present text, that where Freud translated quotations from English into German, Brill was in the habit of simply translating them back, if the English text was not readily to hand.

Totem and Taboo

Some correspondences between the psychical lives of savages and neurotics

Preface

The four essays below, first published under the sub-title of this book in the first two volumes of my journal *Imago*, constitute my first attempt to apply the viewpoints and results of psychoanalysis to unresolved problems in social psychology. Consequently they contain on the one hand a methodological contrast with the extensive work of W. Wundt, which places the hypotheses and working methods of non-analytic psychology at the service of the same goal, and on the other with the works of the Zurich psychoanalytic school which, on the contrary, set out to explain problems of individual psychology by introducing material from social psychology.[1] I freely admit that both of these sources formed the initial stimulus for my own works.

I am well aware of their shortcomings. Some of them, because certain areas are being examined for the first time, I need not touch upon. But others require a word of introduction. The four essays brought together here seek to win the interest of a large circle of educated people, but can only really be understood and judged by those few who are not strangers to the peculiar characteristics of psychoanalysis. This work aims to mediate on the one hand between ethnologists, linguists, folklorists and so on, and psychoanalysts on the other, and yet it cannot give to both sides what each one lacks: to the former a satisfactory introduction into psychological technique, and to the latter adequate mastery of the material calling for elaboration. So it will have to content itself with gaining the attention of both sides, and encouraging the expectation that occasional encounters between the two can only yield benefits to research.

The two main subjects which give this little book its title – totem and taboo – are not examined in the same way. In the analysis of taboo, what I consider to be a well-grounded attempt is made to resolve the problem as a whole. The examination of totemism is restricted to an explanation of how psychoanalytic investigation may help to resolve the problems of the totem. This difference has to do with the fact that taboo still persists among us. Although expressed in a negative sense, and directed towards different objects, in its psychological nature it is merely Kant's 'categorical imperative', operating in a compulsive manner and refusing any conscious motivation. Totemism, on the other hand, is a social and religious institution which is strange to our contemporary way of thinking, abandoned a long time ago to be replaced by newer forms. It has left only very slight traces in the religion, customs and practices of the life of contemporary civilized people, and has even undergone great transformations among those peoples still devoted to it. The social and technical advance of human history has been much less damaging to taboo than it has been to totem. In this book I have attempted to guess the original meaning of totemism from the traces that are seen of it in childhood, the hints with which it reappears in the development of our own children. The close connection between totem and taboo points in new directions for the hypothesis set out here, and if that hypothesis in the end appears to be highly unlikely, that still does not exclude the possibility that it might bring us more or less close to a reality that is difficult to reconstruct.

Rome, September 1913

Notes

1. Jung, 'Wandlungen und Symbole der Libido' ['Transformations and symbols of the libido'], *Jahrbuch für psychoanalytische und psychopathologische Forschungen*, vol. IV, 1912; the same author, 'Versuch einer Darstellung der psychoanalytischen Theorie' ['Attempt at an account of psychoanalytic theory'], vol. V, 1913.

I

The Dread of Incest

We know the stages passed through by prehistoric man from the inanimate monuments and utensils that he left behind, from the messages left in his art, his religion and his view of life, which we have preserved either directly or in traditions, in sagas, myths and fairy tales, and in the traces left by his ways of thinking in our own customs and practices. But that aside he is still, in a certain sense, our contemporary; there are people alive whom we think of as being still very close to primitive man, much closer than we are ourselves, and for this reason we see them as the direct descendants and representatives of earlier human beings. This is our view of the so-called primitive and semi-primitive peoples in whose psychical life we take a particular interest, recognizing them as a well-preserved preliminary stage of our own evolution.

If this premise is correct, a comparison between the 'psychology of primitive peoples', such as that supplied by anthropology, and the psychology of the neurotic, as it has become known through psychoanalysis, is bound to show numerous correspondences and enable us to see in a new light things familiar to us in both fields.

For reasons both external and internal I am choosing for the purposes of this comparison those tribes of peoples whom the ethnographers have described as the most poor and backward of savages, the primeval inhabitants of the youngest continent, Australia, which has preserved for us, in its people but also in its fauna, so much that is archaic and that has disappeared everywhere else.

The aborigines of Australia are considered as a distinct people, displaying no physical or linguistic relationship with their nearest neighbours, the Melanesian, Polynesian and Malay peoples. They build no houses or permanent huts, they do not till the soil, they keep no domestic animals apart from dogs, they do not even know the art of pottery. They live solely on the flesh of whatever animals they hunt, and on roots that they dig up. Kings or chiefs are unknown to them, and the assembly of adult males makes decisions on communal matters. It is most doubtful whether one would be right in attributing to them traces of religion in the form of the worship of higher beings. The tribes in the interior of the continent, who are forced to struggle with the most severe living conditions because of the lack of water, seem in all respects to be more primitive than those who live near the coast.

We will certainly not expect these poor, naked cannibals to be moral in their sexual lives in our sense of the term, or to have imposed a high degree of restriction upon their sexual drives. And yet we learn that they have taken upon themselves, with the most elaborate care and the most painstaking rigour, the aim of preventing incestuous sexual relationships. Indeed, their entire social organization appears to serve this purpose, or to be connected in some way with its accomplishment.

Among the Australians, the place of all absent religious and social institutions is occupied by the system of totemism. The Australian tribes break down into smaller clans, each of them named after its totem. So what is a totem? Generally an animal, whether edible and harmless or dangerous and feared, more rarely a plant or a force of nature (rain, water), which stands in a particular relation to the whole clan. The totem is first and foremost the ancestral father of the clan, but also its protecting spirit and helper. He sends them oracles and, while he may be dangerous in other respects, he knows his children and spares them. The members of the totem, or clansmen, on the other hand, stand under a holy, self-imposed and punishable obligation not to kill (destroy) their totem, and to abstain from its flesh (or any enjoyment that it might otherwise offer). The characteristic of the totem does not adhere to an individual creature or an individual being, but to all individuals of the species. From time to time festivals are celebrated, at which clansmen depict or copy the movements and characteristics of their totem in ceremonial dances.

The totem is inherited down either the maternal or the paternal line; the former was probably the original form in all cases, and was only subsequently replaced by the latter. Membership of the totem is the basis of all the social obligations for the Australians, both extending beyond membership of the tribe and pushing blood relationships into the background.[1]

The totem is not bound to soil or locality; the clansmen live separately from one another, and peacefully with the members of other totems.[2]

And now we must finally turn our attention to the singular feature of the totemistic system that attracts the interest of the psychoanalyst. In almost all places where the totem applies, there also exists a law to the effect that *members of the same totem may not engage in sexual relationships with one another, which is to say that they may not marry one another*. This is totemic *exogamy*.

This prohibition, which is rigorously imposed, is very curious. Nothing that we have previously learned about the concept or the properties of the totem prepares us for it; so we cannot understand how it entered the system of totemism. Hence we should not be surprised if some researchers effectively assume that exogamy originally – at the beginning of time and in terms of its meaning – had nothing to do with totemism, but was added at some point without any deeper underlying connection when marriage restrictions proved necessary. Be that as it may, the association of totemism and exogamy exists and has proven to be very solid.

Let us try and gain a clearer understanding of the significance of this prohibition with the help of some further considerations.

a) Violation of this prohibition is not followed by what we might call an automatically imposed punishment of the guilty parties, as occurs with other totemic prohibitions (such as killing the totem animal), but is most energetically punished by the whole clan, as though it were a matter of averting a danger that threatened the entire community, or a guilt that oppressed it. Some sentences from Frazer's book[3] may show how seriously such transgressions are dealt with by these people who are otherwise, by our standards, quite immoral savages.

'In Australia the regular penalty for sexual intercourse with a person of a forbidden clan is death. It matters not whether the woman be of the same local group or has been captured in war from another tribe; a man of the wrong clan who uses her as his wife is hunted down and killed by his clansmen, and so is the woman; though in some cases, if they succeed in eluding capture for a certain time, the offence may be condoned. In the Ta-Ta-thi tribe, New South Wales, in the rare cases that occur, the man is killed but the woman is only beaten or speared, or both, till she is nearly dead; the reason given for not actually killing her being that she was probably coerced. Even in casual amours the clan prohibitions are strictly observed, any violations of these prohibitions "are regarded with the utmost abhorrence and are punished by death" (Howitt).'

b) As the same severe punishment is also imposed upon fleeting affairs that have not led to procreation, other motives, such as practical ones, seem unlikely.

c) Since the totem is hereditary and is not altered by marriage, the consequences of this prohibition in the case of maternal inheritance are easily grasped. If the man belongs, for example, to a clan with the Kangaroo totem and marries a woman from the Emu totem, then the children, boys and girls, are all Emu. Consequently a son of this marriage is prohibited by the totem rule from having incestuous intercourse with his mother and his sisters, who are Emu just as he is.[4]

d) A little more reflection shows that the exogamy associated with the totem achieves more, and thus aims to achieve more, than the prevention of incest with mother and sisters. Where men are concerned, it also rules out sexual intercourse with all women of their own clan, which is to say a number of women who are not related to them by blood, by treating all those women as blood relations. The psychological justification of this great restriction, which goes far beyond anything comparable among civilized peoples, is not at first apparent. All we seem to understand is that the role of the totem (the animal) as an ancestor is taken very

8

seriously. Everyone descended from the same totem is related by blood, they are all a family, and in this family the most remote degrees of relationship are acknowledged as an absolute obstacle to sexual congress.

Thus these savages reveal to us an unusually intense dread of incest or sensitivity towards it, along with the curious fact, which we do not clearly understand, that they substitute the totem relationship for the real blood relationship. We should not, however, exaggerate this opposition, and should bear in mind that the totemic prohibitions include real incest as a special case.

The manner in which the totem clan was substituted for the real family remains a riddle whose solution may coincide with the explanation of the totem itself. Of course it should be remembered that with a certain freedom of sexual intercourse, beyond the strictures of matrimony, the blood relationship, and thus the prevention of incest, becomes so uncertain that another basis for the prohibition is required. Thus it might be worth pointing out that the customs of Australians acknowledge social conditions and formal occasions on which there are breaches in a man's exclusive conjugal right to his wife.

The linguistic practice of these Australian tribes[5] reveals one curious feature that beyond a doubt belongs in this context. The terms that they use to designate kinship do not in fact cover the relationship between two individuals, or between an individual and a group; rather they belong, in L. H. Morgan's phrase, to the 'classificatory system'. That is to say that a man uses the term 'father' not only for his progenitor, but also for any other man who could, according to the statutes of the tribe, have married his mother and thus become his father; the people whom he calls 'brothers' and 'sisters' are not only the children of his real parents, but also the children of all the named people who are in a parental group relationship with him. Thus the kinship terms that two Australians apply to each other do not necessarily refer to a blood relationship between them, as our linguistic customs would dictate; they refer rather to social than to physical relationships. Something not unlike this classificatory system appears in our own culture in the nursery, when the child is encouraged to greet all of its parents' friends as 'Uncle' and 'Aunt', or in the extended sense, when we speak of 'brothers in Apollo' or 'sisters in Christ'.

We can easily explain this linguistic custom, so disconcerting to us, if we see it as a residue and indication of that marital institution which the Revd L. Fison has called 'group marriage', according to which a certain number of men practise marital rights over a certain number of women. The offspring of this group marriage would then rightly consider each other as siblings, despite the fact they were not all born to the same mother, and see all the male members of the group as their fathers.

Although some authors, such as Westermarck in his *History of Human Marriage*,[6] resist the conclusions that others have drawn from the existence of group-relationship names, the most eminent authorities on Australian savages all agree that the classificatory relationship names should be regarded as a leftover from the days of group marriage. Indeed, according to Spencer and Gillen[7] a certain form of group marriage can still be observed in existence today among the tribes of the Urabunna and the Dieri. According to this view, then, group marriage in these peoples preceded individual marriage and did not disappear without leaving clear traces in language and customs.

But if we replace individual marriage with group marriage, we will be able to grasp the apparent excess of incest avoidance that we have encountered among the same peoples. Totemic exogamy, the prohibition on sexual intercourse between members of the same clan, appeared as the appropriate means for the prevention of group incest, which was then fixed and long outlasted its original motivation.

While we believe that we understand the motivation behind the marriage restrictions among the savages of Australia, we still go on to learn that real relationships reveal a far greater complexity, and one which appears baffling at first sight. There are, in fact, only a few tribes in Australia that have no prohibition other than the totemic restriction. Most are organized in such a way that they at first break down into two divisions, which have been called marriage classes, or phratries. Each of these marriage classes is exogamous and includes several totem clans. Usually, each phratry is divided into two sub-classes (sub-phratries), which means that the tribe as a whole is divided into four; the sub-classes thus standing between the phratries and the totem clans.

The typical diagram of the organization of an Australian tribe thus has the following appearance:

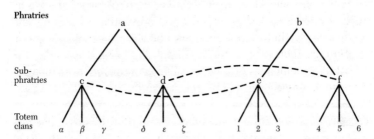

The twelve totemic groups are divided into four sub-phratries and two phratries. All the divisions are exogamous.[8] Sub-phratry *c* forms an exogamous unit with *e*, as does sub-class *d* with *f*. The consequence of these arrangements is quite clear: they introduce a further restriction of marriage choice and sexual freedom. If only these twelve totem clans existed, each member of a clan – assuming the same number of people in each – would be able to choose from eleven-twelfths of all the women in the tribe. The existence of the two phratries restricts this number to six out of twelve, or one half; a man from totem *a* may only marry a woman of clans 1 to 6. With the introduction of the two sub-phratries the selection drops to three-twelfths, or one quarter; a man from totem *a* can choose his wife only from the women of totems 4, 5 and 6.

The historical relationships between phratries – which number as many as eight in some tribes – and the totem clans are very unclear. We can see only that these arrangements seek to achieve the same thing as totemic exogamy, and that they attempt to do even more than that. But while totemic exogamy creates the impression of a sacred statute that has come about in ways that remain unknown, and is thus a custom, the complicated institutions

11

of the phratries, their sub-divisions and the conditions attached to them appear to derive from deliberate legislation, which perhaps assumed the task of preventing incest because the influence of the totem was in decline. And while the totemic system is, as we have seen, the basis of all other social obligations and customary restrictions of the tribe, the phratries do not go beyond the regulation of marriage choice.

In the further development of the system of phratries, there is an apparent tendency to go beyond the prevention of natural and group incest, and to forbid marriages between more distant group relations, much as the Catholic Church did when it extended the prohibitions on marriage between siblings to cousins, even going so far as to invent the concept of spiritual kin.[9]

It would not greatly serve our purposes to go into the extraordinarily intricate and unresolved discussions of the origin and significance of marriage classes and their relationship to totemism. It is enough to point out the great care that the Australians as well as other savage peoples apply to the prevention of incest.[10] We must say that these savages are even more sensitive to incest than we are. In all likelihood the temptation is more immediate for them, and consequently requires more substantial protection against it.

The dread of incest in these peoples does not, however, content itself with the erection of the institutions described, most of which seem to us to be directed against group incest. We must add to this a series of 'customs' which safeguard against intercourse between close relations, which are applied with almost religious severity, and of whose intention there can hardly be any doubt. These customs or customary prohibitions may be called 'avoidances'. Their distribution extends far beyond the Australian totemic peoples. But here again I will have to ask readers to be content with a fragmentary excerpt from the wealth of material.

In Melanesia such restrictive prohibitions are directed against intercourse with mother and sisters. Thus, for example, on Lepers' Island, one of the New Hebrides, at a certain age a boy will leave the maternal home and move to the 'clubhouse', where from that point onwards he will sleep and have his meals. He may still visit his home to ask for food; but if his sister is at home he must leave before he has eaten; if no sister is present, he may sit down to eat near the door. If brother and sister happen to meet in the open, they must run away from each other or hide on either side of the path. If the boy recognizes certain footprints in the sand as being his sister's, he will not follow them, any more than she will follow his. Indeed, he will not even utter her name and will be careful not to use any current word if it forms part of her name. This avoidance, which begins with the ceremony of puberty, is maintained throughout the whole of his life. Reserve between a mother and her son increases with the years, and is, incidentally, more obligatory on the mother's side. If she brings him something to eat, she does not hand it to him herself, but places it in front of him, and addresses him in a formal rather than a familiar way. Similar practices prevail in New Caledonia. If brother and sister happen to meet, she escapes into the bushes, and he walks past without turning his head towards her.[11]

On the Gazelle Peninsula in New Britain a sister may not speak to her brother from her marriage onwards, and nor may she utter his name, only referring to him in a roundabout way.[12]

On the island of New Mecklenburg cousins (although not of all kinds) are affected by such restrictions, as are brothers and sisters. They may not approach one another, shake hands or give each other presents, but they may talk to one another at a distance of several paces. The punishment for incest with a sister is death by hanging.[13]

These rules of avoidance are particularly severe in the Fiji Islands, where they apply not only to blood relations but also to group-sisters. It would seem all the stranger to us to hear that these savages have sacred orgies in which these very forbidden degrees of kinship seek sexual congress with one another, if we did not prefer to make use of this contradiction to explain the prohibition rather than being surprised by it.[14]

Among the Batta of Sumatra, laws of avoidance apply to all close family relationships. It would be most offensive for a Batta, for example, to accompany his own sister to an evening party. A Batta brother will feel ill at ease in the company of his sister, even if other people are also present. If one of them comes into the house, the other prefers to leave. A father will not stay alone in the house with his daughter, any more than will a mother with her son. The Dutch missionary who reported on these customs adds that he must unfortunately consider them to be very well founded. Among these people it is assumed without question that a man and a woman left alone together will indulge in improper intimacy, and since they expect all possible punishments and bad consequences from intercourse between close blood relations, they are right to avoid all temptations with such prohibitions.[15]

Among the Barongo of Delagoa Bay in Africa, the most rigorous precautions are applied, strangely enough, to the sister-in-law, the wife of one's own wife's brother. If a man should happen to meet this woman who is so dangerous to him, he carefully lets her pass. He does not dare to eat from the same bowl with her, he will speak to her only hesitantly, he does not dare to enter her hut, and greets her only with a trembling voice.[16]

Among the Akamba (or Wakamba) in British East Africa there is a law of avoidance which one would have expected to encounter more often. Between puberty and marriage a girl must take care to avoid her own father. She hides if she meets him along the road, she tries never to sit down next to him, and behaves like this until the moment of her engagement. From marriage onwards no obstacle is placed in the way of her social intercourse with her father.[17]

The most widespread, strict and, for civilized peoples, interesting avoidance is the one that restricts intercourse between a man and his mother-in-law. In Australia this avoidance is quite universal, but it is also in force among Melanesians, Polynesians and the Negro populations of Africa, as far as the traces of totemism and group kinship extend, and probably even further than that. Among some of these peoples, similar prohibitions exist against harmless social intercourse of a woman with her father-in-law, but these are not nearly so constant or so strict. In individual cases both parents-in-law become the object of avoidance.

Since we are less interested in ethnographic distribution than in the content and purpose of mother-in-law avoidance, I shall limit myself to a few examples.

On the Banks Islands these prohibitions are very strict and painstakingly precise. A man will avoid the proximity of his mother-in-law just as she will avoid his. If the two of them meet by chance on a path, the woman steps aside and turns her back to him until he has passed, or he will do the same.

In Vanua Lava (Port Patteson), a man will not even walk along the beach behind his mother-in-law before the rising tide has washed away her footprints in the sand. But they are allowed to talk to one another from a certain distance. It is quite unthinkable for him ever to utter the name of his mother-in-law or she that of her son-in-law.[18]

In the Solomon Islands the husband may neither see nor speak to his mother-in-law from his marriage onwards. If he meets her, he does not act as though he knows her, but runs away from her as quickly as he can, and hides.[19]

Among the Zulu custom decrees that a man should be ashamed of his mother-in-law, and that he should do all that he can to avoid her company. He does not enter a hut where she is present, and if they meet one another, one of them will step aside, she hiding behind a bush, for example, while he holds his shield over his face. If they are unable to avoid one another and the woman has nothing else to conceal herself with, she will at the very least wrap a tuft of grass around her head to satisfy the ceremonial requirements. Any social intercourse between them must be mediated by a third party, or else they may shout at each other from a certain distance, as long as there is some barrier between them, such as the enclosure of a kraal. Neither of them may utter the name of the other.[20]

Among the Basoga, a Negro tribe around the sources of the Nile, a man may only speak to his mother-in-law if she is in another room in the house and he is unable to see her. Incidentally, these people have such a horror of incest that they punish it even among domestic animals.[21]

While the purpose and significance of the other avoidances between close relations are beyond a doubt, so much so that they can be understood by all observers as protective measures against incest, the prohibitions applying to intercourse with one's mother-in-law have been differently interpreted in some quarters. It was rightly considered incomprehensible that all these peoples should show such fear of the temptation which appears in the form of an older woman who could be, but was not, one's mother.[22]

This objection was also raised against the view of Fison, who pointed out that there is a discrepancy in certain phratry systems, in that they do not make marriage between a man and his mother-in-law impossible in theory, and that a special guarantee was therefore required to guard against such a possibility.

In his book *The Origin of Civilisation*, Sir J. Lubbock traces the behaviour of the mother-in-law towards the son-in-law back to the 'marriage by capture' of former times. 'When the capture was a reality, the indignation of the parents would also be real; when it became a mere symbol, the parental anger would be symbolized also, and would be continued after its origin had been forgotten.' Crawley easily shows how little this tentative explanation accords with the details of actual observation.

E. B. Tylor is of the opinion that the treatment of the son-in-law by the mother-in-law is nothing but a form of non-acknowledgement, or 'cutting', on the part of the woman's family. The man is seen as a stranger, and remains so until the first child is born. But apart from those cases in which the latter condition does not erase the prohibition, one may object to this explanation by pointing out that it sheds no light on the custom affecting relations between son-in-law and mother-in-law, thus ignoring the sexual factor, and that it does not take into account the element of religious horror expressed in the laws of avoidance.[23]

A Zulu woman who was asked about the basis of the prohibition showed great delicacy in her reply: 'It is not right that he should see the breasts that suckled his wife.'[24]

It is well known that the relationship between son-in-law and mother-in-law is one of the most awkward aspects of family organization, even among civilized peoples. There may no longer be any rules of avoidance for them among the white peoples of Europe and

America, but much quarrelling and displeasure would often be avoided if they still existed as a custom, and did not have to be re-erected by isolated individuals. Many Europeans will see an act of the highest wisdom in the laws of avoidance that the savage peoples have established to exclude the possibility of social contact between people who have become so closely related. There can hardly be any doubt that there is something in the psychological situation of mother-in-law and son-in-law that encourages hostility between them and makes it difficult for them to live together. The frequency among civilized peoples of jokes revolving around the theme of the mother-in-law seems to me to indicate that emotional relations between son-in-law and mother-in-law are governed by ingredients which are sharply opposed to one another. I believe that this relationship is actually an 'ambivalent' one, made up of conflicting impulses of affection and hostility.

A certain amount of these impulses is clearly apparent: on the part of the mother-in-law the disinclination to renounce ownership of her daughter, mistrust of the stranger to whom her daughter has been handed over, and the tendency to maintain the dominant role to which she had become accustomed in her own house. On the husband's part there is the determination not to be subjected to the will of another, jealousy towards everyone who possessed his wife's affection before he did and – last but not least – a disinclination to have his illusion of sexual overvaluation interfered with. This interference usually emanates from the mother-in-law herself, who reminds him of her daughter through so many common features, and yet who lacks all the charms of youth, beauty and psychological freshness that make his wife precious to him.

The knowledge of hidden psychical impulses that we have attained through the psychoanalytic examination of individuals enables us to add other motives to those mentioned above. Where the psychosexual needs of the woman are supposed to be satisfied in marriage and family life, there is always the danger of dissatisfaction through the premature termination of the marital relationship, and monotony in the woman's emotional life. The ageing mother protects herself by living through her children, by identifying with

17

them, by making their emotional experiences her own. Parents are said to stay young with their children; that is in fact one of the most valuable psychical gains that parents draw from their children. Childlessness eliminates one of the best opportunities to bear the resignation imposed by one's own marriage. In the mother, this empathy with her daughter can often go so far that she too actually falls in love with the man her daughter loves, and in extreme cases, because of the violent psychical resistance against this set of feelings, this may lead to serious forms of neurotic illness. At any event, this tendency to infatuation occurs very frequently in mothers-in-law, and either the infatuation itself or the opposing tendency joins the chaos of conflicting forces in the mother-in-law's psyche. Very often the unaffectionate, sadistic component of the excitement of love is turned upon the son-in-law, the better to suppress forbidden, tender feelings.

As to the husband, his relationship with his mother-in-law is complicated by similar impulses, although these derive from other sources. The path of object-choice has regularly led him via the image of his mother, or perhaps of his sister, to his love-object. His fondness for these two beloved people from his childhood was deflected by the incest barrier, so that he was able find their image in an object from outside the family. He now sees his mother-in-law taking the place of his own and his sister's mother. He has an impulse to return to his original choice, but everything within him resists this. His dread of incest requires him not to be reminded of the genealogy of his choice of a love-object. This rejection is facilitated by the fact that his mother-in-law is a figure from his present whom he has not known for ever, unlike his mother, whose image has been preserved unaltered in his unconscious. A certain quantity of ill-temper and animosity added to the emotional mix would lead us to suspect that the mother-in-law actually does represent an incestuous temptation to the son-in-law, just as it frequently happens that the husband at first falls manifestly in love with his future mother-in-law, before transferring his affection to her daughter.

I can see no objection to the assumption that it is precisely this incestuous factor in the relationship that motivates the avoidance between son-in-law and mother-in-law among savages. In order to explain the 'avoidances' so rigidly enforced among these primitive peoples, we would therefore prefer to accept the opinion originally expressed by Fison, which sees these laws only as a protection against possible incest. The same applies to all other avoidances between those related either by blood or marriage. The only difference is that in the former case the incest is direct, and the aim of prevention may be conscious; in the latter case, which includes the relationship with the mother-in-law, incest seems to be a fantasy temptation brought about through unconscious intermediate connections.

In this outline we have had little opportunity to show that the facts of social psychology can be given a fresh understanding by the application of psychoanalytical examination, because the dread of incest among savages has been acknowledged as such for a long time now and requires no further interpretation. What we can add for a better understanding of the dread of incest is the observation that it is a subtle infantile trait in striking correspondence with the psychical life of the neurotic. Psychoanalysis has taught us that the boy's first sexual object-choice is an incestuous one, directed at forbidden objects, his mother and his sister, and it has also made us acquainted with the ways in which the growing boy frees himself from the attraction of incest. But in most cases the neurotic represents to us a piece of psychical infantilism; either he has not succeeded in freeing himself from the infantile relations of psychosexuality, or he has returned to them (in inhibited development and regression). Hence the incestuous fixations of the libido still – or once again – play a major part in his unconscious life. We have even declared the idea that the relationship with the parents is dominated by incestuous longings to be the core complex of neurosis. This discovery of the significance of incest for neurosis naturally meets with a great deal of incredulity among normal adults. The works of Otto Rank, for example, which reveal even more extensively the degree to which the theme of incest is central to poetic interest and the way in which, in countless variations and distortions, it supplies poetry with its material, have been similarly rejected. We cannot help believing that such rejection is above all a product of man's profound distaste for his former incestuous desires, which have since been repressed. So it is of some importance for us to be able to show that these incestuous desires, later destined to become unconscious, are still felt by savage peoples to be threatening, and considered worthy of the harshest defensive measures.

Notes

1. [J. G.] Frazer, *Totemism and Exogamy*, vol. I, p. 53. 'The totem bond is stronger than the bond of blood or family in the modern sense.'
2. This highly condensed abstract of the totemic system cannot be left without explanations and reservations: the name totem was introduced, in the form *totam*, by the Englishman J. Long, who borrowed it from the redskins of North America. The object itself has gradually attracted great interest in science and provoked a wealth of literature, from which I should select the four-volume book by J. G. Frazer, *Totemism and Exogamy*, 1910, and books and papers by Andrew Lang (*The Secret of the Totem*). The merit of recognizing the importance of totemism for man's primeval history is owed to the Scotsman J. Ferguson McLennan (1869–70). Aside from the Australians, totemistic institutions have been, or remain today, observable among the Indians of North America, among the peoples of the Oceanic archipelago, in the East Indies and in much of Africa. But some traces and remnants which are otherwise difficult to interpret allow us to conclude that totemism once also existed among the primeval Aryan and Semitic peoples of Europe and Asia, so that many researchers are inclined to see it as a necessary and universal phase of human development.

How did prehistoric men come to attach themselves to a totem, that is, to make the descent from one animal or another the basis of their social obligations and, as we shall hear, also of their sexual restrictions? There are many theories on this subject, an overview of which the German reader can find in [W.] Wundt's *Völkerpsychologie* [Folk Psychology] (vol. II, *Mythus und Religion* [Myth and Religion]), but there is no agreement between them. I promise in the near future to make totemism the object of a particular study in which I shall attempt to resolve this question through the application of psychoanalytic ideas. (Cf. the fourth essay in this volume.)

But while there are great divergences of thought concerning the theory of totemism, we may also say that the facts relating to it can barely be set out in general propositions, as I have attempted to do above. There is hardly a statement to which one would not have to add exceptions or contradictions. But we should not forget that even the most primitive and conservative peoples are in a sense ancient peoples, and have a long past in the course of which their most primitive practices have undergone a great deal of development and distortion. Thus, for example, totemism is still encountered today among people who demonstrate it in the most diverse stages of decadence, of fragmentation, of transition to other social and religious institutions, or else in stationary forms that may have moved quite far from the original nature. The difficulty, then, lies in the fact that it is not very easy to decide what we may see, in contemporary conditions, as a faithful picture of the meaningful past, and what as a secondary distortion.

3. Frazer, op. cit., vol. I, p. 54.

4. However the father, who is Kangaroo, is free – at least according to this prohibition – to practise incest with his daughters, who are Emu. With paternal inheritance of the totem the father becomes Kangaroo, and the children are also Kangaroo. The father would then be prohibited from incest with his daughters, while the son would still be allowed to practise incest with his mother. These consequences of the totem prohibition suggest that maternal inheritance is older than paternal, because there is reason to assume that the totem prohibitions are directed above all at the incestuous desires of the son.

5. Like those of most totemic peoples.

6. 2nd edn, 1902.

7. *The Native Tribes of Central Australia*, London, 1899.

8. The number of totems is chosen at random.

9. The article 'Totemism' in *Encyclopaedia Britannica*. Eleventh Edition, 1911 (A. Lang).

10. In his study *'Zur Sonderstellung des Vatermordes'* ['On the special status of patricide'], *Schriften zur angewandten Seelenkunde*, Issue 12, Vienna 1911, Storfer recently referred emphatically to this point.

11. R. H. Codrington, 'The Melanesians', in Frazer, *Totemism and Exogamy*, vol. I, p. 77.

12. Frazer, op. cit, vol. II, p. 124, after Kleintitschen, *Die Küstenbewohner der Gazellen-Halbinsel* [The coast-dwellers of the Gazelle Peninsula].

13. Ibid., vol. II, p. 131, after P. G. Peckel in *Anthropos*, 1908.

14. Ibid., vol. II, p. 147, after Revd L. Fison.

15. Ibid., vol. II, p. 189.

16. Ibid., vol. II, p. 388, after Junod.

17. Ibid., vol. II, p. 424.

18. Ibid., vol. II, p. 76.
19. Ibid., vol. II, p. 117, after C. Ribbe, *Zwei Jahre unter den Kannibalen der Salomo-Inseln* [Two Years Among the Cannibals of the Solomon Islands], 1903.
20. Ibid., vol. II, p. 385.
21. Ibid., vol. II, p. 461.
22. V. Crawley, *The Mystic Rose*, London, 1902, p. 405.
23. Ibid., p. 407.
24. Ibid., p. 401, after Leslie, *Among the Zulus and Amatongas*, 1875.

II

Taboo and the Ambivalence
of the Emotions

1

'Taboo' is a Polynesian word which is difficult for us to translate because we no longer have the concept to which it refers. It was still current among the ancient Romans, their *sacer* was the same as the taboo of the Polynesians. And the ἀγος of the Greeks and the *kodesh* of the Hebrews must also have meant the same thing as the Polynesians express through their word 'taboo', and which many peoples in America, Africa (Madagascar), North and Central Asia express using similar terms.

For us, the meaning of taboo branches off in two opposite directions. On the one hand it means: sacred, consecrated; on the other: uncanny, dangerous, forbidden and unclean. The opposite of taboo in Polynesian is designated by the word *noa*, meaning ordinary, universally accessible. Thus there is something in the taboo that is like the concept of reserve; it also expresses itself to a large extent in prohibitions and restrictions. Our own phrase 'holy dread' would also in many cases coincide with the meaning of taboo.

Taboo restrictions are different from religious or moral prohibitions. They do not derive from a commandment from a god, but actually impose their own prohibitions; they are distinguished from moral prohibitions by the fact that they are not part of a system which declares the necessity of abstinences in general while at the same time explaining that necessity. No explanation is given for taboo prohibitions: they are of unknown origin; incomprehensible to us, they seem quite natural to those under their sway.

Wundt calls taboo mankind's oldest unwritten legal code. It is generally assumed that taboo is older than the gods, and goes back to an age before any religions.

As we need an impartial account of taboo before we subject it to psychoanalytic consideration, I shall now cite an excerpt from the article 'Taboo' in the *Encyclopaedia Britannica*,[1] by the anthropologist Northcote W. Thomas.

'Properly speaking taboo includes only *(a)* the sacred (or unclean) character of persons or things, *(b)* the kind of prohibition which results from this character, and *(c)* the sanctity (or uncleanness) which results from a violation of the prohibition. The converse of taboo in Polynesia is *noa* and allied forms which mean "general" or "common" . . .

'Various classes of taboo in the wider sense may be distinguished: (i) natural or direct, the result of *mana* (mysterious power) inherent in a person or thing; (ii) communicated or indirect, equally the result of *mana* but *(a)* acquired or *(b)* imposed by a priest, chief or other person; (iii) intermediate, where both factors are present, as in the appropriation of a wife to her husband. The term taboo is also applied to ritual prohibitions of a different nature; but its use in these senses is better avoided. It might be argued that the term should be extended to embrace cases in which the sanction of the prohibition is the creation of a god or spirit, i.e., to religious interdictions as distinguished from magical, but there is neither automatic action nor contagion in such a case, and a better term for it is religious interdiction.

'The objects of the taboo are many: (i) direct taboos aim at *(a)* the protection of important persons – chiefs, priests, etc. – and things against harm; *(b)* the safeguarding of the weak – women, children and common people generally – from the powerful *mana* (magical influence) of chiefs and priests; *(c)* the provision against the dangers incurred by handling or coming in contact with corpses, by eating certain food, etc.; *(d)* the guarding of the chief acts of life – births, initiation, marriage and sexual functions, etc., against interference; *(e)* the securing of human beings against the wrath or power of gods and spirits;[2] *(f)* the securing of unborn infants and young children, who stand in a specially sympathetic relation with

24

one or both parents, from the consequence of certain actions, and more especially from the communication of qualities supposed to be derived from certain foods. (ii) Taboos are imposed in order to secure against thieves the property of an individual, his fields, tools [. . .].'

Originally, the punishment for the violation of a taboo was probably left up to an internal, automatic arrangement. The violated taboo avenges itself. Wherever the taboo is related to the idea of gods and demons, an automatic punishment is expected from the power of the deity. In other cases, probably as a result of a further development of the concept, the community assumes responsibility for the punishment of the wrongdoer, whose crime has put his companions in danger. Thus humanity's first systems of punishment are also connected to taboo.

'The violation of a taboo makes the offender himself taboo [. . .].' Certain dangers arising out of the violation of a taboo can be exorcized through acts of penance and purification ceremonies.

A peculiar magical power which attaches to people and to spirits, and which can be transmitted from them to inanimate objects, is seen as the source of the taboo. 'Persons or things which are regarded as taboo may be compared to objects charged with electricity; they are the seat of tremendous power which is transmissible by contact, and may be liberated with destructive effect if the organisms which provoke its discharge are too weak to resist it; the result of a violation of a taboo depends partly on the strength of the magical influence inherent in the taboo object or person, partly on the strength of the opposing *mana* of the violator of the taboo. Thus, kings and chiefs are possessed of great power, and it is death for their subjects to address them directly; but a minister or other person of greater *mana* than common, can approach them unharmed, and can in turn be approached by their inferiors without risk. [. . .] So too, indirect taboos depend for their strength on the *mana* of him who opposes them; if it is a chief or a priest, they are more powerful than those imposed by a common person.'

The fact of a taboo being transmissible is probably what has led to attempts to remove it through expiatory ceremonies.

There are permanent and temporary taboos. Those connected to priests and chiefs are the former, along with the dead and everything that belonged to them. Temporary taboos attach to certain conditions such as menstruation and confinement, the status of the warrior before and after the expedition, the activities of fishing and hunting and so on. A general taboo can also be imposed, like an ecclesiastical interdiction, upon a whole district, and may last for years.

If I am correct in my assessment of my readers' impressions, I shall now venture to assert that they do not know, after all that has been said about taboo, what to think of it, and where they should store it in their thoughts. This is certainly down to the inadequate information that they have received from me, and the omission of any discussion of the relationship between taboo and superstition, animism and religion. On the other hand, however, I fear that a more profound description of what we know about taboo would have had an even more confusing effect, and I may assure the reader that the situation is entirely opaque.

These, then, are a series of restrictions to which these primitive peoples subject themselves; this thing and that are forbidden, they do not know why, it does not even occur to them to ask the question. Rather, they submit to the restrictions as a matter of course, and are convinced that a violation will be punished most severely. Reliable accounts suggest that the inadvertent violation of these prohibitions is in fact automatically punished. The innocent wrongdoer who, for example, has eaten of a forbidden animal, becomes severely depressed, awaits his death and then actually dies. The prohibitions generally relate to matters involving the capacity for enjoyment, freedom of movement and social intercourse; in some cases they appear ingenious, and are clearly supposed to signify abstinences and renunciations, while in other cases their content is entirely incomprehensible, relating to worthless trivia, and seems to be merely ceremonial.

All of these prohibitions seem to be based on something resembling a theory, as though the prohibitions were necessary because certain persons and objects possessed a dangerous power transmitted by contact with the object so charged, almost like a contagion. The quantity of this dangerous property is also taken into consideration. Some persons or things have more of it than others, and the danger varies precisely according to the difference in the charges. The strangest thing about this is probably the fact that anyone violating such a prohibition himself assumes the character of the forbidden object, as though he has absorbed the whole of the dangerous charge. This power, then, attaches to all more or less prominent persons, such as kings, priests or newborn children, and all exceptional states, physical conditions such as menstruation, puberty and birth, everything uncanny, such as illness and death, and everything that is connected to them by contagion or dissemination.

But 'taboo' refers to everything, to the people and the places, objects and temporary states that are the bearers or the source of this mysterious property. Taboo also refers to the prohibition derived from this property, and lastly taboo, in the literal sense, encompasses something that is at once holy, elevated above the ordinary, and at the same time dangerous, unclean and mysterious.

This word, and the system to which it refers, express a piece of psychical life which we do not really appear to understand. Above all, one would think that one could not come near any such understanding without examining the characteristic belief in spirits and demons so characteristic of these low cultures.

Why should we be at all interested in the mystery of taboo? Not only, I think, because every psychological problem is inherently worth trying to solve, but also for other reasons. We might surmise that the taboo of the savages of Polynesia is not so far removed from ourselves as we at first wished to believe, that the moral and customary prohibitions which we obey might be essentially connected to this primitive taboo, and that the explanation of the taboo might be able to cast a light on the obscure origin of our own 'categorical imperative'.

So we listen with particularly keen attention when a researcher such as W. Wundt tells us of his conception of the taboo, particularly since he promises 'to go back to the very roots of taboo ideas'.[3]

As regards the concept of the taboo, Wundt says that it 'incorporates all those customs which express the fear of particular objects connected with cult ideas, or the activities related to them'.[4]

Elsewhere: 'If we take the term (taboo), in accordance with the general meaning of the word, to mean that prohibition, established in usage and custom or in expressly formulated laws, against touching an object, taking it for one's own use, or using certain proscribed words . . .' then no people, no stage of civilization, has escaped the harmful effects of taboo.

Wundt then shows why he finds it more effective to study the nature of taboo in the primitive conditions of the savages of Australia than in the higher culture of the Polynesian peoples. In the case of the Australians, he arranges the taboo prohibitions into three classes, according to whether they apply to animals, people or other objects. The taboo on animals, which consists essentially in the prohibition on killing and eating, forms the core of totemism.[5] The second kind of taboo, which takes man as its object, is significantly different in character. From the very first, it is restricted to conditions which bring about an unusual situation in the life of the person tabooed. Thus young men are taboo at their initiation ceremony, as are women during menstruation and immediately after childbirth; newborn children, sick people and above all the dead. The constantly used property of any person, such as his clothes, tools and weapons, is permanently taboo for anyone else. In Australia, the new name that a boy receives upon his initiation into manhood becomes part of his most personal property; it is taboo, and must be kept secret. Taboos of the third kind, which apply to trees, plants, houses and places, are more flexible, and seem only to follow the rule that anything which for any reason provokes fear, anything uncanny, is subject to taboo.

Wundt himself is obliged to declare that the changes that taboo undergoes in the richer culture of the Polynesians and the people of the Malay Archipelago are not very profound. The stronger social differentiation of these peoples is manifested in the fact that chiefs, kings and priests exert a particularly effective taboo, and are themselves exposed to the strongest compulsion of taboo.

But the actual sources of taboo lie deeper than in the interests of the privileged classes: 'they arise where the most primitive and at the same time the most lasting human impulses find their source, *in the fear of the effect of demonic powers*.'[6] 'Taboo is originally nothing other than the objectified fear of the demonic power thought to lie concealed within the tabooed object. It prohibits anything that may provoke that power, and commands, where it is knowingly or unknowingly violated, that the demon's revenge be averted.'

Gradually, taboo becomes an autonomous force that has freed itself from the demonic. It becomes a compulsion of custom and tradition, and finally of law. 'But the commandment that lies hidden behind taboo prohibitions which vary according to place and time is originally one and one alone: Guard against the wrath of demons.'

Wundt, therefore, teaches us that taboo is the expression and product of the belief of primitive people in demonic powers. Later taboo detached itself from this root, and remained a force simply by virtue of a kind of psychical persistence; in this way, Wundt says, it became itself the root of our customs and laws. While there are few objections that one might raise to the first of these propositions, I still think I will be voicing the impression of many readers if I call Wundt's explanation disappointing. It does not reach down to the sources of taboo ideas, or uncover their roots. Neither fear nor demons can be treated by psychology as ends in themselves which require no further deductive reasoning. It would be a different matter if the demons really existed; but we know that, like gods, they are themselves creations of the psychical powers of man; they have been created from and out of something.

Wundt expresses significant but not entirely clear views about the double meaning of taboo. In the primitive beginnings of taboo, in his view, there is not yet any division between *sacred* and *unclean*. For that reason those concepts lack the significance which they would only be able to assume through opposition to one another. The animal, the person, the place to which a taboo applies are demonic, not sacred, and for that reason they are not yet unclean in the later sense of that term. The expression 'taboo' is ideally suited to this undifferentiated and intermediate meaning of the demonic, since it stresses a characteristic which finally attaches, as it has done through the ages, both to the sacred and the unclean: fear of contact. But the persistence of this major common feature also points to the existence of an original correspondence between the two spheres, which only made way for a differentiation as the result of further conditions through which they finally developed into opposites.

The belief, associated with the original taboo, in a demonic power hidden within the object, which avenges contact with it or forbidden use of it by bewitching the offender, is still an entirely objectified fear. This has not yet separated into the two forms that it assumes at a developed stage: *veneration* and *revulsion*.

But how does this separation come about? According to Wundt, it is through the transfer of taboo prohibitions from the demonic sphere into that of theistic views. The opposition of the sacred and the unclean coincides with the sequence of two mythological stages, the first of which does not completely disappear once the next has been reached, but persists in the form of lowered esteem, which gradually turns into contempt. It is a general law in mythology that an earlier stage, precisely because it has been overcome and pushed back by a superior one, continues to exist side by side with it in a debased form, so that its objects of veneration turn into objects of dread.[7]

Wundt's further elucidations deal with the relationship of taboo to purification and sacrifice.

2

Anyone who approaches the problem of taboo from psychoanalysis – from the examination of the unconscious part of the psychical life – needs only to reflect for a moment before saying that these phenomena are not unfamiliar to him. He knows individuals who have created such taboo prohibitions for themselves, and who obey them just as strictly as savages obey those common to their tribe or their society. Were he not accustomed to describing these individuals as 'obsessive neurotics', he would surely find the term 'taboo illness' appropriate to their condition. But he will have learned so much about the clinical aetiology and the psychical mechanism of obsessive illness through psychoanalytic investigation, that he will be unable to resist using what he has learned in that field to illuminate the equivalent phenomenon within the field of social psychology.

There is one warning that we shall have to heed as we make this undertaking. The resemblance of taboo to obsessive illness may be purely external, applying only to the appearance of both without extending any further into their essence. Nature likes to use the same forms in the most divergent biological contexts, in the case, for example, of coral stems and plants, and indeed of certain crystals or in the formation of some chemical precipitates. It would clearly be over-hasty and short-sighted of us to reach conclusions based on these correspondences, which are based solely on shared mechanical conditions. We will bear this warning in mind, although we do not intend to abandon our intended comparison on account of it.

The first and most striking such correspondence between obsessive prohibitions in neurotics and those in taboo lies in the fact that they are equally unmotivated and mysterious in their origins. They have at some point appeared, and must now be maintained because of an unconquerable anxiety. The threat of external punishment is superfluous because there is an inner certainty (a moral conviction) that violation would lead to an unbearable disaster. The most that obsessive neurotics can tell us is their vague sense that harm would come to a certain person from their immediate surroundings if they were to violate the prohibition. What that violation might be is not acknowledged, and this inadequate information is more likely to be received during later discussions of expiatory and defensive actions than it is when the prohibitions themselves are being spoken of.

The chief core prohibition of neurosis is, as in the case of taboo, the act of touching, hence its name: 'touching phobia' or '*délire de toucher*'. The prohibition does not only extend to direct contact with the body, but assumes the latitude of the figurative phrase 'to come into contact with'. Anything that leads the thoughts towards the forbidden, provoking mental contact, is prohibited just as much as direct physical contact; the same extension is also found in taboo.

Some prohibitions are immediately understood from their purpose, while others appear incomprehensible, foolish and senseless. We describe these prohibitions as 'ceremonials', and find that taboo practices show the same variation.

Obsessive prohibitions have an extraordinary capacity for displacement, they exploit all kinds of connections between one object and another and make the new object, as one of my patients tellingly puts it, 'impossible'. By the end, impossibility has placed an embargo upon the whole world. Obsessive neurotics behave as though the 'impossible' people and things were bearers of a dangerous contagion that was about to spread through contact to everything around it. We stressed the same characteristics of contagion and transference at the beginning of this account, with our description of taboo prohibitions. We also know that anyone who has violated a taboo by touching something taboo becomes himself taboo, and no one may come into contact with him.

I shall compare two examples of the transference (or rather displacement) of the prohibition; one from the life of the Maori, the other from my observation of a woman suffering from an obsessive neurotic illness.

'[A] Maori chief would not blow on a fire with his mouth; for his sacred breath would communicate its sanctity to the fire, which would pass it on to the meat in the pot, which would pass it on to the man who ate the meat which was in the pot, which stood on the fire, which was breathed on by the chief; so that the eater, infected by the chief's breath conveyed through these intermediaries, would surely die.'[8]

My patient demands that a utensil which her husband had bought and brought home be removed, as it would make the room in which she lives impossible. For she has heard that this object was bought in a shop which is located, let us say, in Hirschgasse. But 'Hirsch' is now the name of a friend of hers who lives in a far-off town, and who knew her in her youth, under her maiden name. This friend is now 'impossible' for her, taboo, and the object bought here in Vienna is just as taboo as the friend herself, with whom the patient does not wish to come into contact.

Obsessive prohibitions, like taboo prohibitions, involve great renunciation and restrictions in life, but some of them can be removed by the performance of certain actions which must now occur, which have an obsessive character – compulsive acts – and whose nature as penance, expiation, defensive measures and purification is beyond a doubt. The most habitual of these compulsive acts is washing with water (compulsive washing). A part of the taboo prohibitions can also be replaced like this, or rather their violation can be put right by such 'ceremonials', and here too lustration with water is the preferred way.

Let us now sum up the points at which the correspondences of taboo customs with the symptoms of obsessive neuroses are most distinctly expressed: 1) In the unmotivated nature of the prohibitions; 2) in their enforcement by internal coercion; 3) in their capacity for displacement and the danger of contagion by the prohibited object; 4) in the causation of ceremonial actions, commandments issuing from the forbidden.

However, psychoanalysis has made us familiar with both the clinical history and the psychical mechanism of obsessive neurosis. In a typical case of touching phobia, the clinical history would read as follows: at the very beginning, in very early childhood, a strong desire to touch was expressed, the whole of which was far more specialized than one would have been inclined to expect. This desire soon encountered a prohibition *from without* against performing this precise kind of touch.[9] The prohibition was accepted because it was supported by strong internal forces;[10] it proved to be stronger than the drive that sought to find expression in touching. But because of the child's primitive psychical constitution, the prohibition was unable to abolish the drive. The consequence of the prohibition was only to suppress the drive – the desire to touch – and to banish it into the unconscious. The prohibition and the drive were both preserved; the drive because it was only repressed and not abolished, and the prohibition because if it had ceased the drive would have broken through into consciousness and been put into effect. What had been created was an unresolved situation, a psychical fixation, and henceforth everything else emanates from the continuing conflict between prohibition and drive.

The chief characteristic of the psychological constellation thus fixed lies in what we might call the *ambivalent* attitude of the individual towards the particular object, or rather an action performed upon it.[11] It wants to repeat this action – touching – over and over again, [and sees in it the highest pleasure, but may not carry it out,][12] while at the same time it abhors it. The opposition between the two currents cannot simply be balanced out, because – we can only say – their location within the psyche means that they cannot collide. The prohibition becomes fully conscious, while the lasting pleasure in touching is unconscious, and the subject knows nothing of it. If this psychological factor did not exist, an ambivalence could neither maintain itself for so long nor lead to such subsequent manifestations.

In the clinical history of the case we have stressed the appearance of the prohibition so early in childhood as the principal determinant; for its further development the role falls to the mechanism of repression, which comes into play at this age. Because of this repression, which is connected with forgetting – amnesia – the motivation for the prohibition, now conscious, remains unknown, and all attempts to dissect it intellectually are doomed to failure, since the point of attack cannot be found. The prohibition owes its strength – its obsessive character – to its relation with its unconscious opponent, the hidden undiminished desire, an inner necessity inaccessible to consciousness. The prohibition's capacity for transference and its power to reproduce itself reflects a process that coincides with unconscious desire, and is particularly facilitated by the psychological conditions of the unconscious. The instinctual desire is constantly displaced to elude whichever barrier it faces, and seeks to acquire surrogates – substitute objects and substitute actions – for that which is forbidden. For the same reason the prohibition also shifts about and extends to the new goals of the forbidden impulse. The prohibition responds to each new advance on the part of the repressed libido with fresh severity. The mutual inhi-bition of the two conflicting forces creates a need for discharge, for an easing of the prevailing tension, which one can recognize as the motivation for the compulsive actions. In neurosis, these are clearly compromise acts, which may be regarded as proofs of remorse and attempts at expiation, etc., while at the same time they can be seen as substitute acts that compensate the drive for that which is for-bidden. It is a law of neurotic illness that these compulsive actions are placed increasingly at the service of the drive, and come ever closer to the originally forbidden acts.

Let us now attempt to deal with taboo as though it were of the same nature as an obsessive prohibition among our patients. From the very first we should make it clear to ourselves that many of the taboo prohibitions that we can observe are secondary, displaced and distorted in nature, and that we must content ourselves with casting some light on the most original and significant taboo prohibitions. Further, that the divergences between the situation of savages and that of neurotics might be great enough to exclude complete corre-spondence, a transference from one to the other, which would be possible if they were exact copies of one another.

First of all it should be said that there is no point in asking the savages about the real motivation of their prohibitions, the genesis of the taboo. According to our hypothesis, they would be incapable of telling us anything about it, because the motivation is 'uncon-scious' to them. But let us construct the history of the taboo as follows, on the model of obsessive prohibitions. Taboos are ancient prohibitions, imposed from without upon a generation of primitive people at some point in time, that is, they were probably forced upon them by the previous generation. These prohibitions affected activities which there was a strong inclination to carry out. The pro-hibitions were maintained from generation to generation, perhaps merely as a product of tradition, by parental and social authority. But it may be that in later generations they have already organized themselves as a piece of inherited psychical property. Whether such 'innate ideas' exist, whether they caused the fixation of the taboo alone or in connection with upbringing, it is impossible to say for

the case presently under discussion. The persistence of taboo, however, teaches us one thing, that the original desire to perform that
forbidden act persists among the taboo peoples. This means that
they have an *ambivalent attitude* to their taboo prohibitions; in their
unconscious they would like nothing more than to violate them, but
they are also afraid to do so; they are afraid precisely because they
wish to do it, and their fear is stronger than their desire. But in each
individual member of this particular people the desire is unconscious, just as it is in the neurotic.

The oldest and most important taboo prohibitions are the two
fundamental laws of totemism: not to kill the totem animal, and to
avoid sexual intercourse with totem companions of the opposite sex.

These must, therefore, be the oldest and strongest desires of
mankind. We cannot understand this, and therefore cannot test our
hypotheses against these examples, while the meaning and the
source of the totemistic system remain so completely unknown to
us. But the wording of these two taboos, and the fact that they occur
together, will remind anyone familiar with the results of the psychoanalytic examination of individuals of something quite specific,
which psychoanalysts call the central point of infantile wish-life, and
the nucleus of the later neurosis.[13]

The other varieties of taboo phenomena, which have led to the
attempts at classification outlined above, come together for us as
follows to form a single entity: the basis of taboo is a forbidden
action for which there is a strong inclination in the unconscious.

We know, without understanding it, that anyone who does what
is forbidden, anyone who violates the taboo, becomes himself taboo.
But how are we to reconcile this with the fact that taboo adheres not
only to people who have done that which is forbidden, but also to
those who are in particular conditions, to those conditions themselves and also to impersonal objects? What kind of dangerous
property could that be, which always remains the same under all
these different conditions? Only one thing: the aptitude to arouse
man's ambivalence and tempt him to violate the prohibition.

The individual who has violated a taboo becomes himself taboo
because he possesses the dangerous aptitude of tempting others

into following his example. He arouses envy; why should he be allowed to do things that are forbidden to others? So he is really *contagious* in so far as each example provokes imitation, and he must therefore be avoided himself.

But an individual need not have violated a taboo, and can still be permanently or temporarily taboo because he is in a condition apt to stir the forbidden desires of others and arouse the ambivalent conflict within them. Most exceptional positions and exceptional conditions are of this kind and have this dangerous power. The king or chief arouses envy of his privileges; perhaps everyone would like to be king. The dead, newborn children, incapacitated women, all act as incitements because of their specific forms of helplessness, and the individual who has just reached sexual maturity incites with the promise of fresh pleasure. For that reason all these individuals and all these states are taboo, because temptation must not be yielded to.

Now we also understand why it is that the *mana* forces of various individuals are able to neutralize one another, and can partially cancel one another out. The taboo of a king is too strong for his subject because the social difference between them is too great. But a minister, for example, can act as a harmless mediator between them. Translated from the language of taboo into that of normal psychology, this means that the subject who fears the tremendous temptation that comes from contact with the king, is able to endure dealings with the official whom he does not need to envy so much, and whose position may even seem to be attainable for him. The minister, for his part, is able to moderate his envy towards the king by bearing in mind the power that has been bestowed upon him. In this way minor differences in the magic power that leads into temptation are less to be feared than unusually large differences.

It is equally clear why the violation of certain taboo prohibitions represents a social danger that must be punished or expiated by all members of society if it is not to damage everyone. This danger really exists, if we replace unconscious desires with conscious impulses. It consists in the possibility of imitation, in consequence of which society would quickly collapse. If others did not punish the violation, they would be forced to acknowledge that they wanted to do the same thing as the evil-doer.

We should not be surprised to discover that contact plays a similar role in the taboo prohibition as it does in *délire de toucher*, although the secret meaning of the prohibition in the taboo cannot be so specific as it is in neurosis. Contact is the beginning of act of possession, of all attempts to put a person or a thing to one's own use.

We have translated the contagious power within the taboo into the aptitude to lead into temptation, to incite imitation. This does not seem to accord with the fact that the contagious quality of taboo is expressed above all in its transference to objects which thus become bearers of the taboo themselves.

This transferability of taboo reflects the inclination, seen in neurosis, of the unconscious drive to be displaced along associative channels to constantly new objects. In this way we are made aware that the dangerous magic power of *mana* corresponds to two real faculties, the aptitude of reminding man of his forbidden desires, and the apparently more significant one of leading him to violate the prohibition in the service of his desires. But these two functions combine into a single entity if we assume that it is in accord with the life of the primitive mind for the awakening of a memory of the forbidden action to be connected with an awakening of the inclination to perform that action. In that case memory and temptation coincide once again. One would also have to admit that if the example of a person who has violated a prohibition seduces another to do the same, then disobedience of the prohibition has propagated itself like a contagion, just as the taboo is transferred from a person to an object and from that object to another.

If the violation of a taboo can be made good by an atonement or act of penance, which would mean the *renunciation* of a certain possession or a freedom, this proves that compliance with the taboo regulation was itself a renunciation of something keenly desired. The omission of one renunciation was cancelled out by another renunciation elsewhere. This would lead us to conclude that, as far as the taboo ceremonial is concerned, penance is more primal than purification.

Let us now summarize the understanding of taboo that we have reached by equating it with the obsessive prohibition of the neurotic: taboo is an ancient prohibition, imposed (by an authority) from without, and directed against the strongest wishes of mankind. The desire to violate it strongly persists in the unconscious; people who comply with a taboo have an ambivalent attitude towards that which is affected by it. The magical power attributed to the taboo can be traced to the ability to lead people into temptation; it behaves like a contagion because the example is contagious, and because the forbidden desire is displaced on to something else in the unconscious. Atonement for the violation of a taboo by a renunciation proves that renunciation is the basis of observance of the taboo.

3

We should now like to examine what validity there may be in our equation of taboo with obsessive neurosis, and in the conception of taboo based on this comparison. Clearly, our conception is valid only if it offers us an advantage that could not be had in any other way, if it permits a greater understanding of taboo than would otherwise be possible. We might perhaps be inclined to assert that we have already delivered this proof of usability in what we have said above; but we shall have to attempt to reinforce it by continuing the explanation of individual taboo prohibitions and practices.

But another path is also open to us. We can examine whether some of the preconditions that we have transferred from neurosis to taboo, or some of the conclusions that we have reached in the process, might not be demonstrated directly in taboo phenomena. We need only decide what it is that we wish to look for. The assertion that the origin of taboo lies in an ancient prohibition, which was once imposed from without, is of course impossible to prove. So we shall instead attempt to confirm the psychological conditions for taboo with which we have become acquainted in relation to obsessive neurosis. How did we acquire our knowledge of these psychological factors in neurosis? Through the analytical study of symptoms, above all of compulsive actions, defensive measures and obsessive commands. It was here that we found the strongest indications of their origin in *ambivalent* impulses or tendencies, whereby they represented either the wish and the counter-wish simultaneously, or predominantly in the service of one of two opposing tendencies. If we now succeeded in demonstrating the prevalence of ambivalence, of opposing tendencies, in taboo regulations as well, or in finding some among them which simultaneously expressed both currents after the fashion of compulsive acts, we should almost have established what is effectively the most important part of the psychological correspondence between taboo and obsessive neurosis.

As I have mentioned above, the two fundamental taboo prohibitions are inaccessible to our analysis because they belong to totemism; another part of the taboo regulations is of secondary origin, and not useful for our purposes. Taboo has in fact become the general form of legislation among the peoples in question, and has been placed at the service of social tendencies which are certainly younger than taboo itself, as, for example, the taboos imposed by chiefs and priests in order to acquire property and privileges. But this leaves a large group of laws upon which we can perform our investigation; from these I would select the taboos attached *a)* to enemies, *b)* to chiefs, and *c)* to the dead, and will take the material for examination from J. G. Frazer's excellent collection in his great work *The Golden Bough*.[14]

a) The treatment of enemies

Inclined as we may have been to attribute to the savage and semi-savage peoples uninhibited and remorseless cruelty towards their enemies, we may be very interested to learn that the killing of a human being forces even these peoples to follow a series of laws that are considered to be among the taboo customs. These laws are easily divided into four groups: they require 1) the propitiation of the murdered enemy, 2) restrictions and 3) acts of expiation, purification of the slayer and 4) certain ceremonial undertakings. Our imperfect information makes it impossible for us to tell how universal or individual such taboo customs may be among these peoples, although at the same time the issue is irrelevant to our interest in these matters. We may still assume that these are widespread customs rather than isolated peculiarities.

Propitiation customs on the island of Timor, after the return of a victorious expeditions with the severed heads of the defeated foe, are of particular importance because the leader of the expedition is also subject to severe restrictions (see below): 'from another account of the ceremonies performed on the return of a successful head-hunter in the same island we learn that sacrifices are offered on this occasion to appease the soul of the man whose head has been taken; the people think that some misfortune would befall the victor were such offerings omitted. Moreover, a part of the ceremony consists of a dance accompanied by a song, in which the death of the slain man is lamented and his forgiveness is entreated. "Be not angry," they say, "because your head is here with us; had we been less lucky, our heads might now have been exposed in your village. We have offered the sacrifice to appease you. Your spirit may now rest and leave us at peace. Why were you our enemy? Would it not have been better that we should remain friends? Then your blood would not have been spilt and your head would not have been cut off."'[15]

Similar observances are seen among the Paloo in Celebes; the Galla sacrifice to the spirits of their slain enemies before they enter their home village. (From Paulitschke: *Ethnographie Nordostafrikas* ['The Ethnography of North-East Africa'].)

Other peoples have found the means to turn their former enemies into friends, guards and protectors after their death. It consists in the affectionate treatment of the severed heads, as boasted by certain savage tribes in Borneo. When the Sea Dyaks of Sarawak bring home a head from a warlike expedition, it is treated with the most exquisite kindness for several months, and addressed with the most tender names in the language. The best morsels from the people's meals are placed in its mouth, as are delicacies and cigars. The head is repeatedly implored to hate its former friends, and to give its love to its new hosts, since it is now one of them. We would be very much mistaken in attributing any of this treatment, appalling as it seems to us, to mockery.[16]

Observers of several of the savage tribes of North America have been struck by the mourning of the slain and scalped enemy. When a Choctaw had killed an enemy, he began a period of mourning lasting several months, during which he subjected himself to severe restrictions. The Dakota Indians mourned in a similar way. When the Osaga, a source observes, had mourned their own dead, they then mourned the enemy as though he had been a friend.[17]

Before we go into the other classifications of taboo customs concerning the treatment of enemies, we must respond to a pertinent objection. The motivation behind these propitiatory laws, some will argue with Frazer and others, is simple enough, and has nothing to do with 'ambivalence'. These people are governed by a superstitious fear of the spirits of the slain, a fear which was not alien to the people of classical antiquity, and which the great British dramatist brought on to the stage in the hallucinations of Macbeth and Richard III. We may confidently deduce all propitiatory laws from this superstition, as well as the restrictions and expiations that we shall discuss below; this view finds support in the ceremonies brought together in the fourth group, which can be interpreted only as attempts to drive away the spirits of the slain which are pursuing their slayers.[18] The savages willingly admit their fear of the spirits of the slain enemies, and trace back the taboo customs to that fear.

This objection is indeed a pertinent one, and if it were also adequate, we could spare ourselves the trouble of attempting to find an explanation. We shall postpone consideration of it, and for the time being only contrast it with the view that derives from the assumptions of our previous discussions of taboo. From all these laws we may conclude that they express impulses towards the enemy which are not purely hostile in nature. They allow us to glimpse manifestations of remorse, of esteem for the enemy, of a guilty conscience at having killed him. It seems to us in fact as though the commandment 'Thou shalt not kill', which cannot be violated with impunity, was alive even among these savages long before any legislation was received from the hands of a god.

Let us now return to the other kinds of taboo regulations. The *restrictions* placed upon the victorious murderer are uncommonly frequent and generally severe. In Timor (cf. the propitiatory customs mentioned above) the expedition leader may not return to his house under any circumstances. A special hut is erected for him, in which he spends two months obeying various purification laws. During that time he may not see his wife, or feed himself; another person must put his food in his mouth.[19] In some Dyak tribes, men returning from a successful warlike expedition must spend a few days apart from everyone else, and abstain from certain foodstuffs. They may not touch iron, and must stay away from their wives. In Logea, an island near New Guinea, men who have killed the enemy or have witnessed their killing, lock themselves in their houses for a week. They avoid any contact with their wives and their friends, they do not touch food with their hands and eat only plants that are boiled up for them in special vessels. The reason given for this last restriction is that they may not smell the blood of the slain; otherwise they would fall ill and die. Among the Toaripi or Motumoto tribe in New Guinea a man who has killed another may not come near his wife or touch food with his fingers. He receives special food from the hands of others. This lasts until the next new moon.

I shall not, as Frazer does, give a full list of the cases of restrictions imposed upon the victorious murderer, and will single out only those examples in which the taboo character is particularly striking, or the restriction is associated with penance, purification and ceremonial.

Among the Monumbo of German New Guinea, anyone who has killed an enemy in battle is 'unclean'; the word used for this is the same as the one applied to women during menstruation or confinement. He is not permitted to leave the men's clubhouse for a long time, while his fellow villagers gather around him and celebrate his victory with songs and dances. He is not allowed to touch anyone, not even his own wife and his children; if he did so, they would be afflicted with boils. He is then purified by washing and other ceremonials.

Among the Natchez in North America, young warriors who had captured their first scalp were required to undergo certain deprivations for six months. They were not allowed to sleep with women or eat meat, and were fed only on fish and maize pudding. If a Choctaw had killed and scalped an enemy, a month-long period of mourning began for him, during which he was not permitted to comb his hair. If his head itched, he was not allowed to scratch it with his hand, but used a small stick.

If a Pima Indian had killed an Apache, he had to submit to severe ceremonies of purification and expiation. During a six-day fast, he was not permitted to touch meat and salt, look at a burning fire or talk to a single human being. He lived alone in the forest, served by an old woman who brought him small amounts of food, he bathed often in the nearest river and wore – as a sign of mourning – a clump of mud on his head. On the seventeenth day the public ceremony of solemn purification of the man and his weapons took place. As the Pima Indians took the taboo on the killer much more seriously than their enemies did, and were not inclined, as their enemies were, to put off atonement and purification until after the end of the campaign, their military prowess suffered greatly from their moral rigour or, if one prefers, their piety. Despite their extraordinary courage, they proved to be unsatisfactory allies to the Americans in their battles against the Apaches.

As interesting as the details and variations in the atonement and purification ceremonies following the killing of an enemy might be for a more searching study, I shall say no more about them here because they cannot give us any fresh points of view. Perhaps I should add that the temporary or permanent isolation of the professional hangman, which has persisted into our modern age, belongs in this context. The position of the public executioner in medieval society actually gives a good idea of the 'taboo' of savages.[20]

The current explanation of all these laws of propitiation, restriction, atonement and purification is based on two principles: the extension of taboo from the dead to everything that has come into contact with him, and fear of the spirit of the slain man. How these two elements should be combined in order to explain the ceremonial, whether they should be seen as being of equal status, whether one might be primary and the other secondary, and which is which, is not stated anywhere, and the question would be difficult to resolve. On the other hand, we stress the unified nature of our interpretation by deducing all of these regulations from the ambivalence of emotional impulses towards the enemy.

b) *The taboo of rulers*

The behaviour of primitive peoples towards their chiefs, kings and priests is governed by two principles which seem to complement rather than to contradict one another. 'He must not only be guarded, he must also be guarded against.'[21] Both of these precepts are fulfilled through a large number of taboo regulations. We have already seen why one must guard against rulers: because they are the bearers of that mysterious and dangerous magic power which is conveyed through touch like an electric charge, and which brings death and decay to anyone unprotected by a similar charge. One therefore avoids any direct or indirect contact with this dangerous holiness, and where such contact is unavoidable a ceremonial is found in order to avert the feared consequences. The Nuba of East Africa, for example, believe that they will die if they enter the house of their priest-king, but that they will escape this danger if they bare their left shoulder upon entry, and cause the king to touch it with his hand. This sees the introduction of the curious notion that the king's touch becomes a means of healing and protection against the dangers that come from the king's touch, but this probably has to do with the healing power of deliberate touch on the part of the king, as against the danger of touching him, in other words, the conflict between passivity and activity towards the king.

Where the healing effect of the royal touch is concerned, we do not need to seek our examples among savages. Not so long ago, the kings of England practised this power upon scrofula, which for that very reason bore the name 'The King's Evil'. Queen Elizabeth did not shirk this piece of her royal prerogative any more than did any of her later successors. In 1633, Charles I is said to have healed a hundred sick people at one stroke. It was under his dissolute son Charles II, after the defeat of the great English Revolution, that royal healings of scrofula enjoyed their greatest vogue.

Charles II is said to have touched a hundred thousand scrofulous people in the course of his reign. On such occasions, the crowd of those in search of healing tended to be so great that once instead of being cured, six or seven of them were crushed to death. The sceptical William III of Orange, who became king of England after the banishment of the Stuarts, refused to practise this magic; the only time he deigned to touch a patient in this way, he did so with the words, 'God give you better health and more sense.'[22]

The following account may bear witness to the terrible effect of touch when, even inadvertently, one becomes active *against* the king or against that which belongs to him. A chief of high rank and great holiness in New Zealand once left the remains of his meal by the roadside. Along came a slave, a strapping young hungry fellow, saw the leftovers and set about eating them. Hardly had he finished when a shocked onlooker told him that what he had just devoured had been the chief's meal. This man had been a strong and courageous warrior, but as soon as he had heard this news he collapsed, suffered terrible spasms and died around sunset the following day.[23] A Maori woman had eaten certain fruits and then learned that they came from a place with a taboo upon it. She cried out that the spirit of the chief whom she had insulted in this way would certainly kill her. That happened in the afternoon, and the following day at twelve o'clock she was dead.[24] A Maori chief's cigarette lighter was once responsible for the deaths of several people. The chief had lost it, other people found it and used it to light their pipes. When they learned who the lighter belonged to, they died of fright.[25]

It should come as no surprise if there was felt to be a need to isolate such dangerous individuals as chiefs and priests from everyone else, to erect a wall around them, behind which they were out of reach of the others. We may be dimly aware that this wall, originally built out of taboo regulations, continues to exist today in the form of court ceremonial.

But perhaps the greater part of this taboo of rulers is not

traceable to the need of guarding *against* them. The other point of view in the treatment of privileged individuals, the need to guard them against the dangers which threaten them, very clearly played a part in the creation of the taboo and thus in the origin of court etiquette.

The need to protect the king against all conceivable dangers arises from his very great importance for the weal and woe of his subjects. Strictly speaking, it is his person that regulates the running of the world; his people have him to thank not only for the rain and sunshine that allow the fruits of the earth to flourish, but also for the wind that brings ships to their coast and the solid ground upon which they place their feet.[26]

These savage kings are equipped with an abundance of power and an ability to bestow fortune that is the innate property only of gods; in later stages of civilization, only the most servile of their courtiers would pretend to believe in such qualities.

It seems an obvious contradiction that individuals who possess such absolute power themselves require the greatest care to be protected against the dangers that threaten them, but it is not the only contradiction which appears in the treatment of royal individuals by savages. These peoples also consider it necessary to watch over their kings in order to ensure that they use their powers in the right way; they are by no means certain of their good intentions or their conscientiousness. There is a hint of mistrust mixed in with the motivation of the taboo regulations concerning the king. 'The idea that early kingdoms are despotisms', writes Frazer[27] 'in which the people exist only for the sovereign, is wholly inapplicable to the monarchies we are considering. On the contrary, the sovereign in them exists only for his subjects; his life is only valuable so long as he discharges the duties of his position by ordering the course of nature for his people's benefit. So soon as he fails to do so, the care, the devotion, the religious homage which they had hitherto lavished on him cease and are changed into hatred and contempt; he is dismissed ignominiously, and may be thankful if he escapes with his life. Worshipped as a god one day, he is killed as a criminal the next. But in this changed behaviour of the people there is nothing capricious or inconstant. On the contrary, their conduct is entirely of a piece. If their king is their god, he is or should be also their pre-server; and if he will not preserve them, he must make way for another who will. So long, however, as he answers their expecta-tions, there is no limit to the care which they take of him, and which they compel him to take of himself. A king of this sort lives hedged in by a ceremonious etiquette, a network of prohibitions and obser-vances, of which the intention is not to contribute to his dignity, much less to his comfort, but to restrain him from conduct which, by disturbing the harmony of nature, might involve himself, his people and the universe in one common catastrophe. Far from adding to his comfort, these observances, by trammelling his every act, annihilate his freedom and often render the very life, which it is their object to preserve, a burden and sorrow to him.'

One of the most glaring examples of this binding and paralysis of a holy ruler by the taboo ceremonial appears to have been achieved by the life of the Mikado of Japan as it was lived in former centuries. One description, that is now over two hundred years old,[28] relates: '(The Mikado) thinks that it would be very prejudicial to his dignity and holiness to touch the ground with his feet; for this reason, when he intends to go anywhere, he must be carried thither on men's shoulders. Much less will they suffer that he should expose his sacred person to the open air, and the sun is not thought worthy to shine on his head. There is such a holiness ascribed to all the parts of his body that he dares to cut off neither his hair, nor his beard, nor his nails. However, lest he should grow too dirty, they may clean him in the night when he is asleep; because, they say, that which is taken from his body at that time, hath been stolen from him, and that such a theft doth not prejudice his holiness or dignity. In ancient times, he was obliged to sit on the throne for some hours every morning, with the imperial crown on his head, but to sit altogether like a statue, without stirring either hands or feet, head or eyes, nor indeed any part of his body, because, by this means, it was thought that he could preserve peace and tranquillity in his empire; for if, unfortunately, he turned himself on one side or the other, or if he looked a good while towards any part of his dominions, it was apprehended that war, famine, fire or some other great misfortune was near at hand to desolate the country.'

Some of the taboos to which barbarian kings are subject vividly recall the restrictions imposed upon murderers. On Shark Point near Cape Padron in Lower Guinea (West Africa), a priest-king, Kukulu, lives alone in a forest. He is not allowed to touch a woman, or to leave his house, or even to rise from his throne, on which he must sleep sitting down. Were he to lie down, the wind would cease and navigation would be disturbed. It is his function to keep storms in check, and in general to ensure an evenly healthy condition in the atmosphere.[29] The more powerful a king of Loango is, according to Bastian, the more taboos he must observe. The successor to the throne is also bound to them from childhood, but they accumulate around him as he grows; at the moment when he ascends the throne he is suffocated by them.

We do not have sufficient space, and our interest does not require us, to go any further in our description of the taboos attached to the status of king or priest. Let us add that restrictions on freedom of movement and diet play the most important part among them. But two examples of taboo ceremonial, which are taken from civilized peoples, and therefore from far higher stages of civilization, demonstrate the extent to which association with these privileged individuals tends to preserve ancient customs.

The Flamen Dialis, the high priest of Jupiter in ancient Rome, had to observe an extraordinarily large number of taboo commandments. He was not permitted to ride, to see a horse or an armed man, to wear a ring that was not broken, have a knot in his garments, touch wheat-flour or leavened bread, or even call a goat, a dog, raw meat, beans or ivy by their name. His hair could only be cut by a free man with a bronze knife, his hair and nail-clippings had to be buried under a lucky tree; he was not permitted to touch a corpse, stand bare-headed under the open sky, and so on. In addition his wife, the Flaminica, had her own prohibitions: she was not allowed to climb more than three steps up a particular kind of stair, or comb her hair on certain feast days; the leather in her shoes could not be taken from an animal that had died a natural death, but only from one that had been slaughtered or sacrificed; if she heard thunder, she was unclean until she had made an expiatory sacrifice.[30]

The ancient kings of Ireland were subject to a series of very strange restrictions, the maintenance of which was expected to provide all blessing, while their infringement would bring evil upon the land. The complete list of these taboos is contained in the *Book of Rights*, the oldest manuscript copies of which bear the dates 1390 and 1418. The prohibitions are extremely detailed, concerning certain activities in certain places and at particular times; the king may not stay in a particular town on a particular weekday, may not cross a river at a particular hour, may not camp on a particular plain for a full nine days, and so on.[31]

For many savage peoples, the harshness of the taboo restrictions for priest-kings had a consequence which is both historically significant and particularly interesting from our point of view. The status of priest-king ceased to be something desirable; those about to attain it often used any means available to them to escape it. Thus in Cambodia, where there are fire and water kings, force is often required to compel successors to accept the honour. On Niue or Savage Island, a coral island in the Pacific Ocean, the monarchy actually came to an end because no one could be found who was prepared to assume the responsible and dangerous office. In some parts of West Africa, a secret council is held after the death of the king, to determine his successor. The person chosen is grabbed and bound and held in custody in the fetish-house until he has declared himself willing to accept the crown. Sometimes the presumptive successor to the throne finds ways and means to escape the honour planned for him; it is said of one chief, for example, that he used to carry weapons day and night in order to resist any attempt to put him on the throne.[32] Among the Negroes of Sierra Leone, refusal to accept regal status became so great that most tribes were obliged to recruit their kings from outside.

It is to this situation that Frazer traces the fact that as history evolved the original priest-kingship was divided into a spiritual and a secular power. The kings, oppressed by the burden of their sanctity, became incapable of exerting their rule where real matters were concerned, and had to leave that role to inferior but executive individuals who were prepared to renounce the honours of royalty. From these there then arose the secular rulers, while the now effectively insignificant spiritual overlordship remained with the former taboo kings. The extent to which this arrangement is confirmed in the history of old Japan is well known.

Consideration of the picture of relations between primitive people and their rulers suggests that it will not be difficult to advance from a description to a psychoanalytic interpretation. These relations are very complex in nature, and are not without their contradictions. Rulers are granted great privileges, which almost perfectly complement the taboo prohibitions imposed on everyone else. They are privileged individuals; they are allowed to do or consume that which is withheld from others by taboo. But this freedom is restricted by other taboos which do not oppress ordinary individuals. Here, then, is the first conflict, almost a contradiction, between an increase in freedom and an increase in restrictions for the same individuals. They are believed to have extraordinary magical powers, and for that reason people fear contact with them or their property, while at the same time expecting the most beneficial effect from that contact. The touch that comes from the king himself, with benevolent intent, is healing and protecting; but when the common man touches the king and regal things, his touch is a dangerous one, probably because it might suggest a tendency towards aggression. Another contradiction, and one not so easily resolved, is expressed in the attribution to the ruler of great power over natural processes, and in the fact that his subjects still feel obliged to protect him with particular care against any dangers that might threaten him, as though his own power, which is capable of so much, were unable to do that. The situation is rendered even more difficult by the fact that the ruler is not trusted to use his vast power correctly, to the advantage of his subjects as well as for his own protection; consequently he is mistrusted, and it is believed that watch must be kept over him. All of these intentions, exerting one's will over the king, protecting him against dangers and protecting his subjects against the danger that he brings to them, are at the same time served by the taboo etiquette to which the king's life is subject.

The most obvious way to explain the complicated and contradictory attitude of primitive people to their rulers would seem to be the following: for superstitious and other reasons, many different tendencies are expressed in the treatment of kings, each of them taken to an extreme without regard for the others. This then gives rise to all the contradictions, by which, incidentally, the savage intellect is no more repelled than is the intellect of highly civilized people when dealing solely with relations established by religion or 'loyalty'.

That is fine as far as it goes, but psychoanalytic technique enables us to penetrate more deeply into these relations, and will be able tell us more about the nature of these different tendencies. In order to subject the facts described to analysis, as though they were, so to speak, part of the symptomatology of a neurosis, we will turn first of all to the excess of anxious concern that is used to explain the taboo ceremonial. In neurosis, and particularly in the obsessive neurosis which is our primary point of comparison, the appearance of such excessive tenderness is very common. We have reached a very good understanding of its origin. It appears wherever, alongside the predominant tenderness, there is an opposite, unconscious current of hostility, and the typical case of an ambivalent emotional attitude is produced as a result. Then hostility is drowned out by an exaggerated intensification of tenderness, which is manifested as anxiety, and which becomes compulsive because it would not otherwise be able to keep the unconscious counter-current in a repressed state. Every psychoanalyst has experienced the certainty with which this anxious excess of tenderness, in the most improbable situations (between mother and child, or among affectionate married couples) can be explained in this way. Applied to the treatment of privileged individuals, it would reveal that their veneration, indeed their deification, is opposed by an intense hostile current in the unconscious, and it is consequently here, as we expected, that the situation of the ambivalent emotional attitude comes into being. According to this interpretation, the mistrust which seems inevitably to contribute to the motivation of the royal taboo, is another, more direct manifestation of the same unconscious hostility. Indeed, the final outcomes of such conflicts display such diversity among different peoples that there is no shortage of examples in which such hostility would be more easily demonstrated. The savage Timme of Sierra Leone, we read in Frazer,[33] claim the right to thrash their chosen king the evening before his coronation, and they adhere so thoroughly to this constitutional privilege that on occasion the unfortunate ruler does not survive his elevation to the throne by very long, so that the elders of the people have made it a rule, if they bear a grudge against a particular man, to choose him as their king. Nonetheless, even in such glaring cases the hostility will not be acknowledged as such, but will be treated as part of the ceremonial.

Another aspect of the attitude of primitive people towards their rulers brings to mind a process which, generally widespread in neurosis, becomes clearly apparent in so-called delusions of persecution. Here the significance of an individual is elevated to an extraordinary degree, and his omnipotence increased to an improbable level so that responsibility for anything adverse which occurs to the patient may be placed upon his shoulders. Savages are, in fact, treating their kings in a similar fashion by attributing to them power over rain and sunshine, wind and weather, and then dethroning or killing them because nature has disappointed their expectations of a good hunt or a rich harvest. The model which the paranoiac recreates in delusions of persecution lies in the child's relationship to its father. Such an abundance of power is regularly attributed to the father in the son's vision of him, and it becomes apparent that mistrust of the father is profoundly connected with the high esteem in which he is held. If the paranoiac identifies an individual connected to his life as his 'persecutor', he is thus elevating that person to the position of father, placing him in the conditions that allow him to hold him responsible for every misfortune that he experiences. Thus this second analogy between the savage and the neurotic may allow us to gauge how much in the relationship of the savage towards his ruler derives from the infantile attitude of the child to its father.

But we will find the strongest grounds for our view, seeking comparisons between taboo prohibitions and neurotic symptoms, in the taboo ceremonial itself, whose importance for the position of the king was discussed above. This ceremonial unmistakably reveals a double meaning and an origin in ambivalent tendencies, as long as we are willing to accept that it intended the effects that it produces from the very beginning. It not only distinguishes kings and elevates them above all ordinary mortals, it also makes their life a torment and an unbearable burden, and forces them into a kind of serfdom which is far worse than that of their subjects. It thus seems to us to be the correct counterpart to the compulsive activity of neurosis, in which the suppressed drive and the drive suppressing it meet in a simultaneous and common satisfaction. The compulsive act is supposedly a protection against the forbidden act; but we should say that it is actually the repetition of the forbidden. Here the 'supposedly' addresses itself to the conscious, the 'actually' to the unconscious agency of psychical life. Thus the taboo ceremonial of kings is supposedly their highest honour and safeguard, and actually punishment for their elevation, the revenge that their subjects take upon them. The experiences that Cervantes' Sancho Panza undergoes as governor on his island have clearly led him to recognize this understanding of court ceremonial as the only appropriate one. It is quite possible that this point would receive corroboration if we were able to make today's kings and rulers speak on the subject.

Why the emotional attitude towards rulers should contain so powerful an unconscious share of hostility is a very interesting problem, but one that goes beyond the scope of this paper. We have already referred to the infantile father complex; let us add that an investigation of the early history of kingship would bring us the crucial explanations. According to Frazer's impressive, but, by his own admission, not entirely convincing considerations, the first kings were outsiders, destined after a short period of rule to a sacrificial death at solemn feasts as representatives of the deity.[34]

According to this account, the myths of Christianity are touched by the after-effect of this history of the evolution of kings.

c) *The taboo of the dead*

We know that the dead are powerful rulers; we will perhaps be surprised to learn that they are thought of as enemies.

The taboo of the dead demonstrates, if we may stick to the comparison with illness, a particular virulence among most primitive peoples. It is expressed first of all in the consequences that touching the dead entails, and in the treatment of those mourning the dead. Among the Maori, anyone who had touched a corpse or taken part in its burial was extremely unclean, and effectively cut off from all intercourse with his fellow men; he was, so to speak, boycotted. He could not enter a house, or approach a person or a thing, without infecting it with the same quality. Indeed, he was not even permitted to touch food with his hands, which had become effectively unusable because of his unclean status. His food was placed on the floor in front of him, and all he could do was to try and consume it as best he could with his lips and teeth, while holding his hands bent behind his back. On occasion it was permitted for another person to feed him, and that person would do so with his arms outstretched, careful not to touch the wretched man himself. This helper was then himself subject to restrictions not much less oppressive than the man's own. In every village there was a very dissolute character, cast out of society, who lived in the most miserable fashion on the small amount of alms he was given. This creature alone was permitted to approach, at arm's length, the person who had performed the final duty towards a deceased person. But once the period of exclusion was past, the person rendered unclean by the corpse was once again permitted to mingle among his comrades, all the crockery that he had used during that dangerous time was broken, and all the clothing he had worn discarded.

The taboo customs following physical contact with the dead are identical throughout Polynesia, Melanesia and in a part of Africa;

their most consistent aspect is the prohibition on touching food oneself, and the need, arising from this, to be fed by others. It is curious that in Polynesia, or perhaps only in Hawaii,[35] priest-kings were subjected to the same restrictions during the performance of sacred acts. Among the taboos of the dead in Tonga, the decline and gradual suspension of prohibitions through the power of the person's own taboo becomes very clearly apparent. Anyone who had touched the corpse of a dead chief was unclean for ten months; but if he himself was a chief, only for three, four or five months, according to the rank of the deceased; but if the corpse in question belonged to the deified supreme chief, even the most important chiefs became taboo for ten months. The savages firmly believed that anyone infringing such taboo regulations would inevitably fall gravely ill and die; they believed this so firmly that in the opinion of one observer no one had ever dared to discover whether the contrary might be the case.[36]

Essentially similar, but more interesting from our point of view, are the taboo restrictions on those individuals whose contact with the dead is to be understood in the extended sense, the mourning relatives, the widowers and widows. If we see the restrictions mentioned above merely as a typical expression of the virulence of the taboo and its capacity to spread, in those that we are about to discuss, the motives for the taboo glimmer through, both their supposed motives and those which we may see as being more profound, the real motives.

Among the Shuswap in British Columbia, widows and widowers must live apart from everyone else during their period of mourning; they may touch neither their own bodies nor their heads with their hands; no one else may employ any of the crockery that they use. No hunter will wish to approach the hut in which such mourners live, because that would bring him misfortune; if the shadow of a mourner fell upon him, he would fall ill. Mourners sleep on thornbushes, and surround their beds with them. The purpose of this last measure is to keep the spirit of the deceased away, and plainer still is probably the custom of the widow, reported of other North American tribes, to wear a piece of clothing made of dry grass for a while after her husband's death, in order to make herself inaccessible to the approach of the spirit. In this way the idea suggests itself to us that contact 'in the extended sense' is only understood as physical contact, as the spirit of the deceased does not shun his relatives, and does not cease to 'hover around' them during the period of mourning.

Among the Agutainos on Palawan, one of the Philippines, a widow may not leave her hut for the first seven or eight days after her husband's death, except at night when she does not expect to meet anyone. Anyone who looks at her runs the risk of dying immediately, and for that reason she herself warns people of her approach by striking the trees with a wooden staff every time she takes a walk; but those trees wither. The danger posed by such a widow may be explained by another observation. In the Mekeo district of British New Guinea a widower loses all rights as a citizen, and lives for a time as an outcast. He may not plant a garden, show himself in public, or walk in the village or on the road. He creeps around like a wild animal in the high grass or in the bushes, and must hide in the undergrowth if he sees anyone, but particularly a woman, approaching. This latter suggestion makes it easy for us to trace the danger of the widower or the widow back to the danger of *temptation*. The man who has lost his wife is supposed to avoid desiring a substitute; the widow has to battle against the same wishes, and may, besides, arouse the desires of other men as a stray woman. Any such substitute satisfaction runs counter to the meaning of mourning; it would inflame the wrath of the spirit.[37]

One of the most disconcerting, but also most informative, taboo customs of mourning among primitive people is the prohibition on uttering the *name* of the deceased. It is unusually widespread, it has undergone many different interpretations and had significant consequences.

Aside from the taboo practices of the Australians and Polynesians, where they tend to be seen in their best-preserved state, this prohibition is encountered among peoples so remote from one another, and so alien to each other, as the Samoyeds in Siberia and the Toda in South India, the Mongols of Tartary and the

Tuaregs of the Sahara, the Aino in Japan and the Akamba and Nandi in Central Africa, the Tinguans of the Philippines and the inhabitants of the Nicobar Islands, of Madagascar and Borneo.[38] Among some of these peoples, the prohibition and the consequences arising from it apply only during the period of mourning; among some it remains permanent, but in all cases it appears to pale the further away it is from the time of death.

The avoidance of the name of the deceased is generally enforced with extraordinary severity. Among some South American tribes it is considered the most serious insult to the bereaved to utter the name of their deceased relative in their presence, and the punishment imposed on this is no less than that set for an actual murder.[39] Why the mention of a name should be so abhorred is at first not easy to guess, but the dangers associated with it have allowed a whole series of sources of information to come into being, which are interesting and significant in a number of respects. Thus, for example, the Masai in Africa have hit upon the evasive strategy of changing the name of the deceased immediately after his death; he may now be mentioned by his new name without inhibition, while all prohibitions remained linked to the old name. It seems to be assumed that the spirit does not know his new name, and will not learn it. The Australian tribes of Adelaide and Encounter Bay are so consistent in their caution that after a death all individuals who had the same name or a similar one to that of the deceased change their name for another. Sometimes, as among certain tribes in Victoria and Northwest America, in a highly extended form of the same consideration, name-changes are undertaken by all relatives of the deceased, regardless of any similarity in their names. Indeed, among the Guaycuru in Paraguay, the chief tended to give new names to all members of the tribe on such sad occasions, which they then remembered as though they had borne them for ever.[40]

Furthermore, if the name of the deceased was the same as the term used for an animal, an object, etc, it seemed necessary to some of the peoples mentioned to rename those objects as well, so that they would not be reminded of the deceased when the words were used. That inevitably meant that vocabulary was constantly being changed, and this produced considerable difficulties for the missionaries, particularly where the prohibition of a name was permanent. In the seven years that the missionary Dobrizhoffer spent among the Abipon in Paraguay, the name for jaguar was changed three times, and the words for crocodile, thorns and the slaughter of animals had similar fates.[41] But the fear of uttering a name that previously belonged to a dead person also extends towards the avoidance of any mention of anything to do with that deceased, and one significant consequence of this process of suppression is that these peoples have no tradition or historical memories, and very great obstacles lie in the way of any investigation of their early history. But many of these primitive peoples have developed compensatory customs, reviving the names of the deceased after a long period of mourning by giving them to children who are considered as reincarnations of the dead.

The disconcerting aspect of this taboo on names fades when we bear in mind that where savages are concerned the name is a significant part and an important possession of the personality, and that they give the word full object status. Our children, as I have suggested elsewhere, do the same thing, in that they are never satisfied with the assumption of an insignificant verbal similarity, but consistently conclude that this resemblance must indicate a deep-rooted similarity between the name and its object. Even the civilized adult may guess from some peculiarities of his behaviour that he is not as far as he imagined from attributing the status of object to names, and feeling that his name has in a very particular way grown together with his personality. This is borne out by the fact that psychoanalytical practice often finds cause to refer to the meaning of names in unconscious thought.[42]

As we might have expected, then, obsessive neurotics behave exactly like savages in regard to names. Like other neurotics, they show all the 'complex sensitivity' to the utterance and hearing of certain words and names, and derive from their treatment of their own name a large number of inhibitions, often strict in nature. One such taboo patient whom I knew had taken to avoiding writing her name down, for fear that it might fall into the hands of someone who would thus come into possession of part of her personality. In the convulsive faithfulness with which she had to protect herself against the temptations of her imagination, she had established the commandment 'not to give anything of herself away'. This included first of all her name, and by extension her handwriting, and for that reason she finally abandoned writing altogether.

So we are no longer startled by the fact that savages consider the name of the dead person to be a piece of his personality, and make it the object of the taboo of the dead. The naming of the dead person can also be traced back to contact with him, and we may turn to the more comprehensive problem of why this contact is subject to such a strict taboo.

The most obvious explanation would refer to the natural horror that the corpse inspires, and the changes that are soon noticed in it. Mourning of the dead man must also be considered as a motive for everything connected with him. But clearly horror of the corpse does not account for every detail of the taboo regulations, and mourning can never explain to us why it is that any mention of the dead person is a severe insult to those left behind. Mourning prefers to deal with the deceased, to develop his memory and keep it alive for as long as possible. Something other than mourning must be made responsible for the unique features of taboo customs, something that clearly follows different intentions from mourning. Name taboos reveal this still unknown motive to us, and if the customs did not tell us as much, we would learn it from the statements of the mourning savages themselves. In fact they make no secret of the fact that they are *afraid* of the presence and the return of the spirit of the deceased; they practise a large number of ceremonies to keep it hence, to drive it away.[43] Uttering the name of the deceased seems to them to be a spell that will soon be followed by his presence.[44] For that reason they consistently do everything within their power to avoid such a spell, and such an awakening. They disguise themselves so that the spirit will not recognize them,[45] or else they distort his name or their own. They rage against the reckless stranger who has set the spirit upon its survivors. It is impossible to avoid reaching the conclusion that, as

Wundt puts it, they are suffering from the fear 'of his soul, which has become a demon'.[46]

This insight would have led us to a confirmation of Wundt's view, which, as we have heard, locates the essence of taboo in fear of demons.

The premise of this theory, that at the moment of his death the beloved family member becomes a demon from whom the survivors can expect nothing but hostility, and against whose evil desires they must protect themselves with all the means at their disposal, is so strange that one will at first find it difficult to believe. But almost all reliable authors agree in attributing this view to primitive people. Westermarck, who in my view does not pay nearly enough attention to taboo in his work *The Origin and Development of the Moral Ideas*, states in the section 'Regard for the Dead': 'Generally speaking, my collection of facts has led me to the conclusion that the dead are more commonly regarded as enemies than as friends,[47] and that Professor Jevons and Grant Allen are mistaken in their assertion that, according to early beliefs, the malevolence of the dead is for the most part directed against strangers only, whereas they exercise a fatherly care over the lives and fortunes of their descendants and fellow clansmen.'

Rudolf Kleinpaul, in an impressive book, has used the remains of ancient animist beliefs among civilized peoples to represent the relationship between the living and the dead.[48] According to Kleinpaul, this climaxes in the conviction that the dead murderously draw the living to them. The dead kill; the use of the skeleton to represent death in our own times demonstrates that death is only a dead person. The living person does not feel safe from the pursuit of the dead until he has put a separating stretch of water between them. For that reason the dead tended to be buried on islands, or were brought to the other side of a river. This is the source of our expressions such as 'here' and 'beyond'. A later modification restricted the malevolence of the dead to those categories that gave a particular right to a grievance, to the victims of murder, who pursue their murderer as evil spirits, and to those who died in unsatisfied longing, like brides. But originally, according to Kleinpaul, the dead were all vampires, they all bore grievances against the living and tried to harm them, to rob them of their life. It was the corpse that first supplied the concept of an evil spirit.

The assumption that the most beloved deceased transformed themselves into demons after death clearly leaves another question open. What led primitive people to attribute such a change of meaning to their beloved dead? Why did they turn them into demons? Westermarck believes this question is easily answered.[49] 'Death is commonly regarded as the gravest of all misfortunes; hence the dead are believed to be exceedingly dissatisfied with their fate. According to primitive ideas a person only dies if he is killed – by magic if not by force – and such a death naturally tends to make the soul revengeful and ill-tempered. It is envious of the living and is longing for the company of its old friends; no wonder, then, that it sends them diseases to cause their death. [. . .] But the notion that the disembodied soul is on the whole a malicious being constantly watching for an opportunity to do harm to the living is also, no doubt, intimately connected with the instinctive fear of the dead, which is in its turn the outcome of the fear of death.'

The study of psychoneurotic disorders refers us to a more comprehensive explanation, which also incorporates that of Westermarck.

If a woman has lost her husband, or a daughter her mother through death, in many cases the survivor may be afflicted with tormenting doubts, which we call 'obsessive reproaches', about whether she herself might not have been guilty of the death of the beloved person through carelessness or neglect. No memory of how carefully she tended the patient, no objective refutation of the claimed bestowal of guilt can put an end to the torment, which represents something like the pathological expression of mourning, and gradually fades away over time. The psychoanalytical examination of such cases has taught us about the secret mainsprings of this illness. We have learned that these obsessive reproaches are in a certain sense justified, and are only for that reason protected against refutation and objection. It is not as though the mourning woman really was responsible for the death, or really was guilty of the neglect, as the obsessive reproach claims; but there was something within her, a desire unconscious to her, which was not displeased by the death, and which would have brought it about if it had had the upper hand. The reproach of the loved one's death now reacts against this unconscious wish. Such hostility concealed behind tender love exists in almost all cases of intense emotional connection to a particular person, it is the classic case, the model for the ambivalence of human emotional impulses. Such ambivalence will be present in a person's disposition to varying degrees; normally there is not so much of it that it can give rise to the obsessive reproaches described above. But where it is present in abundance, it will manifest itself precisely in relation to the most beloved individuals, or where one would least expect it. We believe that the predisposition to obsessive neurosis, with which we have drawn such frequent comparisons in our discussion of taboo, is distinguished by a particularly high degree of such original emotional ambivalence.

We have now identified the factor that can explain the supposedly demonic nature of recently deceased souls, and the need to protect oneself against their hostility by means of taboo regulations. If we assume that the emotional lives of primitive people have a similarly high level of ambivalence to that which we attribute to people suffering from compulsive disorders on the basis of psychoanalytic study, it becomes understandable that after a painful loss a similar reaction against the latent hostility in the unconscious is necessary, as was demonstrated in this regard by obsessive reproaches. But this hostility, felt painfully in the unconscious as satisfaction about the death, has a different fate in primitive man; he defends himself against it by displacing it on to the object of hostility, the deceased. We call this defensive process, which occurs so frequently both in normal and in pathological mental life, a *projection*. The survivor is denying that he ever harboured hostile impulses against the late beloved; but the soul of the deceased harbours them now, and will struggle to activate them throughout the entire period of mourning. The punitive and penitential characteristic of this emotional reaction will be manifested, despite the fact that it has been successfully defended against through projection, in the patient being frightened, imposing renunciations upon himself and subjecting himself to restrictions, some of which are disguised as protective measures against the hostile demon. Conversely, we find that the taboo has grown up on the basis of an ambivalent emotional attitude. The taboo of the dead also derives from the opposition between the conscious pain and the unconscious satisfaction over the death. Given this origin of the grievances held by spirits, it is natural that the closest and formerly the most beloved surviving relatives have the most to fear.

Here again, taboo regulations behave in just as conflicting a manner as neurotic symptoms. On the one hand, through their restrictive character they express mourning, while on the other they very clearly reveal what they seek to conceal, the hostility towards the dead, which is now seen as self-defence. We have come to understand a certain proportion of the taboo prohibitions as a fear of temptation. The dead person is defenceless, that must prompt the hostile desires towards him, and this temptation must be countered by the prohibition.

But Westermarck is right in saying that in the conception of savages there is no difference between a violent and a natural death. For unconscious thought, even someone who has died a natural death is a murdered person; evil wishes killed him. (Cf. the next essay in this series: 'Animism, magic and the omnipotence of thoughts'.) Anyone interested in the origin and meaning of dreams of the death of dear relations (parents and siblings) will be able to observe, in the dreamer, the child and the savage, a perfect correspondence in the attitude towards the dead person, based on the same emotional ambivalence.

Above, we contradicted a view of Wundt's which located the essence of the taboo in the fear of demons, and yet we have just agreed with the explanation that traces the taboo of the dead back to a fear of the soul of the deceased which has now become a demon. That would seem to be a contradiction: but it will not be difficult for us to resolve it. We have indeed accepted demons, but we have not allowed them to remain something final which psychology is unable to analyse. We have, so to speak, got behind the demons by recognizing them as projections of the hostile emotions that survivors harbour against the dead.

The emotions which, according to our well-founded hypothesis, we have identified as conflicting – tender and hostile – towards the deceased attempt to bring both of these to the fore at the time of the loss, as mourning and as satisfaction. There must be a conflict between these two opposites, and since one part of this opposition, hostility, is either entirely or for the most part unconscious, the outcome of the conflict cannot consist in a subtraction of the two intensities one from another with the difference being used by consciousness, as one might, for example, forgive a beloved person an illness they had suffered. Rather, the process occurs through a particular psychical mechanism, which in psychoanalysis we are accustomed to calling *projection*. But the hostility about which we know nothing, and about which we wish to know nothing, is cast from inner perception into the outside world, freed in the process from the subject and laid upon others. It is not we, the survivors, who are now pleased to be free of the deceased; no, we mourn for him, but in a strange way he has become a wicked demon to which our misfortune would bring satisfaction, and who seeks to bring us death. The survivors must now defend themselves against this evil foe; they are relieved of their inner oppression, but have only swapped it for a distress from without.

It cannot be denied that this process of projection, which turns the deceased into evil enemies, borrows from real hostilities that we remember from them, and can really reproach them for. These could be their harshness, overbearing behaviour, unfairness or whatever else forms the background to even the most affectionate relationships between human beings. But this factor cannot simply help us to understand the projected creation of demons all on its own. The wrongs done by the deceased certainly contain part of the motivation for the hostility of the survivors, but they would not be effective if the latter did not develop this hostility all by themselves, and the moment of their death would certainly be the most inappropriate occasion to awaken a memory of the reproaches that one was justified in making towards them. We cannot do without unconscious hostility as the actual regularly active driving motive. This hostile current towards the nearest and dearest relatives could remain latent while they were alive, that is, it did not reveal itself to consciousness either directly or indirectly through some kind of substitute formation. With the demise of the individuals who were simultaneously loved and hated this was no longer possible, and the conflict became acute. The mourning that arose out of intensified tenderness became on the one hand more impatient with the latent hostility, while on the other hand it could allow a feeling of satisfaction to arise out of it. This led to the repression of unconscious hostility along the route of projection, in the formation of that ceremonial which expresses fear of punishment by demons, and as mourning progresses over time the conflict also loses intensity, so that the taboo of the dead is allowed to fade or to sink into oblivion.

4

Having thus cleared the ground on which the richly informative taboo of the dead has grown up, we are determined not to miss adding a few observations that might be significant for our understanding of taboo in general.

The projection of unconscious hostility on to demons in the taboo of the dead is only one individual example from a series of processes in which we must see the greatest influence on the formation of the psychical life of primitive people. In the case under consideration, projection serves to resolve an emotional conflict; it finds the same use in a large number of psychical situations leading to neurosis. But projection is not made for defence, it also comes into being where there are no conflicts. The outward projection of inner perceptions is a primitive mechanism upon which, for example, our sensory perceptions are based, and which thus normally has a large part to play in the formation of our outside world. Under conditions that have not yet been sufficiently well established, internal perceptions are also projected outwards by processes of thought and feeling, like sensory perceptions, and employed to arrange the outside world when they should remain within the inner world. This may at root have to do with the fact that the function of attentiveness was not originally turned towards the inner world, but towards stimuli flowing in from the outside world, and from endopsychical processes received only information about developments of pleasure and displeasure. Only with the formation of an abstract language of thought, by linking sensual remnants of verbal ideas with internal processes, did this itself gradually become amenable to perception. Until then, primitive man developed a picture of the outside world through the projection of internal perceptions, which we must now, with a stronger conscious perception, translate back into psychology.

The projection of the subject's own evil impulses on to demons is only one part of a system that has become the 'world-view' of primitive people, and with which we will become familiar in the next essay in this series as the 'animistic'. We will then have to establish the psychological characteristics of the formation of such a system, and in turn find our clues in the analysis of those system-formations that neuroses make available to us. We will provisionally guess only that the so-called 'secondary treatment' of the dream content is the model for all these system-formations. At the same time, let us not forget that from the stage of system-formation onwards there are two kinds of derivation for each act assessed by the consciousness, the systematic and the real but unconscious.[50]

Wundt[51] observes that 'among the effects that myth everywhere attributes to demons, first of all the *ominous* predominate, so that in the belief of these peoples, the evil demons are visibly older than the good ones'. Now it is very possible that the concept of the demon in general was gained from such a meaningful relationship with the dead. Over the further course of human development, the ambivalence within this relationship has then been expressed in the fact that it allowed two completely opposite psychical formations to emerge from a single root: a fear of demons and ghosts on the one hand, and ancestor worship on the other.[52] That the demons are always seen as the ghosts of the recently deceased confirms more than anything else the influence of mourning on the emergence of belief in demons. Mourning has a very particular psychical task to perform: it is to free the memories and expectations of the survivors from the dead. Once this work has taken place, the pain yields, and with it repentance and reproach, and for that reason also fear of the demon. But the same spirits that were initially feared as demons are now redefined in a more friendly sense, worshipped as ancestors and appealed to for help.

If we consider the relationship of survivors towards the dead over the changing course of time, it is unmistakably clear that their ambivalence has declined to an extraordinary degree. It is now easy to keep down the unconscious and still demonstrable hostility towards the dead, and no particular psychical effort is required for this. Where satisfied hatred and painful tenderness have been battling with one another, piety now rises like the formation of a scar, and demands this: *De mortuis nil nisi bonum*. It is only neurotics who are made gloomy by mourning over the loss of one of their dear ones through attacks of obsessive reproach, which, in psychoanalysis, reveal their secret to be the old ambivalent emotional attitude. Along which route this change is wrought, and the extent to which constitutional change and real improvement in family relationships play a part in their origin, need not be discussed here. But one could be led by this example to the hypothesis that *a higher degree of ambivalence should be attributed to the psychical impulses of primitive people than is to be found among civilized people living today. With the decline in this ambivalence the taboo, the symptom of compromise of the conflict of ambivalence, also slowly faded*. Of neurotics, who are compelled to reproduce this struggle and the taboo emerging from it, we would say that they have brought with them an archaistic constitution as an atavistic remnant, compensation for which forces them to such terrible psychical efforts in the service of the advance of civilization.

Let us at this point recall the information, confusing in its vagueness, which Wundt offered to us about the twofold meaning of the word taboo: sacred and unclean (see above). Originally the word taboo did not yet mean sacred and unclean, but referred to the demonic which must not be touched, and thus stressed an important feature shared by these two extreme terms, but the persistence of this shared property proves that between the two fields of the sacred and the unclean an original agreement prevails, which only later made way for a differentiation.

In contrast, we have no difficulty in deriving from our reflections the idea that the word 'taboo' has this double meaning from the very first, that it serves to describe a particular ambivalence and everything that has grown on the soil of this ambivalence. 'Taboo' itself is an ambivalent word, and in retrospect we think we might have been able to guess from the established meaning of the word something that was revealed as the result of lengthy investigation, namely that the taboo prohibition should be understood as the result of an emotional ambivalence. The study of the most ancient languages has taught us that there were once many such words which contained opposites within themselves, and which were, in a certain sense – if not entirely the same sense – as the word taboo, ambivalent.[53] Small modifications in the pronunciation of the antiphrastic primal word have later been used to create a separate linguistic expression for the two opposites united here.

The word 'taboo' had a different fate; with the declining importance of the ambivalence to which it refers, the word itself, or words similar to it, have vanished from the vocabulary. I hope, in a later context, to be able to show that behind the fate of this term there probably lurks a tangible historical transformation, that the word first attached to very particular human relationships, which included great emotional ambivalence, and that it was extended from here to other, similar relationships.

If we are not mistaken, the understanding of taboo also casts a light on the nature and origin of *conscience*. We can speak, without stretching the terms too far, of a taboo conscience and a taboo sense of guilt after an infringement of the taboo. The taboo conscience is probably the oldest form in which the phenomenon of conscience appears to us.

For what is 'conscience'? Linguistically it refers to that which one knows most consciously; in some languages the word is almost coterminous with consciousness.

Conscience is the inner perception of the repudiation of a wishful impulse within us; but the stress is on the fact that this repudiation needs to refer to nothing else, that it is conscious of itself. This becomes even clearer in the sense of guilt, the perception of the internal condemnation of such acts through which we have accomplished certain wish-impulses. An explanation here appears superfluous; anyone with a conscience must feel the justification of the condemnation, the reproach for the action performed within himself. But the same characteristic is apparent in the attitude of savages towards taboo; taboo is a commandment of conscience, its violation causes a terrible sense of guilt to arise, which occurs as a matter of course, while its origin remains unknown.[54]

So in all likelihood conscience also arises out of an emotional ambivalence, quite particular human relationships to which that ambivalence is attached, and under the conditions that we have shown to apply to taboo and to obsessive neurosis, that one part of the opposition is unconscious, and is preserved by the obsessive domination of the other. Much that we have learned from the analysis of neurosis bears out this conclusion. First of all, that in the character of the obsessive neurotic a trait of painful conscientiousness emerges as a reactive symptom against the temptation that lurks in the unconscious, and that as the illness intensifies the patient's sense of guilt reaches its highest levels. In fact we might dare to state that if we cannot explain the origin of the sense of guilt in obsessive neurotics, we have no prospect of discovering it at all. The task can be successfully resolved in the case of the neurotic individual; where whole peoples are concerned, we might expect to reach a similar solution.

Secondly, it must strike us that the sense of guilt has many of the qualities of anxiety; we are right in describing it as 'conscience anxiety'. But this anxiety directs us towards unconscious sources; we have learned from the psychological study of neuroses that if wishful impulses are subjected to repression, their libido is transformed into anxiety. We should also like to point out that there is something unknown and unconscious in the sense of guilt, namely the reasons for repudiation. The anxiety within the sense of guilt corresponds to just this unknown.

If taboo is expressed primarily in prohibitions, we might conceive an underlying positive current of desire, quite obvious and
requiring no extensive proof from analogy with neurosis. Because if
no one desires to do something, there is no need to prohibit it, and
in any case that which is most emphatically forbidden must be an
object of desire. If we were to apply this plausible thesis to our
primitive people, we would inevitably conclude that it is among
their strongest temptations to kill their kings and priests, to practise
incest, to mistreat their dead and so on. That hardly seems likely;
but we will encounter the most resolute contradiction if we measure
the same thesis against those cases in which we ourselves believe we
most clearly hear the voice of conscience. We would then maintain,
with the most complete certainty, that we do not feel the slightest
temptation to transgress any of these commandments, such as the
one to 'commit no murder', and that we would feel nothing but
revulsion at the idea of doing so.

But if we were to grant credence to the claims insisted upon by
our conscience, the prohibition would become superfluous – both
the taboo and our moral prohibition – while at the same time the
fact of conscience would be left unexplained and the connections
between conscience, taboo and neurosis would be absent; hence
we would be returned to the state of knowledge that pertains
today as long as we do not apply psychoanalytic viewpoints to the
problem.

If, on the other hand, we were to take into account what the
psychoanalysis of the dreams of healthy people has shown, that
the temptation to kill is stronger and occurs more frequently than
we imagine, even within ourselves, and that it expresses psychical
effects even where it does not announce its presence to our consciousness; and if, in the obsessive rules of certain neurotics, we
have also discerned the guarantees and self-punishments designed
to counter the intensified impulse to murder, we will attach even
greater importance to the thesis posited above: where a prohibition
is present, a desire must lie behind it. We shall take it that this
desire to murder is actually present in the unconscious, and that
taboo, like the moral prohibition, is psychologically by no means

superfluous, rather that it is explained and justified by the ambivalent attitude towards the murderous impulse.

The feature of this ambivalent attitude, which is as frequent as it is fundamental, that the positive, desiring current is unconscious, gives us a glimpse of further connections and possible explanations. The psychical processes in the unconscious are not entirely identical with the ones that we know from our conscious psychical life, but enjoy certain noteworthy freedoms that the latter now lack. An unconscious impulse need not necessarily have come into being where it finds its expression; it may come from somewhere else entirely, it may originally have related to other individuals and relationships, and reached the place where we notice it through the mechanism of *displacement*. Also, because of the indestructibility and lack of susceptibility to correction of unconscious processes, it may have survived from very early times, to which it was appropriate, into later times and conditions in which all of its manifestations are bound to seem strange. These are all merely hints, but a thorough account of them would show how important they can be for our understanding of the development of civilization.

To conclude these discussions, we cannot neglect to make an observation that will prepare for our further investigations below. While we may maintain the essential similarity between taboo prohibitions and moral prohibitions, we will not dispute that there must be a psychological difference between the two. An alteration in the conditions of the underlying ambivalence must explain why the prohibition no longer appears in the form of taboo.

So far, in our analytic consideration of taboo phenomena, we have taken our bearings from the demonstrable analogies that exist with obsessive neurosis. Taboo, however, is not a neurosis, but a social institution; thus we also find ourselves presented with the task of showing where it is that we might seek the principal difference between neurosis and a cultural form such as taboo.

Here again I should like to take a single fact as my starting-point. Primitive people generally fear that the transgression of a taboo will lead to punishment, usually a severe illness or death. The punishment threatens the person responsible for the transgression. This is not the case in obsessive neurosis. If the patient should carry out an action forbidden to him, he fears the punishment not for himself, but for another person who is generally left undefined, but can easily be shown, through analysis, to be one of those people dearest and closest to him. So the neurotic behaves as an altruist, and primitive man as an egoist. Only when the transgression of the taboo has not been spontaneously avenged in the wrong-doer does a collective feeling arise among the savages that they were all threatened by the crime, and they hurry to carry out the omitted punishment themselves. The mechanism behind this solidarity is easily explained. What is at work here is fear of the infectious example, of the temptation to imitate, of the contagious power of the taboo. If a single individual has succeeded in satisfying the repressed desire, all the other members of the community must feel the same desire. In order to suppress this temptation, the person who is actually envied for his satisfaction must be stripped of the fruit of his audacity, and the punishment itself often gives those imposing it the opportunity to commit the same sacrilegious act themselves. This is one of the foundations of the human penal code, and it is based, no doubt correctly, upon the similarity between the prohibited impulses in the criminal and those of the avenging society. Here psychoanalysis confirms what pious people tend to say, that we are all miserable sinners.

How then are we to explain the unexpected nobility of neurosis, which fears nothing for itself and everything for a loved one? Analytical investigation shows that it is not primary. Originally, which is to say, at the beginning of the illness, the threat of punishment hung over the individual himself, just as it did among primitive people; in both cases the subject feared for his own life; only later was the fear of death displaced on to another loved one. The process is relatively complex, but it can be grasped none the less. Underlying the formation of the prohibition there is regularly a bad impulse – a death-wish – directed against a beloved person. This is repressed by a prohibition, and the prohibition is linked to a certain act which effectively stands in, through displacement, for the hostile act against the beloved person, and the performance of this act is threatened with punishment by death. But the process goes further, and the original death-wish against the beloved other is then replaced by a fear of that person's death. So if neurosis proves to be so tenderly altruistic, it is only *compensating* for the opposite, underlying attitude of brutal egoism. We may use the term 'social' for those emotional impulses which are defined by care for another person without taking him as a sexual object. The recession of these social factors may be stressed as a fundamental trait of neurosis which is later concealed by over-compensation.

Without lingering over the origin of these social impulses and their relationship to other fundamental traits in man, we wish to reveal the second main feature of neurosis with reference to another example. In its manifestations, taboo has the greatest similarity with the fear of touching found among obsessive neurotics – *délire de toucher*. Now, in neurosis the prohibition regularly relates to sexual contact, and psychoanalysis has shown as a general rule that the drive-forces diverted and displaced in neurosis are sexual in origin. In taboo, the prohibited contact clearly has not only a sexual meaning, but the more general one of attack, of control, of self-assertion. If one is forbidden to touch the chief or anything that has been in contact with him, the same impulse is supposed to have imposed upon it an inhibition that is expressed on other occasions in keeping a suspicious watch upon the chief, indeed in his physical mistreatment before his coronation (see above). *Consequently the predominance of the sexual over the social drives is the characteristic feature of neurosis*. But the social drives have themselves arisen out of a merging of egoistic and erotic components into special entities.

From this single example, comparing taboo with obsessive neurosis, we can already guess the relationship between the individual forms of neurosis and cultural institutions, and in what respects the study of the psychology of neurosis is important for an understanding of the development of civilization.

On the one hand neuroses show striking and deep-rooted correspondences with the great social productions of art, religion and philosophy, while at the same time appearing as distortions of them. One might dare to suggest that hysteria is a distorted picture of an artistic creation, and obsessive neurosis a distorted picture of a philosophical system. This divergence can be traced back, in its final resolution, to the fact that neuroses are asocial formations; they attempt to achieve with private means something that has arisen in society through collective labour. In the analysis of the drives at work in neuroses we learn that it is drive-forces of sexual origin that exert the crucial influence, while the corresponding cultural formations are based on social drives, which have emerged from the fusion of egoistic and erotic elements. Sexual needs are not capable of bringing people together in the same way as the requirements of self-preservation; sexual satisfaction is primarily a private affair for the individual.

Genetically, the asocial nature of neurosis arises out of its most original tendency to flee from an unsatisfactory reality into a more pleasurable fantasy world. This real world, the one avoided by the neurotic, is dominated by the society of human beings and the institutions collectively created by them: to turn one's back on reality is at the same time to leave the human community.

Notes

1. Eleventh Edition, 1911. This article also includes the most important references.
2. This application of the taboo can be omitted as not originally belonging in this context.
3. In *Völkerpsychologie* [Folk Psychology], vol. II, '*Mythus und Religion*' [Myth and Religion], Part II, p. 301 ff.
4. Ibid., p. 237.
5. Cf. the first and the last essays in this book. [Essays I and IV of *Totem and Taboo*]
6. Wundt, op. cit., p. 307.
7. Ibid., p. 313.
8. [J. G.] Frazer, *The Golden Bough*, Part II, *Taboo and the Perils of the Soul*, 1911, p. 136.
9. Both, pleasure and prohibition, referred to touching one's own genitals.
10. The relationship with the loved ones who had issued the prohibition.

11. From an excellent expression of Bleuler's.

12. [The phrase in square brackets was left out from 1920 onwards, probably inadvertently.]

13. Cf. my study on totemism, already mentioned several times in these essays. (Chapter IV of this book.) [Essay IV of *Totem and Taboo*]

14. [Frazer, *The Golden Bough*] Third edition, Part II, *Taboo and the Perils of the Soul*, 1911.

15. Frazer, op. cit., [Part II] p. 166.

16. Frazer, [Part IV] *Adonis Attis, Osiris*, 1907, p. 248 – After Hugh Low, *Sarawak*, London, 1848.

17. J.O. Dorsey in Frazer, *Taboo* etc., [i.e. Part II] p. 181.

18. Frazer, *Taboo*, p. 169ff., p. 174. These ceremonies consist in beating with shields, shouting, roaring and creating noise with instruments, etc.

19. Frazer, *Taboo*, p. 166, after S. Müller, *Reizen en Onderzoekingen in den Indischen Archipel* [Travels and investigations in the Indian Archipelago], Amsterdam, 1857.

20. On these examples, see Frazer, *Taboo*, pp. 165–90, 'Manslayers tabooed'.

21. Frazer, *Taboo*, p. 132.

22. Frazer, [*The Golden Bough*, Part I] *The Magic Art*, p. 368.

23. *Old New Zealand*, by a Pakeha Maori, London 1884, in Frazer, *Taboo*, p. 135.

24. W. Brown, *New Zealand and its Aborigines*, London 1845, in Frazer, op. cit. [Part II].

25. Ibid.

26. Frazer, *Taboo*, 'The Burden of Royalty', p. 7.

27. Ibid.

28. [E.] Kaempfer, *History of Japan* [1727], in Frazer, op. cit. [Part II], p. 3.

29. A. Bastian, *'Die deutsche Expedition an der Loangoküste'* ['The German expedition along the Loango coast'], Jena 1874, in Frazer, op. cit. [Part II], p. 5.

30. Ibid., p. 13f.

31. Ibid., p. 11f.

32. A. Bastian, *'Die deutsche Expedition an der Loangoküste'*, in Frazer, op. cit. [Part II], p. 17f.

33. Ibid., p. 18, after [J.] Zweifel and [M.] Moustier, *Voyage aux sources du Niger* [Journey to the sources of the Niger], 1880.

34. Frazer, op. cit. [*The Golden Bough*, Part II], *The Magic Art and the Evolution of Kings*, 2nd vol., 1911.

35. Frazer, *Taboo*, p. 148ff.

36. W. Mariner, '[An Account of] The Natives of the Tonga Islands', 1818, in Frazer, op. cit. [Part II], p. 140.

37. The same patient whose 'impossibilities' I compared above (p. 32f.) with taboo, confessed that she was outraged every time she met someone dressed in mourning in the street. Such people should be forbidden to go out!

38. Frazer, op. cit. [Part II], p. 353.

39. Ibid., p. 352.

40. Ibid., p. 357, according to an old Spanish observer, 1732.

41. Ibid., p. 360.

42. [W.] Stekel [1911], [K.] Abraham [1911].

43. Frazer, op. cit. [Part II], p. 353, presents the Tuaregs of the Sahara as an example of such a declaration.

44. Perhaps we should add the condition: as long as something of his physical remains still exists. Frazer, op. cit. [Part II], p. 372.

45. In the Nicobars, in Frazer, op. cit. [Part II], p. 382.

46. Wundt, *Mythus und Religion*, vol. II, p. 49.

47. [E.] Westermarck, *The Origin and Development of the Moral Ideas*, vol. II, p. 424. The footnote and the continuation of the text contain an abundance of confirmatory, often highly characteristic evidence. For example: the Maoris believed that 'the nearest and most beloved relatives were supposed to have their natures changed by death, and to become malignant, even towards those they formerly loved'. The Negroes of Australia believe that their departed ancestors remain malevolent for a long time; the closer the kinship, the greater the fear. The Central Eskimo are governed by the idea that the dead delay coming to rest, but are at first to be feared as malevolent spirits, who frequently roam around the village causing sickness, death and other mischief.

48. R. Kleinpaul, *Die Lebendigen und die Toten in Volksglauben, Religion und Sage* [The Living and the Dead in Folk Belief, Religion and Saga], 1898.

49. Westermarck, op. cit., p. 426.

50. Close to the projected creations of primitive people are the personifications through which the poet personifies the opposing drive-impulses as separate individuals.

51. *Mythus und Religion*, II, p. 129.

52. In the psychoanalytic treatment of neurotic individuals who suffer from fear of ghosts, or who have suffered from such a fear during childhood, it is often not difficult to unmask these ghosts as the patient's parents. On this subject, cf. also the paper called 'Sexualgespenster' ['Sexual ghosts'] by P. Haeberlin (*Sexualprobleme*, February 1912). Here the person involved was not the subject's father, who had died, but someone else erotically significant to him.

53. Cf. my reference to Abel's 'Gegensinn der Urworte' ['The antithetical meaning of primal words'] in the *Jahrbuch für psychoanalyt. und psychopathol. Forschungen*, vol. II, 1910 (*Gesammelte Werke*, vol. VIII).

54. It is an interesting parallel that the sense of guilt in taboo is not at all diminished if the transgression occurred unwittingly (see examples above), and that in Greek myth the guilt of Oedipus is not erased by the fact that it was acquired without, indeed against, his knowledge and will.

III

Animism, Magic and the Omnipotence of Thoughts

1

It is an inevitable shortcoming of works seeking to apply the viewpoints of psychoanalysis to the moral sciences that they are unable to offer the reader enough of either. For that reason they do nothing more than offer suggestions to the expert, which he can then use in his work. This shortcoming will make itself felt to an extreme extent in an essay that attempts to deal with the vast field that we call animism.[1]

Animism in the narrower sense means the theory of ideas of the soul, and in the extended sense the theory of imaginary beings in general. One sub-division is called *animatism*, the theory that what we see as inanimate nature is in fact animate, and it includes animalism and manism. The name animism, previously applied to a particular philosophical system, seems to have been given its present meaning by E. B. Tylor.[2]

What prompted the creation of these terms is the insight into the very curious conception of nature and the universe of the primitive peoples that are known to us, both from history and those alive today. They populate the world with a huge number of spirit creatures which are either benevolent or malevolent towards them; they attribute the cause of natural processes to these spirits and demons, and consider not only animals and plants but also the inanimate objects of the world to be animated by them. A third, and perhaps the most important, part of this primitive 'natural philosophy' seems much less strange to us because we ourselves are not yet far enough removed from it, despite the fact that we have greatly restricted the existence of spirits and explain natural processes on the basis of impersonal physical forces. Primitive people actually believe in a similar 'animation' of human individuals as well. Human beings receive souls which can leave their dwelling-place and migrate to other people; these souls are the vehicles of spiritual acts, and are to a certain degree independent of the 'bodies'. Originally souls were imagined as being very similar to the individuals, and only over the course of a long development did they shed the characteristics of the material world to attain a high level of 'spiritualization'.[3]

Most authors incline towards the hypothesis that these ideas of the soul form the original core of the animistic system, that the spirits only correspond to souls that have become autonomous, and that the souls of animals, plants and objects are conceived in analogy with human souls.

How did primitive man reach the curiously dualistic conceptions upon which this animistic system is based? It is thought that it was the result of observing the phenomena of sleep (in dreams) and death, which it so closely resembles, and of an effort to explain these states which so closely affected every individual. The problem of death above all must have become the starting-point for the formation of the theory. For primitive man the continuation of life – immortality – was considered quite natural. The idea of death is something that was received rather late and only hesitantly, and even for us it remains empty of content and 'impossible'. Very lively but inconclusive discussions have taken place concerning the contribution that other observations and experiences may have made to the basic theories of animism, those concerning dream-images, shadows, reflections and so on.[4]

If primitive man's reaction to the phenomena that stimulated his reflection was to form conceptions of the soul, and then transfer those conceptions to the objects of the outside world, his behaviour will be considered thoroughly natural, and not condemned as mysterious. In view of the fact that the same animistic ideas have appeared among the most diverse peoples and in all ages, they are 'the necessary psychological product of the mythologizing consciousness, and primitive animism might be considered the spiritual expression of *man's natural state*, in so far as this is access-ible to our observation.'[5] In his *Natural History of Religion*, Hume already provided the justification for the animation of the inani-mate, writing: 'There is an universal tendency among mankind to conceive all beings like themselves and to transfer to every object those qualities with which they are familiarly acquainted and of which they are intimately conscious.'[6]

Animism is a system of thought, it not only provides the explana-tion of an individual phenomenon, but permits an understanding of the whole world as a vast continuity, based on a single point. If we are to follow the authors who have written on the subject, mankind has produced three such systems of thought, three great world-views over the course of the ages: the animistic (mythological), the religious and the scientific. Of these, the first to be created, animism, is perhaps the most consistent and exhaustive, the one that fully explains the nature of the world. This first world-view of mankind is a psychological theory. It is beyond our scope to show how much of it is still demonstrable in present-day life, either in the devalued form of superstition, or in a living form, as a foundation of our speech, beliefs and philosophies.

With reference to the sequence of the three world-views we might say that animism itself is not actually a religion, but that it con-tains the preconditions upon which religions are later constructed. It is striking that myth is based on animistic premises; but the relation-ship between myth and animism appears to be unexplained in some essential points.

2

Our psychoanalytical work will, however, take a different starting-point. It would be wrong for us to assume that human beings forced themselves to create their first cosmic system purely out of a spec-ulative thirst for knowledge. The practical need to take possession of the world must have had a share in that effort. For that reason we are not surprised to know that there is something else that goes hand in hand with the animistic system, an indication about how one is to proceed if one is to master people, animals and objects, or their spirits. This indication, known under the names of 'sorcery and magic', is what S. Reinach[7] calls the strategy of animism; I would prefer, along with Hubert and Mauss, to liken it to a technique.[8]

Can one distinguish in principle between sorcery and magic? It is possible, if one rather high-handedly ignores the vacillations of current usage. If we do make this distinction, then sorcery is essentially the art of influencing spirits by treating them as one would treat human beings under the same conditions, which is to say pacifying them, propitiating them, making them look kindly upon one, intimidating them, robbing them of their power, subjecting them to one's will, using the same means that one has found effective with people. But magic is something different: it basically disregards spirits, and uses special means, not banal psychological methods. It will not be difficult for us to guess that magic is the more original and significant piece of animist technique, because the means with which spirits are to be treated include magical ones,[9] and the magic is also applied in cases in which the spiritualization of nature appears not to have taken place.

Magic must serve the most manifold intentions, it must subject natural processes to the will of man, protect the individual against enemies and dangers and give him the power to harm his enemies. But the underlying principle on which magical activity is based – the principle of magic properly speaking – is so obvious that no author could fail to recognize it. It can be expressed most precisely, if one ignores the added value judgement, in the words of E. B. Tylor: *'mistaking an ideal connection for a real one'*. We wish to explain this characteristic in relation to two groups of magical actions.

One of the most widespread magical procedures for the harming of an enemy consists in making an effigy of him out of some material or other. The resemblance is of little importance. One can also 'name' any object as his image. Whatever one then does to this effigy is also done to the hated original; one need only harm a part of the former, for the corresponding part of the latter's body to fall ill. Rather than being used for the satisfaction of a private hostility, the same magical technique can also be put at the service of piety, and thus come to the assistance of gods against evil demons. I quote from Frazer:[10]

'Every night when the sun-god Ra sank down to his home in the glowing west he was assailed by hosts of demons under the leadership of the arch-fiend Apepi. All night long he fought them, and sometimes by day the powers of darkness sent up clouds even into the blue Egyptian sky to obscure his light and weaken his power. To aid the sun-god in this daily struggle, a ceremony was daily performed in his temple at Thebes. A figure of his foe Apepi, represented as a crocodile with a hideous face or a serpent with many coils, was made of wax, and on it the demon's name was written in green ink. Wrapt in a papyrus case, on which another likeness of Apepi had been drawn in green ink, the figure was then tied up with black hair, spat upon, hacked with a stone knife, and cast on the ground. There the priest trod on it with his left foot again and again, and then burned it in a fire made of a certain plant or grass. When Apepi himself had thus been effectually disposed of, waxen effigies of each of his principal demons, and of their fathers, mothers and children, were made and burned in the same way. The service, accompanied by the recitation of certain prescribed spells, was repeated not merely morning, noon and night, but whenever a storm was raging, or heavy rain had set in, or black clouds were stealing across the sky to hide the sun's bright disc. The fiends of darkness, clouds, and rain felt the injuries inflicted on their images as if they had been done to themselves; they passed away, at least for a time, and the beneficent sun-god shone out triumphant once more.'[11]

From the great abundance of similarly founded magical actions I shall stress only two kinds, which have played an important part among primitive peoples in all ages, and which have been partly preserved in the myths and religions of higher stages of development, such as the variants of rain and fertility sorcery. One produces rain in a magical way, by imitating it, or by copying the clouds or the storm that produces it. It looks as though one wished to 'play at

raining'. The Japanese Aino, for example, make rain in the following way; some of them pour water out of big sieves, while others fit
out a large bowl with a sail and oars, as though it were a ship, and
pull them around the village and gardens like that. But the fertility
of the soil was also assured in a magical way, by being shown a sim-
ulation of human sexual intercourse. In this way – to take one example rather than an infinite number – in some parts of Java at the
time of the coming of the rice flower, peasant men and women go
to the fields at night in order to stimulate the rice to fertility by their
own example.[12] Conversely, incestuous sexual relationships, being
the object of loathing, were feared to have an adverse effect on
growth and the fertility of the soil.[13]

Certain negative prescriptions – magical prescriptions – also
form a part of this first group. If one part of the inhabitants of a
Dyak village has gone off to the jungle to hunt wild pigs, those
remaining behind may not touch either oil or water with their hands
before their return, or else the hunters would be 'butter-fingered'
and allow their prey to slip out of their hands.[14] Or, when a Gilyak
hunter is pursuing his game in the forest, his children at home are
forbidden to make drawings on wood or in sand. The paths in the
dense forest could otherwise become as tangled as the lines in the
drawing, and the hunter would be unable to find his way home.[15]

If, in these last examples of magical effect as in so many others, distance plays a part, and telepathy is therefore taken for granted, this
curious feature of magic will be equally easy to understand.

There can be no doubt about what will be seen as the active
ingredient in all of these examples. It is the *similarity* between the
completed action and the expected event. For that reason Frazer
calls this kind of magic *imitative* or *homoeopathic*. If I want it to
rain, I need only do something that looks like rain or that recalls
rain. In a further phase of cultural development, instead of making
this magical rain spell, the people will go in procession to a house of
God and plead with the holy man living there for rain. Finally, even
this religious technique will be abandoned, and instead people will
investigate how rain might be produced by exerting an influence
upon the atmosphere.

In another group of magical actions, the principle of similarity is abandoned in favour of another which will be easily deduced from the examples below.

If one wishes to harm an enemy, there is also another procedure that can be used. One gains possession of some of the enemy's hair, nails, waste products or even a part of their clothing, and treats them in a hostile manner. It is then exactly as though one had gained possession of the actual person, and that which has been done to the things taken from the person will also happen to the person. In the view of primitive people, the significant components of a personality include its name; so if one knows the name of a person or a spirit, one has acquired a certain power over the bearer of the name. Hence the curious precautions and restrictions in the use of names which have been mentioned in passing in the essay on taboo.[16] In such cases similarity is clearly replaced by *contiguity*.

The cannibalism of primitive man derives its more subtle motivation in a similar way. By absorbing parts of a person's body through the act of consuming them, one also appropriates the qualities that belonged to that person. This, in certain circumstances, has produced dietary precautions and restrictions. A pregnant woman will avoid eating the flesh of certain animals because their undesirable qualities, such as cowardice, might in the process be passed on to the child she is feeding. It makes no difference to the magic effect even if the connection is one that has already been abolished, or if it only consisted of a unique and meaningful contact. Thus, for example, belief in a magic bond linking the fate of a wound with that of the weapon which caused it was passed down unchanged over thousands of years. If a Melanesian gains possession of the bow by which he was wounded, he will preserve it carefully in a cool place in order to keep down the inflammation of the wound. But if the bow remains in the possession of his enemies, it will certainly be hung up very close to a fire so that the wound becomes inflamed and burns. In his *Natural History*, XXVIII, Pliny advises that if one regrets injuring someone, one should spit upon the hand that caused the injury; the pain of the injured person will then be immediately eased. In his *Sylva Sylvarum, or, A Natural*

History Francis Bacon mentions the widespread belief that rubbing ointment on a weapon that caused a wound will heal the wound itself. Even today, English peasants are said to act according to this formula, and if they have cut themselves with a sickle, from that moment onwards they keep the instrument painstakingly clean so that the wound does not go septic. In June 1902, according to a local English newspaper, a Norwich woman named Matilda Henry accidentally drove an iron nail into the sole of her foot. Without having the wound examined or even taking off her stocking, she instructed her daughter to oil the nail well, in the expectation that nothing could happen to her. She died of lockjaw a few days later[17] as a result of the postponed antisepsis.

The examples of this last group explain what Frazer calls *contagious* as against *imitative* magic. What is thought to be the active part in them is no longer similarity but their proximity in space, *contiguity*, or at least imagined contiguity, the memory of their presence. But since similarity and contiguity are the two essential principles of associative processes, the preponderance of the association of ideas turns out to be the true explanation for all the madness of magical prescriptions. One sees how accurate Tylor's characterization of magic, quoted above, proves to be: 'mistaking an ideal connection for a real one', or, as Frazer puts it in almost identical terms, 'Men mistook the order of their ideas for the order of nature, and hence imagined that the control which they have, or seem to have, over their thoughts, permitted them to exercise a corresponding control over things.'[18]

We will at first be surprised to note that this illuminating explanation of magic has been rejected as unsatisfactory by some commentators.[19] But upon closer examination one must agree with the objection that the associative theory of magic merely illuminates the paths that magic travels, but not its actual nature, nor, in fact, the misunderstanding that leads it to put psychological laws in the place of natural laws. Here what we clearly need is a dynamic factor, but while the search for such a factor leads critics of Frazer's theory astray, it is easy to give a satisfactory explanation of magic by taking associative theory further and by probing more deeply into it.

Let us first of all consider the simpler and more significant case of imitative magic. According to Frazer this can be practised on its own, while contagious magic generally needs to be supplemented by the imitative kind.[20] The motives leading to the practice of magic are easy to discern, they are the desires of men. We need only assume that primitive man has great confidence in the power of his wishes. Basically everything that he makes in a magical way must only occur because he wishes it to. Thus, at first, the emphasis is on his wish alone.

As regards the child, which is in a similar psychical state but does not yet have the same motor abilities, we have suggested elsewhere that it at first satisfies its wishes in a hallucinatory way, by bringing about the satisfactory situation through centrifugal excitations of its sensory organs.[21] The primitive adult has another way of doing this. His desire is connected to a motor impulse and this impulse – which will later change the face of the earth in the service of the satisfaction of wishes – is now used to represent satisfaction, so that one can experience it, so to speak, through motor hallucinations. Such a *representation* of the satisfied desire is entirely comparable to children's *play*, which produces in children the purely sensory technique of satisfaction. If play and imitative representation are enough for the child and for primitive man, this is not a sign of modesty in our sense, or of resignation at the recognition of their real impotence, but the entirely intelligible consequence of the predominant appraisal of their wish, of the will that is dependent on it and the path that it has taken. Over time the psychical emphasis shifts from the motives for the magical action to their means; to the action itself. It would perhaps be more accurate to say that it is through these means that primitive man comes to recognize his over-valuation of psychical acts. It would also seem that it is the magic act itself which compelled the desired event by virtue of its similarity to that act. At the stage of animistic thinking there is as yet no opportunity to demonstrate objectively the true state of affairs, but such an opportunity exists at later stages, when although these procedures are still practised, the psychical phenomenon of doubt is already beginning to intervene, as a tendency to repression. At that stage men will begin to admit that the invocation of spirits can achieve nothing if belief in them is not present, and the magical power of prayer is useless if there is no piety at work behind it.[22]

The possibility of contagious magic based on associations of contiguity will then show us that the psychical valuation of desire and will has extended to all psychical acts subordinate to the will. This results in a general over-valuation of psychical processes, that is, an attitude to the world which, from what we know of the relation between reality and thought, will appear to us as an over-valuation of the latter. Objects are eclipsed by their ideas; what is done to the latter must also affect the former. The relations that exist between ideas are also taken to exist between objects. As thought knows no distances, and can easily unite in a single act of consciousness things that are spatially and temporally remote from one another, the magic world also telepathically puts itself beyond spatial distance and treats past associations as though they were present. In the animistic age, the mirror image of the inner world must obscure that other image of the world that we think we know.

Incidentally, let us stress that the two principles of association – similarity and contiguity – meet in the higher unity of *contact*. Association by contiguity amounts to contact in the direct sense of the word, and association by similarity is contact in the figurative sense. Another identity within the psychical process which has not yet been grasped is probably confirmed by the use of the same word for both kinds of association. It is the same range of the concept of 'contact' that we found in the analysis of taboo.[23]

To summarize, we might say: the principle that governs magic, the technique of the animistic way of thinking, is that of the 'omnipotence of thoughts'.

3

I have borrowed the phrase 'omnipotence of thoughts' from a highly intelligent man who suffered from obsessive ideas, and who was able to demonstrate his efficiency and intelligence once he had effected a recovery as a result of psychoanalytic treatment.[24] He had coined this phrase in order to explain all those strange and uncanny events which seemed to pursue him as they did others suffering from the same affliction. If he thought of someone, he would see that person coming towards him, as though he had invoked him; if he suddenly inquired after the well-being of an acquaintance whom he had not seen for a long time, he would hear that that person had just died, leading him to believe that they had attracted his attention; if he uttered a half-meant curse about a stranger, he would expect the person to die shortly afterwards, making him responsible for the person's demise. Over the course of his treatment, however, he himself was able to tell me how the deceptive appearance had come about in many of these cases, and what he himself had added in order to reinforce his superstitious expectations.[25] All obsessive neurotics are superstitious in this way, generally against their better judgement.

We most clearly encounter the persistence of the omnipotence of thoughts in the context of obsessive neurosis, and it is here that the results of this primitive way of thinking are closest to consciousness. But we must take care not to see it as a distinguishing feature of this neurosis, because analytic examination reveals the same thing in other neuroses. In all of them, what is crucial for symptom-formation is not the reality of experience, but the reality of thought. Neurotics live in a particular world in which, as I have put it elsewhere, only the 'neurotic currency' is valid: only that which is thought intensely, imagined with affect, is effective in it, while its coincidence with external reality is secondary. The hysteric repeats in his attacks, and fixates though his symptoms, experiences which have only occurred in his imagination, but which can ultimately be shown to be traceable back to real events, or which have been constructed from them. We would be similarly misunderstanding the sense of guilt in neurotics if we were to trace it back to real misdeeds. An obsessive neurotic can be oppressed by a sense of guilt that would be more appropriate to a mass murderer; he will behave as the most considerate and scrupulous companion towards his fellow man, and will have behaved in that way since childhood.

But there is a foundation for his guilt feeling; it is based on the intense and frequent death-wishes that he harbours against others in his unconscious. It has a foundation to the extent that what is in question is unconscious thoughts and not deliberate deeds. Thus the omnipotence of thoughts, the over-valuation of psychical processes as against reality, proves to be limitlessly effective in the neurotic's affective life and everything that follows on from it. But if one subjects him to psychoanalytic treatment which brings his unconscious to consciousness, he will find it impossible to believe that thoughts are free, and will always be afraid to express evil wishes, lest they be fulfilled by virtue of being uttered. But through this attitude, as well as through the superstition that he activates in his life, he shows us how close he is to the savage, who imagines he can change the outside world merely by thinking.

The primary compulsive actions of these neurotics are in fact entirely magic in nature. They are, if not sorcery, then counter-sorcery, designed to defend against the expectations of disaster with which neurosis usually begins. As soon as I was able to penetrate the mystery, it became apparent that the content of these expectations of disaster was death. According to Schopenhauer, the problem of death stands at the portal of every philosophy; we have heard that the formation of ideas of the soul and the belief in demons that characterize animism may be traced back to the impression that death makes upon mankind. It is difficult to judge whether these first compulsive or protective actions obey the principle of similarity or of contrast, because under the conditions of neurosis they are usually distorted by being displaced on to something trivial, an action that is in itself very insignificant.[26] The protective formulae of obsessive neurosis also have their counterpart in magical formulae. But it becomes possible to describe the history of the evolution of compulsive actions if one stresses how these actions, as remote as possible from the sexual sphere, begin as a spell against evil wishes, and end up as a substitute for forbidden sexual activity, which they imitate as faithfully as possible.

If we accept the history of the development of human world-views, as outlined above, in which the *animistic* phase is replaced by the *religious*, and this in turn by the *scientific*, it is not difficult for us to pursue the vicissitudes of the 'omnipotence of thoughts' through these various phases. In the animistic stage man arrogates omnipotence to himself; in the religious stage he has ceded it to the gods, but not seriously abandoned it, because he reserves for himself the power to guide the gods through many different kinds of influence according to his desires. There is no longer any room in the scientific world-view for the omnipotence of man, he has admitted his own smallness and submitted to death with resignation as he has to all other natural necessities. But a piece of the primitive belief in omnipotence survives in the trust in the power of the human spirit, which grapples with the laws of reality,.

In tracing the evolution of libidinous tendencies in the individual human being from their formation in maturity back to their first beginnings of childhood, we first established an important difference, which was expounded in 'Three Essays on Sexual Theory', 1905. The manifestations of the sexual drives are recognizable from the very first, but they are not at first directed towards an external object. The individual drive components of sexuality each strive towards a gain in pleasure, and find satisfaction in the individual's own body. This stage is called *auto-eroticism*, and it is followed by *object-choice*.

Further study has shown it to be appropriate, indeed necessary, to insert a third stage between these two or, if one prefers, to break down the first stage of auto-eroticism into two. In this intermediate stage, the significance of which is coming increasingly to the fore, the previously isolated sexual drives have already combined into a single whole, and also found an object; however, this object is not an external one, alien to the individual, but is the subject's own ego, which is constituted around this time. Taking into account the pathological fixations of this condition, which will be discussed below, we call the new stage *narcissism*. The individual behaves as though he is in love with himself: the ego-drives and libidinous desires are inseparable as far as our analysis is concerned.

Although we are not yet able to characterize with sufficient clarity this narcissistic stage, in which previously dissociated sexual drives come together into a single entity, and invest the ego as an object, we already sense that the narcissistic organization is never completely abandoned. The individual remains narcissistic to a certain degree even after he has found external objects for his libido: the object-investments that he undertakes are, we might say, emanations of the libido that remains attached to the ego, and they can be drawn back into it. The conditions of passionate love, psychologically so curious, and the normal models of psychoses, correspond to the highest state of these emanations, in contrast to the level of self-love.

Primitive people and neurotics attach a high value – we would call it over-valuation – to psychical acts, and this may perhaps be related to narcissism and regarded as a significant component of it. It might be said that among primitive people thought is still sexualized to a high degree, and that this is the source of the belief in the omnipotence of thoughts, the unshakeable confidence of the possibility of mastering the world, and the inaccessibility of the obvious facts which can instruct man of his true place in the world. A considerable share of this primitive attitude has remained as a part of the constitution of neurotics, while at the same time the sexual repression occurring in them has introduced a new sexualization of thought processes. The psychical consequences must be the same in both cases, in original libidinous hyper-investment of thought and in its regressive transformation: this consequence is intellectual narcissism, the omnipotence of thoughts.[27]

If we are right in seeing the demonstration of the omnipotence of thoughts among primitive people as evidence of narcissism, we may venture to compare the stages of the evolution of the human world-view with studies of the libidinous development of the individual. In that case, both in terms of time and content, the animistic phase corresponds to narcissism, the religious phase corresponds to the stage of object-finding as characterized by the parental bond, and the scientific phase has its perfect counterpart in that state of maturity in the individual who, having abandoned the pleasure principle and adapted to reality, seeks his object in the outside world.[28]

There is only one field in which 'omnipotence of thoughts' has been preserved in our civilization, and that is in art. It is only in art that a man consumed by his desires produces something similar to a satisfaction of them, and that this game – thanks to artistic illusion – creates emotional effects as though they were something real. People rightly speak of the magic of art, and liken the artist to a magician. But this comparison is perhaps more significant than it claims to be. Art, which certainly did not begin as *l'art pour l'art* [art for art's sake], originally served tendencies most of which no longer exist. Among these we may assume various magical purposes.[29]

4

Thus the first conception of the world that human beings succeeded in erecting, that of animism, was a psychological one, it did not require science for its foundation, because science only begins once people understand that they do not know the world, and must therefore seek ways of knowing it. But animism was natural and a self-certainty for primitive man; he knew how the things of the world are, which is to say how he himself felt them to be. So we are prepared to find that primitive man transferred structural relations from his own psyche into the outside world,[30] while at the same time we may attempt to transport what animism tells us of the nature of things back to the human soul.

The technique of animism, magic, clearly and unmistakably demonstrates the intention of forcing the laws of psychical life on to real things; in this, spirits need not yet play a part, although they may be taken as objects of magical treatment. The premises of magic are thus older and more primitive than the theory of spirits that forms the core of animism. Here our psychoanalytical view coincides with a theory of R. R. Marett's, according to which animism is preceded by a *pre-animistic* stage whose character is best suggested by the name *animatism* (theory of universal animation). There is little more to be said from experience about pre-animism, since no people has been encountered without a conception of spirits.[31]

While magic still retains full omnipotence of thoughts, animism has surrendered a part of this omnipotence to spirits, and thus started off along the path towards the formation of a religion. What is supposed to have led primitive man to this first renunciation? It could hardly have been an insight into the falseness of his premises, because he retained the technique of magic.

Spirits and demons are, as I have suggested elsewhere, nothing but the projections of primitive man's emotional impulses;[32] he personifies his emotional investments, populates the world with them and now finds his inner psychical processes outside of himself, much like the witty paranoiac Schreber, who found the connections and dissolutions of his libido mirrored in the fates of the 'divine rays' that he had conjured up.[33]

Here, as on an earlier occasion,[34] we should avoid the problem of where the tendency to project psychical processes outwards actually comes from. But we may assume one thing, that this inclination is intensified where the projection brings the advantage of psychical relief. One would definitely expect such an advantage when the impulses striving for omnipotence have come into conflict with one another; in that case they can clearly not all become omnipotent. The process of illness in paranoia actually uses the mechanism of projection in order to resolve such conflicts that have arisen in the psychical life. Now the model case of such a conflict between the two parts of an opposition is the ambivalent attitude which we have minutely dissected in the situation of the mourning person on the occasion of the death of a dear relative. Such a case will strike us as being particularly well-suited to motivate the creation of projection-formations. Here again we concur with those authors who declare the evil spirits to be the first-born among the spirits, and derive the origin of ideas of the soul from the impression that death makes upon the survivors. We differ from them only in that we do not bring to the fore the intellectual problem that death imposes on the living, instead transferring the force that drives man's inquiry into the emotional conflict in which this situation places the survivor.

Thus man's first theoretical accomplishment – the creation of spirits – could be said to spring from the same source as the first moral restrictions that he imposes upon himself, the taboo restrictions. But the identity of their origin does not by any means imply the simultaneity of their appearance. If it really was the relationship of the bereaved towards the deceased that first made primitive man reflective, and required him to yield part of his omnipotence to the spirits and sacrifice a part of the arbitrary power of his actions, these cultural creations would be a first acknowledgement of the ʾΑνάγκη [necessity] that resists human narcissism. Primitive man would thus submit to the superior power of death with the same gesture with which he appears to deny it.

If we have the courage to exploit our hypothesis further, we might ask which essential part of our psychological structure is reflected and returned in the projection-formation of souls and spirits. In that case it is hard to deny that the primitive idea of the soul, however distinct it may be from the later, entirely immaterial soul, nonetheless shares its nature, considering the person or the thing as a duality, with the known properties and modifications of the whole distributed over its two parts. This original duality – to use a term of Herbert Spencer's[35] – is already identical with the dualism familiar to us in the separation of mind and body, and whose indestructible linguistic expressions we find, for example, in the description of someone who faints or raves: 'he is beside himself'.

When, like primitive man, we project into external reality, what must be happening is this: we are acknowledging two states, one in which a thing is given to the senses, is *present*, and another in which the same thing is *latent* but might potentially reappear. What we are acknowledging is the coexistence of perception and memory or, extended into the universal, the existence of *unconscious* psychical processes alongside the *conscious* ones.[36] It might be said that the 'spirit' of a person or a thing is finally reduced to its propensity to be remembered and imagined once it is absent from perception.

It is not, admittedly, to be expected that either the primitive or the contemporary idea of the 'soul' will be separated from the other part of the personality along the line that contemporary science draws between conscious and unconscious psychical activity. Rather, the animistic soul combines within itself definitions from both sides. Its flightiness and its agility, its capacity to leave the body, to take possession of another body either permanently or temporarily, are the features that unmistakably remind us of the essence of consciousness. But the way it remains hidden behind its personal appearance recalls the unconscious; we no longer ascribe its unalterability and indestructibility to conscious processes, but rather to unconscious ones, and we also consider these to be the actual bearers of psychical activity.

Above, we described animism as a system of thought, the first complete theory of the world, and we shall now draw certain conclusions from the psychoanalytic view of such a system. Our everyday experience is able to present us time and again with the chief properties of the system. We dream at night, and have learned to interpret the dream by day. The dream can, without denying its nature, appear confused and disconnected, but it can also, on the other hand, imitate the order of impressions of an experience, deduce one event from another and relate one part of its content to another. The dream appears to do this more or less successfully, but hardly ever so completely that some absurdity or gap in the texture does not become apparent. If we subject dreams to interpretation, we learn that the inconsistent and uneven arrangement of dream components is also of very little importance for the understanding of the dreams themselves. The essential part of the dream is the dream-thoughts, which are meaningful, coherent and orderly. But their order is very different from that which we remember in the manifest dream content. The connection between the dream-thoughts has been abandoned, and may either remain lost or be replaced by the new coherence in the dream content. Apart from the condensation of the dream elements, they have been reordered in a way more or less independent of the earlier arrangement. We should say in conclusion that what the dream-work has made out of the material of the dream-thoughts has been subjected to a new influence, the so-called *secondary elaboration*, the intention of which is clearly to remove the incoherence and unintelligibility resulting from the dream-work in favour of a new 'meaning'. The new meaning achieved as a result of the secondary elaboration is no longer the meaning of the dream-thoughts.

The secondary elaboration of the product of the dream-work is an excellent example of the nature and the claims of a system. An intellectual function within us requires unification, coherence intelligibility from all the material that it has acquired from perception or thought, and is not afraid to create an incorrect connection if it is unable for special circumstances to grasp the correct one. We know such system-formations not only from dreams, but also from phobias, obsessive ideas and the various forms of delusion. System-formation is most easily grasped in the delusory illnesses (paranoia), where it dominates the clinical picture, but neither can it be ignored in other forms of neuropsychosis. In all cases we are able to show that the psychical material has been reordered towards a new goal, often essentially a very violent one, even if it only appears intelligible from the point of view of the system. It then becomes the most dependable distinguishing mark of system-formation that each of its results reveals two motivations, one drawn from the premises of the system – and hence perhaps delusory – and one which is hidden, but which we must acknowledge as the actually effective, real one.

An example from a case of neurosis may serve as an example: in the essay on taboo I mentioned a patient whose obsessive prohibitions coincide very neatly with the taboos of the Maori.[37] This woman's neurosis is directed at her husband, and culminates in a defence against the unconscious wish for his death. But her manifest, systematic phobia applies to any mention of death as such, so her husband is completely left out of it and never becomes the object of conscious concern. One day she hears her husband issuing the instruction for his blunt razor-blade to be taken to a particular shop to be sharpened. Impelled by a curious unease, she herself sets off for this shop, and after her return from this reconnoitre she demands that her husband put all his blades away, because she has discovered that next to the shop in question there is an undertaker's establishment storing coffins, funeral accessories and so on. She insists that he has deliberately and permanently connected the razor-blades with the idea of death. This is now the systematic motivation of the prohibition. We may be sure that the patient would have brought home the prohibition on razor-blades even had she not discovered the sinister proximity of the two businesses, for she would have needed only to encounter a hearse, a person in mourning or a woman carrying a wreath as she made her way to the shop. The net of required conditions was spread far enough to catch its prey in any trap. After that it was up to her whether she wanted to draw it tight or not. It was possible to establish with certainty that she did not activate the conditions leading to the prohibition under other circumstances, and she would then insist that she had had a 'better day'. Of course the true cause of the prohibition on razor-blades was, as we had no difficulty in discovering, her resistance to a pleasurably emphasized idea that her husband might cut his throat with the whetted razor.

A particular motor disorder, abasia or agoraphobia, is completed and detailed in a very similar way once the symptom has managed to bring itself to represent an unconscious desire and the defence against it. Anything else in the way of unconscious fantasies and effective reminiscences that is present in the patient pushes its way towards this or that symptomatic manifestation, and lodges in a functional arrangement in the context of the motor disorder. So it would be both vain and foolish to attempt to understand the symptomatic structure and the details of a case of agoraphobia from its fundamental premise. All the consistency and rigour of the connection is thus only apparent. More intense observation can, as in the formation of dream façades, reveal the most serious inconsistencies and randomness in symptom-formation. The details of such a systematic phobia draw their real motivation from hidden conditions that need have nothing to do with the motor disorder, and it is for that reason the manifestations of such a phobia appear so diverse and so contradictory in different people.

If we now return to the system of animism which concerns us here, we will conclude from the insights that we have gained into other psychological systems that an individual custom or regulation does not need to have a single motivation, even among primitive people, and does not free us from the obligation to seek hidden motives. When an animistic system is in force, it is inevitable that every regulation and every activity will be given a systematic explanation which we would call 'superstitious' today. 'Superstition' is, like 'anxiety', like 'dream', like 'demon', one of the provisional psychological concepts that have dissolved in the face of psychoanalytical investigation. Once we get behind these constructions, which act as screens to fend off understanding, we sense that the psychical and cultural life of savages has not in the past had all the recognition that it deserves.

If we take the repression of drives as a measure of the level of civilization that has been reached, we will be obliged to admit that under the animistic system advances and developments have taken place which are undervalued because they have been motivated by superstition. When we learn that warriors of a savage tribe assume the greatest modesty and purity as soon as they set out on the warpath,[38] we immediately jump to the conclusion that they are removing their refuse so that the enemy will not acquire possession of this part of their person in order to damage them in a magical way, and we are supposed to assume superstitious motivations for their abstemiousness. But the fact of drive-renunciation remains intact, and we will probably reach a better understanding of the situation if we assume that the savage warrior imposes such restrictions on himself as a form of compensation, because he is on the point of allowing himself the complete satisfaction of cruel and hostile impulses which are otherwise forbidden. The same is true of the many instances of sexual restriction, as long as one is concerned with difficult or responsible works.[39] While the explanation of these prohibitions may still be based upon a magical connection, the fundamental idea of acquiring greater power by renouncing drive-satisfaction remains unmistakable, and the hygienic root of the prohibition should not be neglected alongside its magical rationalization. When the men of a savage tribe have gone out to hunt, to catch fish, to wage war, to collect precious plant materials, their wives at home remain subjected to numerous oppressive restrictions, to which the savages themselves attribute a sympathetic effect on the success of the expedition, and one that even remains effective over long distances. But one does not have to be terribly astute to guess that the factor which remains effective over long distances is nothing but thinking about home, a longing for the absent men, and that behind those disguises there lurks the sound psychological insight that the men will only do their best if they are entirely at ease concerning the whereabouts of their unsupervised wives. On other occasions it is stated directly, and without any magical motivation, that marital infidelity on the part of the wife will cause the husband's efforts to fail when he is absent on responsible work.

The countless taboo regulations to which the wives of savages are subject during menstruation are motivated by the superstitious fear of blood, and probably have a real grounding in that fear. But it would be wrong to ignore the possibility that the fear of blood also serves aesthetic and hygienic purposes which would in all cases have to disguise themselves with magical motives.

We may well be laying ourselves open to the accusation of attributing to contemporary savages a degree of delicacy that is highly unlikely. But I think that our attitude towards the psychology of these peoples who have remained at the animistic stage may be very much the same as our attitude towards the psychical lives of children, which we adults no longer understand, and whose richness and delicacy of feeling we have for that very reason so greatly underestimated.

There is one other group of hitherto unexplained taboo restrictions that I should like to mention because they permit an explanation with which the psychoanalyst will be familiar. In many savage peoples it is forbidden under various conditions to keep sharp weapons and cutting instruments in the house.[40] Frazer cites a German superstition to the effect that a knife should not be permitted to lie with its blade upwards, on the grounds that God and the angels might hurt themselves on it. Should we not see in this taboo a sense of certain symptomatic actions for which the sharp weapon could be used by unconscious evil impulses?

Notes

1. The inevitable condensation of the material also means that I am unable to include a detailed bibliography. Let us instead refer to the well-known works of Herbert Spencer, J. G. Frazer, A. Lang, E. B. Tylor and W. Wundt, from which I have drawn all my information about animism and magic. The independence of the author can only be affirmed in the selection he has made of the materials, as well as the opinions that they suggest to him.

2. E. B. Tylor, *Primitive Culture*, vol. I, p. 425, 4th ed., 1903 – W. Wundt, *Mythus und Religion*, vol. II, p. 173, 1906.

3. Wundt, ibid., Chapter IV, 'Die Seelenvorstellungen' ['Ideas of the Soul'].

4. Cf., apart from Wundt and H. Spencer, the helpful articles in the *Encyclopaedia Britannica*, 1911 'Animism', 'Mythology', etc.)

5. Wundt, op. cit., p. 154.

6. In Tylor, *Primitive Culture*, vol. I, p. 477.

7. *Cultes, mythes et religions* [Cults, Myths and Religions], vol. II, Introduction, p. xv, 1909.

8. *Année sociologique*, vol. VII, 1904.

9. If one scares away a spirit with noise and shouting, this is an act of pure sorcery; if one forces the spirit by gaining possession of its name, one has used magic against him.

10. [Frazer, *The Golden Bough*, Part I] *The Magic Art*, [vol.] I, p. 67.

11. The biblical prohibition on making an image of anything living probably did not arise out of a rejection in principle of visual art, but was supposed to remove one tool from the magic loathed by the Hebrew religion. Frazer, [Part I], vol. I, op. cit., p. 87, note.

12. *The Magic Art*, [vol.] II, p. 98.

13. There is an echo of this in Sophocles' *Oedipus Rex*.

14. *The Magic Art*, [vol.] I, p. 120.

15. Ibid., p. 122.

16. Cf. p. 57–61.

17. Frazer, *The Magic Art*, [vol.] I, pp. 201–203.

18. Ibid., p. 420ff.

19. Cf. the article 'Magic' (N.W.T.) [N. W. Thomas] in the 11th edition of the *Encyclopaedia Britannica*.

20. [Frazer, op. cit., vol. I] p. 54.

21. 'Formulierungen über die zwei Prinzipien des psychischen Geschehens' ['Formulations on the two principles of psychical process'], *Jahrb. f. psychoanalyt. Forschungen*, vol. III, 1911, p. 2, *Ges. Werke*, vol. VIII.

22. The king in *Hamlet* (III, 4.): 'My words fly up, my thoughts remain below: Words without thoughts never to heaven go.'

23. Cf. the previous essay in this series [i.e. essay II].

24. 'Bemerkungen über einen Fall von Zwangsneurose' ['Notes upon a Case of Obsessional Neurosis'], *Ges. Werke*, vol. VII.

25. It would appear that we assign the characteristic of the 'uncanny' to those impressions which seek to confirm the omnipotence of ideas and the animist way of thinking, while in our judgements we have already turned away from both long since.

26. One further motive for this displacement on to something trivial will emerge from the discussions below.

27. 'It is almost an axiom with writers on this subject, that a sort of Solipsism or Berkeleïanism (as Professor Sully terms it as he finds it in the child), operates in the savage to make him refuse to recognize death as a fact.' – [R. R.] Marett, 'Pre-animistic Religion', *Folk-Lore*, vol. XI, 1900, p. 178.

28. Here I am only seeking to hint that the original narcissism of the child is crucial for the view of its character development, and excludes the assumption of a primitive feeling of inferiority in it.

29. S. Reinach, '*L'art et la magie*' [Art and magic], in the collection *Cultes, Mythes et Religions*, vol. I., pp. 125–36. Reinach believes that the primitive artists who have left us the scratched or painted pictures of animals in the caves of France wanted not to 'excite pleasure', but to 'charm'. He explains it by saying that these drawings are in the darkest and most inaccessible parts of the caves, and that representations of the feared beasts of prey are absent. '*Les modernes parlent souvent, par hyperbole, de la magie du pinceau ou du ciseau d'un grand artiste et, en general, de la magie de l'art. Entendu au sens propre, qui est celui d'une contrainte mystique exercée par la volonté de l'homme sur d'autres volontés ou sur les choses, cette expression n'est plus admissible; mais nous avons vu qu'elle était autrefois rigoureusement vraie, du moins dans l'opinion des artistes.*' ['The moderns often speak hyperbolically of the magic of the brush or chisel of a great artist and, in general, of the magic of art. Understood in terms of its true meaning, which is that of a mystical constraint exercised by man's will over other wills or over things, this expression is no longer admissible; but we have seen that it was rigorously true in the past, at least in the opinion of artists.'] (p. 136.)

30. Those known through so-called endopsychical perception.

31. R. R. Marett, 'Pre-animistic Religion', *Folk-Lore*, vol. XI, No. 2,

London, 1900. Cf. Wundt, *Mythus und Religion*, vol. II, p. 171ff.

32. We assume that in this early narcissistic stage investments from libidinous and other sources of excitement may perhaps be inseparably interconnected.

33. Schreber, *Denkwürdigkeiten eines Nervenkranken* [Memoirs of my Nervous Illness]. 1903 – Freud, 'Psychoanalystische Bemerkungen über einen autobiographisch beschriebenen Fall von Paranoia' ['Psycho-Analytic Notes on an Autobiographical Account of a Case of Paranoia (Dementia Paranoides)'] (*Ges. Werke*, vol. VIII).

34. Cf. the essay on Schreber quoted above, *Ges. Werke*, vol. VIII.

35. In vol. I of *Principles of Sociology*.

36. Cf. my little essay: 'A Note on the Unconscious in Psycho-Analysis', from the *Proceedings of the Society for Psychical Research*, Part LXVI, vol. XXVI, London, 1912. (*Ges. Werke*, vol. VIII.)

37. p. 55f.

38. Frazer, *Taboo and the Perils of the Soul*, p. 157.

39. Ibid., p. 200.

40. Ibid., p. 238.

IV

The Recurrence of Totemism in Childhood

We need not be concerned that psychoanalysis, the first discipline to uncover the regular over-determination of psychical acts and formations, will be tempted to trace something so complicated as religion back to a single origin. When, out of duty or necessity, it wishes to bring a single one of the wellsprings of this institution to light, it does not claim that it is exclusive or that it occupies the first rank among the other factors. Only a synthesis of various areas of research can decide what relative significance should be assigned to the mechanism under discussion here in the genesis of religion; but such a task exceeds both the scope and the aims of the psycho-analyst.

1

In the first paper in this series we encountered the concept of totemism. We have heard that totemism is a system that occupies the place of a religion among certain primitive peoples in Australia, America and Africa, and provides the basis of their social organiza-tion. We know that the Scotsman McLennan attracted general interest to the phenomena of totemism, which had hitherto only been considered as curiosities, by expressing the hypothesis that a large number of customs and traditions in various societies, ancient and modern, should be seen as remnants of a totemistic era. Since then, science has fully acknowledged the significance of totemism. As one of the opinions most recently expressed on the issue, I should like to quote a passage from W. Wundt's 1912 *Elements of*

Folk Psychology:[1] 'In view of all this, one will very probably reach the conclusion that totemistic culture has everywhere constituted a preliminary stage in later developments, and formed a transitional stage between the state of primitive man and the age of gods and heroes.'

The aims of the preceding essays oblige us to probe more deeply into the characteristics of totemism. For reasons that will later become apparent, I prefer to follow an account by Salomon Reinach, who, in 1900, drew up the following twelve-article *code du totémisme*, what we might call a catechism of totemistic religion:[2]

1) Certain animals may not be killed or eaten, but people rear individual members of these animal species and tend to them.

2) An animal that has happened to die is mourned and buried with the same honours as a member of the tribe.

3) The food prohibition sometimes applies only to a particular part of the animal's body.

4) If an animal that is usually spared must be killed out of necessity, the members of the tribe apologize to it and attempt to mitigate the violation of the taboo, murder, by the use of many kinds of ruses and expedients.

5) If the animal is ritually sacrificed, it is solemnly mourned.

6) On certain solemn occasions, religious ceremonies, the skins of certain animals are worn. Where totemism still pertains, these are the totem animals.

7) Tribes and individuals take the names of animals, the totem animals.

8) Many tribes use pictures of animals as heraldic devices, and decorate their weapons with them; men paint pictures of animals on their bodies, or have them tattooed on to their skin.

9) If the totem is one of the feared and dangerous animals, it is assumed that it spares the members of the tribe named after it.

10) The totem animal protects and warns the members of the tribe.

11) The totem animal predicts the future for its followers, and acts as their leader.

12) The members of a totem tribe often believe that they are related to the totem animal through the bond of common descent.

This catechism of the totemic religion can only be appreciated if we bear in mind that Reinach has also incorporated into it all the signs and remnants from which one can deduce the former existence of the totemic system. One particular attitude of this author towards the problem is apparent in the fact that to a certain extent he ignores the essential traits of totemism. As we shall see, of the two main principles of the totemistic catechism he has forced one into the background, and completely passed over the other.

In order to arrive at a proper conception of the characteristics of totemism, we shall turn to an author who has dedicated four volumes to the subject, combining the most complete collection of the observations on this area with the most far-reaching discussions of the problems thrown up by it. We will remain obliged to J. G. Frazer, the author of *Totemism and Exogamy* (1910) for pleasure and instruction, even if our psychoanalytic investigation should lead to results that take us a long way from his.[3]

A totem, Frazer wrote in his first essay,[4] is a material object for which the savage declares a superstitious respect because he believes that a very particular relationship exists between his own person and each member of this species. The bond between a human being and his totem is a reciprocal one: the totem protects the human being, and the human being demonstrates his respect for the totem in various ways, such as by not killing it if it is an animal, and not plucking it if it is a plant. The totem differs from the fetish in that it is never an individual thing as the fetish is, but always a species, generally a kind of animal or plant, more rarely a class of inanimate object, and yet more rarely of artificially manufactured object.

At least three kinds of totem can be distinguished:

1) The clan totem, which is shared by an entire tribe and passed down from one generation to the next.

2) The sex totem, to which all male or all female members of a tribe belong to the exclusion of the other sex, and

3) The individual totem, which belongs to an individual person, and is not passed down to the following generation. The last two kinds of totem are not as worthy of note as the tribal totem. They are, if I am not mistaken, late formations which are of little significance to the essence of the totem.

The clan totem is the object of veneration of a group of men and women who take their name from it, consider themselves to be blood-related descendants of a common ancestor, and are firmly connected to one another by shared obligations and by a common belief in their totem.

Totemism is both a religious and a social system. On the religious side it consists in the relationships of mutual respect and consideration between a person and his totem, on the social side in the obligations of the clan members towards one another and towards other tribes. In the later history of totemism these two sides show a tendency to part company; the social system often survives the religious one, and conversely remnants of totemism persist in the religions of those countries in which the social system based on totemism has disappeared. Given our ignorance of its origins, we cannot say with any certainty how these two sides of totemism are originally connected to one another. But overall it seems highly likely that the two sides of totemism were initially inseparable. In other words, the further back we go the more clearly apparent it becomes that the clansman sees himself as belonging to the same species as his totem, and does not differentiate his attitude towards the totem from that towards a fellow clansman.

At the beginning of his special description of totemism as a religious system, Frazer states that the members of a clan call themselves after their totem, and as a rule also believe that they are descended from it. The consequence of this belief is that they do not hunt, kill or eat the totem animal, and refrain from any other use of the totem, if it should be something other than an animal. The prohibitions on killing and eating the totem are not the only taboos affecting it; sometimes it is also forbidden to touch it or even to look at it; in a number of cases the totem may not be called by its proper name. Infringement of the taboo prohibitions protecting the totem is automatically punished by serious illnesses or death.[5]

Specimens of the totem animal are sometimes reared by the clan and kept in captivity.[6] If a totem animal is found dead, it is mourned and buried like a fellow clan member. If one has to kill a totem animal, the action is accompanied by a prescribed ritual of apologies and expiatory ceremonies.

The clan expects protection and consideration from its totem. Where it is a dangerous animal (a big cat or a poisonous snake), it is assumed that it would not harm its comrades, and where this assumption is not confirmed, the victim is expelled from the tribe. Oaths, Frazer believes, were originally divine judgements – ordeals. Many tests of descent and authenticity thus rest on the decision of the totem. The totem helps with illnesses, gives the tribe omens and warnings. The appearance of the totem animal in the vicinity of a house was often believed to herald a death. The totem had come to fetch its relative.[7]

In various significant conditions, the clan member seeks to stress his kinship with the totem by making himself appear similar to it, wrapping himself in the skin of the totem animal, scarring himself with its image and the like. On solemn occasions of birth, manhood rituals and funerals, this identification with the totem is enacted in deeds and words. Dances at which all the members of the tribe disguise themselves as their totem and copy its gestures serve many different kinds of magic and religious purposes. Finally there are ceremonies in which the totem animal is solemnly killed.[8]

The social side of totemism is expressed above all in the rigour with which the prohibition is observed, and in the extent and amplitude of the restrictions. The members of a totem clan are brothers and sisters, obliged to help and protect one another; in the case of the killing of a clan member by an outsider, the whole of the perpetrator's clan is held responsible for the killing, and the clan of the victim feels solidarity in its demand for the expiation of the spilled blood. Totemic bonds are stronger than family bonds in our sense; they do not coincide with them since the totem is generally passed on through the maternal line, and since paternal descent may not originally have had any validity at all.

The corresponding taboo restriction consists in the prohibition which states that members of the same totem clan may not marry one another and may certainly not engage in sexual intercourse with each other. This is the famous and mysterious exogamy, which is linked with totemism. We have dedicated the whole of the first essay in this series to it, and here we need therefore say only that it emerges out of the intensified dread of incest among primitive people, that it would become completely intelligible as a guarantee against incest in group marriage, and that it first and foremost preserves the younger generation from incest, and only becomes an obstacle for the older generation as well once it has undergone further developments.[9]

To this account of totemism in Frazer, one of the earliest in the literature on the subject, I should now like to add some extracts from one of the most recent summaries. In his *Elemente der Völkerpsychologie* [Elements of Folk Psychology], published in 1912, W. Wundt[10] says, 'The totem animal is seen as the ancestral animal of the group in question. "Totem" is thus on the one hand a group name, and on the other an ancestral name, and in the latter context the name also has a mythological significance. But all of these uses of the term are intertwined, and the individual meanings can retreat into the background, so that in some cases the totems have almost become a mere nomenclature of the tribal divisions, while in others the idea of descent or even that of the religious significance of the totem is placed in the foreground. [. . .] The concept of the totem is the basis for tribal division and tribal organization. Connected with these norms and the solidification of the belief and feeling of the tribal members is the fact that the totem animal was originally not considered merely as a name for a group of tribal divisions, but that the animal is generally seen as the tribal father of the unit in question. [. . .] This is connected to the fact that these animal ancestors are the object of a cult. [. . .] Apart from certain ceremonies and ceremonial festivities, this cult is manifested above all in the attitude towards the totem animal: not only an individual animal, but every representative of the same species is to a certain degree a sacred animal, the members of the totem are forbidden, or only permitted under certain circumstances, to consume the flesh of the totem animal. This corresponds to the contrary phenomenon, significant in such a context, that in certain circumstances a kind of ceremonial consumption of totemic flesh takes place [. . .]

'However, the most important social side of this totemistic tribal division consists in the fact that certain customary norms for the social intercourse of groups are interconnected. Among these norms is primarily that concerning marital intercourse. Thus this tribal division coincides with an important phenomenon that appears for the first time in the totemistic era; with exogamy.

'If we wish to penetrate to one characteristic of original totemism, ignoring everything that might correspond to later accretions or to decline, we discover the following significant traits: *originally, all totems were animals, which were thought to be the ancestors of the individual clans. The totem was only inherited along the female line; it was forbidden to kill the totem* (or eat it, which by primitive standards amounts to the same thing); *members of a totem were forbidden to have sexual intercourse with one another.*'[11]

We might now be struck by the fact that in the *'code du totémisme'* drawn up by Reinach, one of the main taboos, that of exogamy, does not occur at all, while the premise of the second, descent from the totem animal, is mentioned only in passing. But I have chosen the account of Reinach, an eminent authority on the subject, to prepare for the differences of opinion between these different authors, to which we shall now turn our attention.

2

The more irrefutably apparent it became that totemism formed a regular phase in all cultures, the more urgent the need became to reach an understanding of it, and to cast some light on the mystery at its heart. It would appear that everything about totemism is mysterious; the crucial questions are those concerning the origin of totemic ancestry, the motivation of exogamy (or the incest taboo which it represents) and the relationship between the two, totemic organization and the prohibition on incest. Our understanding was to be both historical and psychological, and supply us with information about the conditions under which this curious institution had developed, and to which needs of the human psyche it gives expression.

At this point my readers will be surprised to learn of the great divergence of viewpoints apparent in attempts to answer these questions, and the extent to which opinions of specialist researchers on the subject differ on the subject. More or less everything that might be generally claimed about totemism and exogamy is called into question; even the earlier conception, from an essay published by Frazer in 1887, lays itself open to the criticism that it represents a random preference on the part of the expert, and would today be rejected by Frazer himself, since he has repeatedly altered his views on the matter.[12]

We should be inclined to assume that the essence of totemism and exogamy might be most easily grasped the closer one came to the origins of the two institutions. But here we should bear in mind the observation of Andrew Lang, to the effect that primitive peoples have not preserved these original forms of institutions and the conditions under which they arose, so that we can rely only upon hypotheses to make up for our want of observation.[13] Among the attempts at explanation presented, some seem inadequate to the judgement of the psychologist from the very first. They are all too rational, and do not take into account the emotional nature of the matters for which an explanation is being sought. Others are based on premises unconfirmed by observation; still others refer to material that really requires a different kind of interpretation. In general it is not difficult to refute the various views; the writers are as usual more united in their criticism of one another than in their own productions. On most of the points under discussion the final result is '*non liquet*' [the case is deferred]. Hence it should not come as a surprise if the most recent literature on the subject, generally ignored here, reveals the unmistakable attempt to dismiss a general solution of totemistic problems as unrealizable. Thus, for example, Goldenweiser in the *Journal of American Folk-Lore*, Vol. XXIII, 1910. (Referred to in *Britannica Year Book*, 1913.) I have taken the liberty, in my account of these contradictory hypotheses, of ignoring the sequence in which they were presented.

a) The Origin of Totemism

The question of the origin of totemism can also be posed as follows: how did primitive people come to name themselves (their tribes) after animals, plants and inanimate objects?[14]

The Scottish anthropologist McLennan, who made the scientific discovery of totemism and exogamy,[15] refrained from publishing any views on the origins of totemism. According to a communication from A. Lang[16] he was inclined for a time to trace totemism back to the custom of tattooing. I should like to present the theories so far presented for the derivation of totemism in three groups, as *α*) nominalistic, *β*) sociological and *γ*) psychological.

α) The nominalistic theories

My accounts of these theories will justify my placing them under this common heading.

Garcilaso del Vega, a descendant of the Peruvian Incas, who wrote the history of his people in the seventeenth century, is already supposed to have traced back what he knew of totemistic phenomena to the needs of the tribes to distinguish themselves from one another by names.[17] The same idea reappears centuries later in A. K. Keane's *Ethnology*: totems arose out of the 'heraldic badges' through which individuals, families and tribes sought to distinguish themselves from one another.[18]

Max Müller voiced the same opinion about the significance of the totem in his *Contributions to the Science of Mythology*.[19] A totem is: 1) A clan badge, 2) a clan name, 3) the name of the ancestor of the clan, 4) the name of the object revered by the clan. Later J. Pikler, writing in 1899: people needed a lasting name for com-

munities and individuals, and one that could be fixed in writing . . .
Thus totemism springs not from religious needs, but from the sober
everyday needs of humanity. The core of totemism, naming, is a
consequence of primitive writing technology. The characteristic of
the totem is also that of the easily drawn pictograph. But once the
savages bore the name of an animal, they inferred from that the idea
of their kinship with that animal.[20]

Herbert Spencer[21] has also identified the act of naming as being
of crucial significance for the origins of totemism. Single individuals,
he explained, had possessed certain qualities which invited their
being called after animals, and had thus acquired honorific names or
nicknames which were passed on to their descendants. Because of
the vagueness and unintelligibility of primitive languages, these
names had been understood by later generations as though they
testified to their descent from those very animals. In this way
totemism had unmistakably come into being as ancestor-worship.

Lord Avebury (better known under his former name of Sir John
Lubbock) assessed the origin of totemism very similarly, although
without the emphasis on misunderstanding: if we wish to explain
the veneration of animals, we cannot forget how often human
names are taken from animals. The children and entourage of a
man who was called Bear or Lion naturally turned it into a tribal
name. The result of this was that the animal itself acquired a certain
respect and finally worship.

Fison has presented what appears to be an irrefutable reservation about tracing back totemic names to the names of individuals
in this way.[22] Referring to conditions in Australia, he shows that the
totem is always the mark of a group of people, never of an individual. If this were not the case, however, and the totem were originally the name of an individual, it could, with the matriarchal
system, never be passed on to the man's children.

The theories communicated so far are, incidentally, clearly inadequate. They may explain the fact of animal names for primitive
tribes, but never the significance that this naming has acquired for
them, the totemistic system. The most remarkable theory in this
group is that developed by Andrew Lang in his books *Social Origins*

(1903) and *The Secret of the Totem* (1905). It still identifies naming as the core of the problem, but it engages with two interesting psychological elements and can thus claim to have led the way towards the definitive solution of the mystery of totemism.

Lang first of all considers the question of how the clans acquired their animal names to be irrelevant. We need only assume that they one day became aware that they bore such a name, and were unable to give an account of where it had come from. The origin of this name had been forgotten. Then they would try to discover its source through speculation, and given their convictions concerning the significance of names, they would inevitably arrive at all the ideas that are contained in the totemistic system. Names are for primitive people – as they are among savages today, and even among our own children[23] – not something indifferent and conventional, as they appear to us, but something significant and essential. A person's name is a major component of his character, perhaps a part of his soul. Having the same name as the totem animal must have led primitive people to assume a mysterious and significant bond between themselves and that species. In such circumstances, what bond might be considered apart from blood kinship? But once this was assumed on the basis of their identical names, all the totemic prescriptions, including exogamy, flowed forth as direct consequences of the blood taboo. 'No more than these three things – a group animal name of unknown origin; belief in a transcendental connection between all bearers, human and bestial, of the same name; and belief in the blood superstitions – was needed to give rise to all the totemic creeds and practices, including exogamy.' (*Secret of the Totem*, p. 125f.)

Lang's explanation is, so to speak, two-sided. It derives the totemistic system with psychological necessity out of the fact of the totemic name, on the assumption that the origin of this act of naming has been forgotten. The other part of the theory now seems to illuminate the origin of these names; we shall see that its character is quite different.

This other part of Lang's theory does not differ greatly from the others that I have called 'nominalistic'. The practical need to be distinguished from one another required the individual clans to take names, and for that reason they settled for the names that each clan was given by the others. This 'naming from without' is the peculiarity of Lang's construction. There is nothing particularly striking about the fact that the names that came into being in this way were borrowed from animals, and there was no need for primitive people to take it as an insult or mockery. Incidentally, Lang also invokes the by no means isolated cases from later historical eras, in which names given from without, and originally meant as mockery, were accepted and willingly borne by those so identified (Gueux, Whigs and Tories). The assumption that the origin of these names was forgotten over the course of time connects this second part of Lang's theory with the first part outlined above.

β) The sociological theories

S. Reinach, who has successfully traced the remnants of the totemistic system in the cults and customs of later periods, but who has from the very first showed little interest in the element of descent from the totem animal, at one point states without reservation that totemism seems to him to be nothing but 'une hypertrophie de l'instinct social [a hypertrophy of the social instinct]'.[24]

The same view seems to be represented by the recent work of Émile Durkheim: *Les formes élémentaires de la vie religieuse. Le système totémique en Australie* [*The Elementary Forms of Religious Life. The Totemic System in Australia*] (1912). The totem is the visible representative of the social religion of these peoples. It embodies the community that is the actual object of veneration. Other authors have sought a more immediate explanation for this involvement of social drives in the formation of totemic institutions. Thus A. C. Haddon hypothesized that all primitive clans lived originally on a particular type of plant or animal, perhaps also trading in that foodstuff and bartering it with other tribes. So it was inevitable that the clan should be known to the others by the name of the animal that played such an important part in its life. At the same time a special familiarity with the animal in question and a kind of interest in it must have developed, although it might have been based on no other psychical motive than the most elementary and urgent of human needs, hunger.[25]

Those who object to this most rational of all theories of the origins of totems would claim that such a state of nutrition among primitive people was not found anywhere, and probably never existed. Savages are omnivorous, the more so the more primitive they are. And it is also impossible to understand how such an exclusive diet should have developed into an almost religious attitude towards the dead, peaking in absolute abstention from the preferred foodstuff.

The first of the three theories that Frazer put forward concerning the origin of totemism was a psychological one; I shall give an account of it elsewhere.

The second of Frazer's theories to be discussed here was produced under the influence of the significant publication by two researchers about the natives of Central Australia.[26]

Spencer and Gillen described a series of curious systems, practices and views in a group of tribes, the so-called Arunta nation, and Frazer agreed with their judgements that these peculiarities should be seen as features of a primal state, and might provide information about the original and actual meaning of totemism.

Among the Arunta tribe itself (a part of the Arunta nation), these curious features are as follows:

1) They are divided into totem clans; however the totem is not hereditary but individually determined (in a way that will be examined below).

2) The totem clans are not exogamous, marriage restrictions are produced through a highly developed division into phratries unrelated to the totems.

3) The function of the totem clans consists in the performance of a ceremony which, in an exquisitely magical way, aims at the increase of the edible totem (this ceremony is called *Intichiuma*).

4) The Arunta have a curious theory of conception and rebirth. They assume that at various places in their country the spirits of the dead of the same totem wait to be reborn, and enter the bodies of

women who pass through those places. If a child is born, the mother states at which spirit place she thinks she conceived her child. The child's totem is determined accordingly. It is also assumed that the spirits (of both the dead and the reborn) are connected to curious stone amulets (called churinga) which are found in those places.

Two factors seem to have led Frazer to the belief that the oldest form of totemism has been found in the institutions of the Arunta. First of all, the existence of certain myths claiming that the ancestors of the Arunta were regularly fed by their totem, and married no women but those from their own totem. Secondly, the apparent neglect of the sexual act in their theory of conception. People who had not yet recognized that conception was the result of sexual intercourse might well be considered as the most backward and primitive of those living today.

While he based his opinion of totemism on the *Intichiuma* ceremony, Frazer came to see the totemic system in a quite different light as a thoroughly practical organization for the satisfaction of the most natural needs of man (cf. Haddon, above).[27] The system was simply a magnificent piece of 'co-operative magic'. The primitive people formed, so to speak, a magical association of production and consumption. Each totem clan had assumed the task of ensuring ample supplies of a particular foodstuff. If this was an inedible totem – dangerous animals, rain, wind and so on – then the duty of the totem clan was to master this piece of nature and fend off its threats. The functions of each clan benefited all the others. As the clan could eat nothing, or very little, of its totem, it acquired that precious commodity for the others, and was in return kept supplied with that which they in turn were bound to provide as their social totemic duty. In the light of this view, as conveyed through the *Intichiuma* ceremony, it seemed to Frazer that the prohibition imposed upon the clan against eating its own totem had blinded people to the more important aspect of the relationship, namely the command to provide as much as possible of the edible totem for the needs of the others.

Frazer accepted the tradition of the Arunta, that each totem clan had originally been fed by its totem without restriction. In that case it was difficult to understand the subsequent development, in which the clan was satisfied with acquiring the totem for others, while itself almost entirely avoiding the consumption of the totem. He then suggested that this tradition had arisen not out of any kind of religious respect, but perhaps from the observation that no animal tends to consume its own species, so that this break in identification with the totem damaged the power that one hoped to achieve over the totem. Or it might have emerged from an effort to win the creature's favour by sparing it. Frazer did not conceal the difficulties presented by this explanation,[28] and neither did he venture to express an opinion on the way in which the custom of marrying within the totem, present in the Arunta myths, had turned into exogamy.

Frazer's theory based on the *Intichiuma* stands and falls with the recognition of the primitive nature of Arunta institutions. But it appears impossible to maintain this recognition against the objections raised by Durkheim[29] and Lang.[30] Rather, the Arunta seem to be the most highly developed of the Australian tribes, and to represent a stage of dissolution rather than a beginning of totemism. The myths that so impressed Frazer, because in contrast to the institutions prevailing today they stress the freedom to eat the totem and to marry within the totem, should rather be seen as wish-fantasies projected into the past, akin to the myth of the Golden Age.

γ) The psychological theories

Frazer's first psychological theory, developed even before he became acquainted with the observations of Spencer and Gillen, was based on belief in the 'external soul'.[31] According to this theory, the totem represented a safe place of refuge for the soul, where it is deposited in order to escape the dangers that threaten it. Once primitive man had lodged his soul in his totem, he himself was invulnerable, and of course he took care not to damage the bearer of his soul. But since he did not know which individual member of the animal species bore his soul, the obvious thing for him to do was to spare the entire species. Frazer himself later abandoned this derivation of totemism from belief in the soul.

When he encountered the observations of Spencer and Gillen, he proposed the other sociological theory of totemism outlined above, but he himself then found that the motive from which he had derived totemism was all too 'rational', and that he had assumed a social organization which was too complex to be called primitive.[32] The magical cooperative societies now seemed to him more like late fruits than like the seeds of totemism. He sought a simpler element, a primitive superstition, from which he could deduce the emergence of totemism. He then found that original element in the Arunta's curious theory of conception.

The Arunta, as we have mentioned above, make no link between conception and the sexual act. If a wife feels herself to be a mother, it means that at that moment one of the spirits waiting to be reborn has entered her body, and is born to her as a child. This child has the same totem as all the spirits lurking in the same spot. This theory of conception cannot explain totemism, being premised upon the totem. But if we take another step back, to assume that the woman originally believed that the animal, the plant, the stone, the object which occupied her imagination at the moment when she first felt herself to be a mother, really did enter her and was then born to her in human form, the identification of a human being with his totem would really be explained by the mother's belief, and all other totemic commandments (apart from exogamy) could be derived from it. The person in question would refuse to eat this animal, this plant, because he would, so to speak, be eating himself. But he would feel sometimes induced to consume something of his totem in a ceremonial fashion, because in that way he would reinforce his identification with the totem, which is the essence of totemism. W. H. R. Rivers' observations of the native of the Banks Islands seemed to demonstrate people's direct identification with their totem on the basis of just such a theory of conception.[33]

The final source of totemism, then, would be the savages' lack of knowledge of the process by which human beings and animals propagate their species, and particularly the lack of awareness of the role played by the male in fertilization. This lack of knowledge must be made easier by the long interval which comes between the fertilizing act and the birth of the child (or the feeling of the child's first movements). Totemism is thus a creation not of the male but of the female mind. Its roots lie in the 'sick fancies' of the pregnant woman. 'Anything indeed that struck a woman at that mysterious moment of her life when she first knows herself to be a mother might easily be identified by her with the child in her womb. Such maternal fancies, so natural and seemingly so universal, appear to be the root of totemism.'[34]

The main objection to this third of Frazer's theories is the same one that has already been raised against the second, sociological one. The Arunta seem to have moved a long way away from the beginnings of totemism. Their denial of paternity does not seem to be based on primitive ignorance; they themselves even know inheritance by the paternal line. They seem to have sacrificed paternity to a kind of speculation that seeks to honour the ancestral spirits.[35] If they elevate the myth of immaculate conception by the spirit to a general theory of conception, we need not expect them to be any more ignorant about the conditions of reproduction than the ancient peoples around the time of the origin of the Christian myths.

Another psychological theory of the origin of totemism has been put forward by the Dutchman G. A. Wilken. It establishes a link between totemism and metempsychosis. 'The animal to which the souls of the dead passed in the general belief became a blood relation, an ancestor, and was venerated as such.' But the belief in the transmigration of souls to animals may be explained by totemism rather than the other way around.[36]

Another theory of totemism is represented by such excellent American ethnologists as Franz Boas, Hill-Tout and others. It is based on observations of totemistic North American Indian tribes, and claims that the totem was originally the protective spirit of an ancestor, which the ancestor had acquired in a dream and passed on to his descendants. We have heard above of the difficulties involved in suggesting that totems are inherited from individuals; besides, the Australian observations do not at all support the idea of tracing the totem back to the tutelary spirit.[37]

For the last of the psychological theories, the one expressed by Wundt, two facts have become crucial: first of all, the original and the most enduringly widespread totemic object is an animal, and that secondly, among the totem animals the earliest coincide with the 'soul animals'.[38] Soul animals, such as birds, snakes, lizards and mice, are ideally suited by their rapid movements, their flight through the air, and by other qualities prompting surprise and fear, to be recognized as the bearers of the soul as it leaves the body. The totem animal is a descendant of the animal metamorphoses of the ethereal soul. Thus it is here, for Wundt, that totemism leads directly to belief in the soul, or animism.

b) and c) The Origin of Exogamy and its Relationship to Totemism

I have quoted the theories of totemism in some detail, and yet I fear that I have not given an adequate idea of them, because I have had to present my ideas in such a condensed form. As regards further questions, in the interests of my readers I shall take the liberty of being even more concise. Discussions of exogamy in totemic peoples are rendered particularly complex and numerous by the nature of the material employed; we might even describe them as confused. The purposes of this paper also allow me to emphasize only a few broad guidelines, and to refer those in search of a more thorough treatment of the subject to the specialist papers that I have cited a number of times.

The position adopted by an author on the problems of exogamy is of course not independent of his support for one theory of totems or another. Some of these explanations of totemism avoid making any connection with exogamy, so that the two institutions fall smoothly apart. Thus two views confront one another, one seeking to maintain the original appearance that exogamy is a significant piece of the totemistic system, and another that disputes any such connection, and believes in a chance coincidence of the two features in the most ancient cultures. In his later works, Frazer resolutely represented the latter point of view. 'I must request the reader to bear constantly in mind that the two institutions of totemism and exogamy are fundamentally distinct in origin and nature, though they have accidentally crossed and blended in many tribes.' (*Totemism and Exogamy*, I, Preface, xii.)

He warns directly against the opposite view as a source of endless difficulties and misunderstandings. By contrast, other authors have found a way of understanding exogamy as a necessary consequence of the fundamental totemistic views. Durkheim[39] has explained how the taboo connected to the totem is bound to imply the prohibition on sexual intercourse with a woman of the same totem. The totem is of the same blood as the human being, and for that reason the blood ban (with reference to defloration and menstruation) prohibits sexual intercourse with a woman of the same totem.[40] A. Lang, who agrees with Durkheim in this respect, goes so far as to say that it does not take the blood taboo to bring the prohibition against women of the same tribe into effect.[41] The general totem taboo which forbids, for example, sitting in the shade of the totem tree, would have been sufficient for that. Incidentally, Lang argues for another derivation of exogamy (see below), and leaves some doubt about the way in which these two explanations relate to one another.

As regards temporal relations, most authors hold the view that totemism is the older institution, and exogamy was a later addition.[42]

Among the theories that seek to explain exogamy independently of totemism, we need mention only a few which explain the various attitudes of the authors towards the problem of incest.

McLennan[43] had ingeniously explained exogamy on the basis of the remnants of customs indicating the former practice of bride theft. He now hypothesized that in primeval times it had been customary to fetch a wife from a strange tribe, and marriage to a woman from one's own tribe had gradually become 'improper because it was unusual'. He sought the motive for the custom of exogamy in a lack of women in those primitive tribes, the result of the practice of killing most female children at birth. This is not the place to examine whether the actual situation confirms McLennan's hypotheses. What interests us far more is the argument that the premises of his argument fail to explain why the male members of the tribe should also have made the few women of their own blood inaccessible, and the way in which the incest problem is here left completely to one side.[44]

In contrast to this, and evidently with more justice, other researchers have seen exogamy as an institution for the prevention of incest.[45]

If we ignore the gradually increasing complexity of Australian marriage restrictions, we can only agree with the view of Morgan, Frazer, Howitt and Baldwin Spencer,[46] that these institutions bear the imprint of what Frazer calls 'deliberate design', and that they are designed to achieve what they have in fact achieved. 'In no other way does it seem possible to explain in all its details a system at once so complex and so regular.'[47]

It is interesting to stress that the first of the restrictions produced by the introduction of marriage classes affected the sexual freedom of the younger generation, which is to say incest between brothers and sisters and sons and mothers, while incest between father and daughter was only abolished by subsequent measures.

But tracing exogamous sexual restrictions back to a legalistic intention does not help us to understand the motive behind the creation of those institutions. In the final analysis, what is the source of the dread of incest that must be acknowledged as the root of exogamy? In order to explain the dread of incest, it is clearly not enough to refer to an instinctive aversion towards sexual intercourse with a blood relation, that is, to refer to the fact of the fear of incest, when social experience demonstrates that, despite this instinct, incest is not a rare occurrence even in our own contemporary society, and when historical experience tells us of cases in which incestuous marriage was obligatory for privileged people.

Westermarck[48] has explained the fear of incest by saying 'that between people who live together from childhood an innate aversion towards sexual intercourse predominates, and that this feeling, since these individuals are generally blood relations, finds natural expression, in custom and law, in aversion towards sexual contact among close relations'. Havelock Ellis may have disputed the instinctive characteristic of this aversion in his *Studies in the Psychology of Sex*, but otherwise he essentially supports the same explanation, saying, 'The normal failure of the pairing instinct to manifest itself in the case of brothers and sisters, or of boys and girls brought up together from infancy, is a merely negative phenomenon due to the inevitable absence in those circumstances of the conditions which evoke the pairing instinct [. . .]. Between those who have been brought up together from childhood all the sensory stimuli of vision, hearing and touch have been dulled by use, trained to the calm level of affection, and deprived of their potency to arouse the erethistic excitement which produces sexual tumescence.'

It strikes me as very curious that Westermarck should see this innate aversion towards sexual intercourse with people with whom one has shared one's childhood as a psychical equivalent of the biological fact that in-breeding is damaging to the species. This would mean biological instinct of this kind having gone so far astray in its psychological expression that rather than affecting blood-relations, with whom intercourse would be damaging to reproduction, it would apply to people who were quite harmless in this respect, because they had merely shared one's home. But neither can I avoid referring to Frazer's excellent criticism in reply to Westermarck's assertion. Frazer finds it incomprehensible that there should be no resistance whatsoever in contemporary sexual feeling to intercourse with people with whom one has shared a home, while the dread of incest, which according to Westermarck's theory is only derived from that other aversion, has increased enormously. Other of Frazer's observations go deeper, however, and I shall set them down here in their complete form, because in essence they coincide with the arguments developed in my essay on taboo:

'It is not easy to see why a deep human instinct should need to be reinforced by law. There is no law commanding men to eat and drink or forbidding them to put their hands in the fire. Men eat and drink and keep their hands out of the fire instinctively for fear of natural not legal penalties, which could be entailed by violence done to these instincts. The law only forbids men to do what their

instincts incline them to do; what nature itself prohibits and pun-
ishes, it would be superfluous for the law to prohibit and punish.
Accordingly we may always safely assume that crimes forbidden by
law are crimes which many men have a natural propensity to commit. If there was no such propensity there would be no such crimes,
and if no such crimes were committed what need to forbid them?
Instead of assuming, therefore, from the legal prohibition of incest
that there is a natural aversion to incest, we ought rather to assume
that there is a natural instinct in favour of it, and that if the law
represses it, as it represses other natural instincts, it does so because
civilized men have come to the conclusion that the satisfaction
of these natural instincts is detrimental to the general interests of
society.'

To these excellent arguments of Frazer's I might add that the
experiences of psychoanalysis utterly exclude the hypothesis of an
innate aversion to incestuous intercourse. On the contrary, they
have taught that the first sexual impulses in the young person are
regularly incestuous in nature, and that such repressed impulses
play a role which can hardly be overestimated as drive-forces
behind later neuroses.

We must abandon the notion of the dread of incest as an innate
instinct. Nor is the situation much better with another explanation
of the prohibition on incest which can claim many supporters, the
hypothesis that primitive peoples noticed at an early stage the dangers emanating from incest which threatened their line, and that it
was for that reason, with deliberate intent, that they declared the
prohibition on incest. The objections to this theory are manifold.[49]
It is not only that the prohibition on incest must be older than cattle
breeding, from which mankind was able to learn about the effects
of incest on the qualities of the breed; the damaging effects of incest
have still not been established beyond all doubt, and are difficult to
demonstrate in humans. Besides, everything we know about contemporary savages makes it appear very unlikely that the thoughts
of their remotest ancestors would have been concerned with the
prevention of harm to their later descendants. It sounds almost
ludicrous to attribute to these childlike and unreflecting human

beings hygienic and eugenic motives that are barely taken into account in our own contemporary culture.[50]

Finally, we shall also have to point out that the prohibition against in-breeding as a factor which weakens the race for practical hygienic reasons seems quite inappropriate as an explanation of the profound aversion towards incest that is apparent in our society. As I have set out elsewhere,[51] this dread of incest seems in fact to be even more vivid and intense among primitive peoples living today than it is among civilized people.

While we might also expect to have a choice between possible sociological, biological and psychological explanations of the derivation of the fear of incest, while psychological motives might perhaps be regarded as a representation of biological forces, at the end of the inquiry we see ourselves obliged to concur with Frazer's resigned conclusion: we do not know the origin of the dread of incest, and do not even know where we should seek it. None of the solutions to the mystery put forward so far seems satisfactory to us.[52]

I must, however, mention one other attempt to explain the origin of the dread of incest, which is quite different in nature from those considered hitherto. It could be described as 'historical'.

This attempt is linked with a hypothesis of Charles Darwin's concerning the primal social state of man. Darwin concluded from the habits of the higher primates that mankind, too, first lived in small hordes within which the jealousy of the oldest and strongest male prevented sexual promiscuity. 'We may indeed conclude from what we know of the jealousy of all male quadrupeds, armed, as many of them are, with special weapons for battling with their rivals, that promiscuous intercourse in a state of nature is extremely improbable. [. . .] Therefore, if we look far enough back in the stream of time, [. . .] judging from the social habits of man as he now exists we may indeed conclude from what we know of the jealousy of all male quadrupeds, [. . .] the most probable view is that primaeval man aboriginally lived in small communities, each with as many wives as he could support and obtain, whom he would have jealously guarded against all other men. Or he may have lived with several wives by himself, like the gorilla; for all the natives "agree that but one adult male is seen in a band; when the youngest male grows up, a contest takes place for mastery, and the strongest, by killing and driving out the others, establishes himself as the head of the community". (Dr Savage, in *Boston Journal of Natural History*, vol. V, 1845–47, p. 423.) The younger males, being thus expelled and wandering about, would, when at last successful in finding a partner, prevent too close interbreeding within the limits of the same family."[53]

Atkinson[54] seems at first to have recognized that these conditions in the Darwinian primal horde must effectively have enforced the exogamy of the young men. Each of these expelled males could form a similar horde, in which the same prohibition on sexual intercourse was enforced by the jealousy of the chief male, and over the course of time this would produce the rule that became a conscious law: no sexual intercourse between those who share a home. With the establishment of totemism, the rule would have assumed another form: no sexual intercourse within the totem.

Lang[55] agrees with this explanation of exogamy. But in the same book he also puts forward the other (Durkheimian) theory, according to which exogamy emerges as a consequence of the totemic laws. It is not entirely easy to harmonize the two conceptions; in the former case exogamy existed prior to totemism, in the latter it is a consequence of it.[56]

3

Psychoanalytical experience casts a single beam of light into this darkness.

The relationship between children and animals is very similar to that between primitive man and animals. Children do not yet show a trace of that arrogance that leads civilized adult men to draw a strict boundary between their own nature and the animal world. Children grant animals complete and unreserved equality; uninhibited as they are in admitting to their bodily needs, they probably feel more closely related to animals than they do to adults, who may well be a mystery to them.

In many cases, however, a curious disturbance occurs in this excellent understanding between children and animals. The child suddenly develops a fear of a particular kind of animal, and begins to guard against touching or even seeing any individual members of the species. The clinical picture of an animal phobia is forming, one of the most frequently occurring of the psychoneurotic illnesses of this age, and perhaps the earliest form of such an illness. The phobia generally applies to animals in which the child had until that point shown a particularly keen interest, and has nothing to do with the individual animal. In urban conditions, the selection of animals that can become objects of phobia is not great. They are horses, dogs, cats, more rarely birds, and strikingly often very small animals such as beetles and butterflies. Sometimes animals with which the child is familiar only from picture-books and fairy tales become objects of the senseless and immoderate fear that is shown in these phobias; we seldom even manage to discover the ways in which an unusual choice of this kind has taken place. So I thank K. Abraham for communicating to me a case in which a child himself explained his fear of wasps by revealing that the colour and stripes of the wasp's body made him think of tigers, which, from all that he had heard, he could legitimately fear.

Animal phobias among children have not yet been the subject of close analytical investigation, although they certainly merit such study. The difficulties involved in the analysis of children of such a tender age probably explain why this should be so. Consequently we cannot claim to know the general meaning of these illnesses, and I myself am of the opinion that it might not turn out to be uniform in nature. But some cases of such phobias applied to larger animals have proven accessible to analysis, and thus revealed their secret to the investigator. In every case it was the same: the fear was basically of the father, where the children under examination were boys, and had merely been displaced on to the animal.

Anyone with any psychoanalytic experience will inevitably have come across such cases, and received the same impression of them.

But I can only refer to a few detailed publications on the subject. This is an accidental fact of the literature, and it should not be thought that we are supporting our conclusions only on a handful of observations. I might mention, for example, one author who has sympathetically treated childhood neuroses, M. Wulff of Odessa. In connection with the account of the illness of a nine-year-old boy he relates that the boy had suffered from a phobia of dogs at the age of four. 'When he saw a dog walk by in the street he wept and cried, "Dear dog, don't touch me, I'll be good." By "being good" he meant, "no longer playing the fiddle" (masturbating).'[57]

The same author later sums up: 'His phobia of dogs is actually fear of his father displaced on to the dogs, because his curious expression, "Dog, I will be good" – that is, not masturbate – actually refers to his father, who forbade masturbation.' In a note he then adds something that coincides just as completely with my own experience, and at the same time bears out the widespread nature of such experiences: 'Such phobias (phobias relating to horses, dogs, cats, chickens and other domestic animals) are, I believe, just as widespread in childhood as *pavor nocturnus* [fear of the dark], and can almost always be revealed in analysis as a displacement of fear from one of the parents on to animals. Whether the common phobia of mice and rats has the same mechanism I should not like to say.'

In the first volume of the *Jahrbuch für psychoanalytische und psychopathologische Forschungen* I published the 'Analysis of the Phobia of a Five-year-old Boy', the material for which the father of the little patient had placed at my disposal. This concerned a fear of horses, in consequence of which the boy refused to go into the street. He expressed the fear that the horse would come into the room and bite him. It turned out that this was to be the punishment for his wish for the horse to fall over (die). Once the boy's fear of his father had been removed with reassurances, it turned out that he was battling against desires whose content involved his father being away (travelling, dying). He perceived his father, as he very clearly revealed, as a competitor for his mother's favours, at which his blossoming sexual wishes were directed in obscure premonitions. So he was in that typical attitude of the male child towards his parents that we call the 'Oedipus complex', and in which we can discern the core-complex of neuroses in general. The new thing that we learn from the analysis of 'little Hans' is the fact valuable to totemism, that in such circumstances the child displaces a proportion of its feelings from his father on to the animal.

Analysis is able to reveal the associative paths, both arbitrary and significant, along which such a displacement occurs. It also allows us to guess the motives behind it. The hatred emerging out of rivalry over the mother may not spread uninhibitedly in the boy's psychical life, it has to battle with the affection and admiration that he has always felt for a single person, and the child finds himself in an ambiguous – ambivalent – emotional position towards his father, and seeks relief in this conflict of ambivalence by displacing his hostile and fearful emotions on to a father surrogate. However, this displacement cannot be accomplished in such a way as to effect a smooth separation between affectionate and hostile emotions. Rather, the conflict persists with regard to the displacement object, and the ambivalence is transferred to that object. It was clear that little Hans was not only afraid of horses, but also respected them and was interested in them. As his fear subsided, he identified with the feared animal, jumped around like a horse and eventually bit his father.[58] In another stage of the resolution of the phobia he had no qualms about identifying his parents with other large animals.[59]

We might observe that in these animal phobias of children certain traits of totemism recur in a negative form. But it is to S. Ferenczi that we owe the lovely and isolated observation of a case that can only be described as positive totemism in a child.[60] In the case of little Árpád, however, as related by Ferenczi, his totemistic interests do not awaken directly in the context of the Oedipus complex, but on the basis of the narcissistic precondition for it, the fear of castration. Anyone who carefully examines the story of little Hans will also find in it ample testimony for the idea that the father is admired as the possessor of large genitals, and feared as a threat to the boy's own genitals. The father plays the same role in the

Oedipus complex as he does in the castration complex, that of the feared opponent of the child's sexual interests. Castration and its substitute, blinding, is his threatened punishment.[61]

When little Árpád was two and a half years old, on a summer holiday he tried to urinate into the chicken-house, whereupon a chicken pecked his member, or pecked at it. A year later, when he returned to the same place, he himself became a chicken, he took a great interest in the chicken-house and everything that happened in it, and he abandoned his human language for clucking and crowing. At the time of the observation (at the age of five), he was speaking once again, but he spoke only of chickens and other types of poultry. He did not play with any other toys, he sang only songs featuring chickens. His behaviour towards his totem animal was exquisitely ambivalent, showing excessive hatred and love. His favourite game was slaughtering fowl. 'The slaughtering of poultry is a celebration for him. He is capable of dancing for hours around the corpses of the animals in a state of great excitement.' But then he would kiss and stroke the slaughtered animal, clean and caress the images of chickens that he himself had mistreated.

Little Árpád himself ensured that the meaning of his strange behaviour could not remain hidden. He sometimes translated his desires out of the totemistic mode of expression back into that of everyday life. 'My father is the cock,' he once said. 'Now I am small, now I'm a little chick. When I grow up I'm going to be a chicken. When I'm even bigger I'll be a cock.' On another occasion he suddenly said that he wanted some 'fricassee of mother' to eat (by analogy with fricassee of chicken). He was very generous with clear threats of castration against other people, just as he himself had experienced them in response to masturbatory activity with his member.

According to Ferenczi there was no doubt about the source of his interest in activity in the chicken-yard: 'The lively sexual intercourse between cock and hen, the laying of eggs and the hatching of the young brood' satisfied his desire for sexual knowledge, which actually applied to human family life. He had based his object-desires on the model of the life of chickens, once saying to his neighbour, 'I will marry you and your sister and my three female cousins and the cook, no, not the cook, my mother.'

At a later point we will be able to assess the worth of this observation; for the time being let us only emphasize two features as valuable correspondences with totemism: complete identification with the totem animal[62] and the ambivalent emotional attitude towards it. On the basis of these observations we consider ourselves justified, in the formula of totemism – where males are concerned – to insert the father in the place of the totem animal. We might then observe that in so doing we have not taken a new or a particularly bold step. Indeed, savages say the same thing themselves, and in so far as the totemistic system is still in force, they describe the totem as their ancestor and forefather. All we have done is to take literally a statement made by these peoples, with which ethnologists were not able to do a great deal, and which they were therefore happy to place in the background. Psychoanalysis, on the other hand, recommends that we seek out this very point and use it to explain totemism.[63]

The first result of our substitution is very curious. If the totem animal is the father, then the two chief commandments of totemism, the two taboo prescriptions which form its nucleus, not to kill the totem and not to have sexual intercourse with any woman belonging to the totem, coincide in their content with the two crimes of Oedipus, who killed his father and took his mother as his wife, and with the two primal desires of the child, insufficient repression or reawakening of which perhaps forms the core of all psychoneuroses. If this equation is more than a misleading trick of chance, it should allow us to cast a light on the distant origins of totemism. In other words, we should succeed in making it appear likely that the totemistic system arose out of the conditions of the Oedipus complex, like the animal phobia of 'little Hans' and the poultry perversion of 'little Árpád'. In order to pursue this possibility, below we shall study one peculiarity of the totemistic system, or, as we might say, of the totemic religion, which we have barely seen mentioned hitherto.

4

W. Robertson Smith, the physicist, philologist, biblical exegete and classical researcher who died in 1894, a man as many-sided as he was clear-eyed and free-thinking, in his book on the religion of the Semites published in 1889[64] put forward the hypothesis that a curious ceremony, the so-called totem meal, had formed an integral part of the totemic system from the very beginning. In support of this supposition he had at the time only a single description of such an act at his disposal, from the fifth century AD, but he was able to elevate his hypothesis to a high level of probability by analysing the institution of sacrifice among the ancient Semites. Since the sacrifice assumes a divine person, it was a matter of constructing the argument back from a superior phase of the religious rite to the lowest phase of totemism.

I shall now attempt to extract from Robertson Smith's excellent book the theses that are crucial to our interest in the origin and significance of the sacrificial rite, omitting all of the often fascinating details, and neglecting all later developments. There is no question, in such an abstract, of conveying anything of the lucidity or convincing force of the account that were present in the original.

Robertson Smith states that sacrifice on the altar was the essential part of the rite of the ancient religion. It plays the same role in all religions, so that its origins must go back to very universal causes, which work in similar ways in all places.

But sacrifice – the sacred act par excellence (sacrificium, ἱερουργία – originally had a meaning other than the one it acquired in later times: an offering to the deity in order to propitiate him or gain his favour. (It was from the subsidiary meaning of self-denial that the secular use of the word emerged.) At first, the sacrifice was demonstrably nothing other than 'an act of social fellowship between the deity and his worshippers', a communion of the faithful with their god.

The materials offered as sacrifices could be eaten or drunk; man sacrificed to his god the things that he ate himself: meat, cereals, fruits, wine and oil. It was only in relation to sacrificial meat that there were any restrictions and deviations. The god fed on the animal sacrifices along with his devotees, while the vegetable sacrifices were left to him alone. There is no doubt that animal sacrifices are older, and were once the only forms of sacrifice. The vegetable sacrifices emerged out of the offering of first fruits, and correspond to a tribute to the lord of the soil and the land. But animal sacrifice is older than agriculture.

From linguistic remnants it is certain that the portion of the sacrifice destined for the god was originally considered really to be his food. As the divine being progressively dematerialized, this idea became a stumbling block; it was avoided by assigning only the liquid part of the meal to the deity. Later, the use of fire, which allowed the sacrificial meat on the altar to go up in smoke, made it possible to prepare human foodstuffs in such a way that they became more appropriate to the divine being. The substance of the drink-sacrifice was originally the blood of sacrificial animals; wine was later substituted for blood. The ancients saw wine as the 'blood of the grape', as our poets call it even today.

So the most ancient form of sacrifice, older than the use of fire and the knowledge of agriculture, was the animal sacrifice, the flesh and blood of which was consumed by both the god and his worshippers. It was essential for each of the participants to receive his share of the meal.

Such a sacrifice was a public ceremony, the celebration of a whole clan. Religion as such was a universal matter, religious duty a piece of social obligation. Sacrifice and festivity coincide in all peoples, every sacrifice involves a feast, and no feast can be celebrated without a sacrifice. The sacrificial feast was an occasion at which people rose joyfully above their own interests, with the emphasis being placed on mutual dependence both among one another and with their god.

The ethical power of the public sacrificial meal was based upon ancient ideas concerning the significance of communal eating and drinking. Eating and drinking with someone else was at the same time a symbol and a reinforcement of social community and the assumption of mutual obligations; the sacrificial meal directly expressed the idea that the god and his devotees share a table, but every other aspect of their mutual relationship was incorporated in this. Practices that are still commonplace among the desert Arabs prove that what is binding about the communal meal is not some religious element but the act of eating itself. Anyone who has eaten the smallest morsel with such a Bedouin, or taken a sip of his milk, no longer needs to fear him as an enemy, and may be sure of his protection and his help. But not for ever; strictly speaking only for as long as the food they have consumed together can be assumed to remain in the body. The bond of unity is conceived as realistically as that; it requires repetition in order to be reinforced and made to endure.

But why is this binding force attributed to communal eating and drinking? In the most primitive societies there is only one bond that unites people unconditionally and without exception, and that is common membership of a clan, or kinship. The members of this community stand by one another, the term 'kin' refers to a group of people whose lives are connected into a physical entity in such a way that they can be considered as pieces of a communal life. In the case of the murder of an individual member of the kin these people do not say: the blood of this or that person has been shed, but: our blood has been shed. The Hebrew phrase with which kinship is acknowledged is: you are my bone and my flesh. Kinship thus means participation in a common substance. That being the case, it is natural for it to be based not only on the fact that a person is a part of the substance of his mother, to whom he was born and on whose milk he was fed, but that the food that he later consumes and with which he renews his body can also allow him to acquire and reinforce kinship. If a person shared the meal with his god, it expressed the conviction that he was of the same material as the god, and if he regarded someone as a stranger, he would not share a meal with him.

So the sacrificial meal was originally a feast of kinsmen, following the law that only kinsmen eat together. In our society the meal brings together the members of the family, but the sacrificial meal has nothing to do with the family. Kinship is older than family life. The most primitive families known to us regularly include people who have different kinship connections. Men take wives from outside clans, children inherit the mother's clan; there is no kinship between the husband and the other family members. In such a family there is no communal meal. Even today savages eat apart and alone, and the religious food prohibitions of totemism often make communal eating with their wives and children impossible.

Let us now turn our attention to the sacrificial animal. There was, as we have heard, no tribal assembly without an animal sacrifice, but – significantly – neither was there any slaughtering of animals except for such solemn occasions. People had no reservations about eating fruits, game and the milk of domestic animals, but religious scruples made it impossible for the individual to kill a domestic animal for his own use. There is not the slightest doubt, says Robertson Smith, that every sacrifice was originally a clan sacrifice, and that the *killing of a sacrificial animal was originally among those actions that are forbidden to the individual and are only justified when the whole tribe assumes shared responsibility*. Among primitive people there is only one class of actions to which this characteristic applies, namely those that involve the sanctity of the tribal blood. A life which no individual is permitted to invade and which can only be sacrificed by the agreement, and with the participation, of all clan members, stands on the same footing as the life of the tribesmen themselves. The rule that every guest at the sacrificial meal must consume the flesh of the sacrificial animal has the same meaning as the law that the execution of a guilty tribe member must be performed by the whole tribe. In other words: the sacrificial animal was treated like a tribal relation, *the sacrificing community, its god and the sacrificial animal were of one blood, members of a single clan*.

Quoting ample evidence, Robertson Smith identifies the sacrificial animal with the old totem animal. In later antiquity there are two kinds of sacrifices, those of domestic animals that were also usually eaten, and unusual sacrifices of animals that were forbidden as unclean. Closer investigation then shows that these unclean animals were sacred animals, that they were offered as sacrifices to the gods to whom they were sacred, that these animals were originally identical with the gods themselves, and that in the act of sacrifice the faithful in some way stressed their blood relationship with the animal and the god. In even earlier times, however, this difference between normal and 'mystical' victims is absent. All animals were originally sacred, their flesh was forbidden and might only be consumed on solemn occasions with the participation of the whole tribe. The slaughter of the animal was equated with the shedding of tribal blood, and had to occur amidst the same precautions and guarantees against reproach.

The taming of domestic animals and the rise of cattle-breeding seems in all places to have put an end to pure, strict totemism.[65] But such sanctity as still attached to domestic animals in the now 'pastoral' religion is clear enough to reveal its originally totemic character. Even in late classical times the rite in various places required the person performing the sacrifice to flee as though to escape a punishment. In Greece the idea that the killing of an ox was actually a crime must once have been universally prevalent. In the Athenian festival of Buphonia, a formal trial was introduced after the sacrifice, in which everyone taking part was interrogated. Finally they agreed to shift guilt for the murder on to the knife, which was then thrown into the sea.

Despite the fear that protects the life of the sacred animal like that of a tribal member, it becomes necessary to kill such an animal in solemn community from time to time, and to distribute its flesh and blood among the clansmen. The motive calling for this deed reveals the underlying significance of the institution of sacrifice. We have heard that in later times every communal meal, a sharing of the same substance entering their bodies, generates a sacred bond between the commensals; in very ancient times this meaning seems only to apply to the sharing of the substance of a sacred victim. *The holy mystery of sacrificial death 'is justified by the consideration that only in this way can the sacred cement be procured which creates or keeps alive a living bond of union between the worshippers and their god'.*[66]

This bond is nothing other than the life of the sacrificial animal, which dwells in its flesh and in its blood, and which is communicated to all participants by the sacrificial meal. Such an idea underlies all blood covenants through which even in later times people commit to one another. The thoroughly realistic conception of blood kinship as an identity of substance helps us to understand the need to renew it at intervals through the physical process of the sacrificial meal.

Let us at this point interrupt our survey of Robertson Smith's reflections, to give a highly compressed summary of what lies at their core: when the idea of private property came into being, the sacrifice was conceived as a gift to the deity, as a transfer from the property of the human being to that of the god. But this interpretation left all the curious features of the sacrificial ritual unexplained. In most ancient times the sacrificial animal itself had been sacred, its life invulnerable; that life could only be taken with the participation and shared responsibility of the whole tribe and in the presence of the god, if it was to supply the sacred substance, consumption of which assured the clansmen of their material identity both with each other and with the deity. The sacrifice was a sacrament, the sacrificial animal itself a member of the clan. It was in fact the old totem animal, the primitive god himself, through the killing and devouring of which the clansmen refreshed and ensured their likeness with the god.

From this analysis of sacrifice Robertson Smith concludes that the periodic killing and consumption of the totem in times *before the worship of anthropomorphic deities* became a significant part of totemic religion. The ceremonial of such a totem meal, he said, had been represented for us in the description of a sacrifice from later times. St Nilus gives an account of a sacrificial custom of the Bedouins in the Sinai Desert around the end of the fourth century AD. The sacrifice, a camel, was bound and laid upon a crude altar of stones; the leader of the tribe made the participants pass singing three times around the altar, inflicted the first wound upon the beast and greedily drank the blood that poured out; then the whole community fell upon the victim, hacked out pieces of its quivering flesh with their swords and devoured it raw in such haste that in the brief interval between the rising of the morning star for which this sacrifice was made, and the fading of the stars before the sun's rays, the whole of the sacrificial animal, its body, bones, skins, flesh and innards had been devoured. This barbaric and clearly very ancient rite was, all indications suggest, not an isolated custom, but the universal and original form of the totemic sacrifice which would later be watered down in various ways.

Many authors have refused to lend credence to the idea of the totem meal because it could not be reinforced by direct observation on the level of totemism. Robertson Smith himself referred to the examples in which the sacramental significance of the sacrifice appears assured, for example in the human sacrifices of the Aztecs, and to others that recall the conditions of the totem meal, the bear sacrifices of the Bear clan of the Ouataouaks in America and the bear festivals of the Ainos in Japan. Frazer has given detailed accounts of these and similar cases in the two last sections of his great work.[67] An Indian tribe in California which worships a large bird of prey (the buzzard) kills the bird in a solemn ceremony once a year, whereupon it is mourned and its skin and feathers preserved. The Zuni Indians in New Mexico treat their sacred tortoise the same way.

One trait that has been observed in the *Intichiuma* ceremonies of the central Australian tribes excellently bears out Robertson Smith's conjectures. Each clan that performs magic for the multiplication of its totem, despite the fact that the clan itself is forbidden to consume it, is obliged to consume something of his totem at the ceremony before the other tribes are given access to it. According to Frazer, the finest example of otherwise forbidden totem is supposed to be found among the Bini in West Africa, in connection with the funeral ceremonial of those tribes.[68]

But we will follow Robertson Smith in his conjecture that the sacramental killing and communal consumption of the otherwise forbidden totem animal was a significant feature of totemic religion.[69]

5

Let us now imagine the scene of one such totem meal, and equip it with some of its probable features which we have not hitherto been able to appreciate. The clan cruelly kills its totem animal on a solemn occasion and consumes it raw, blood, flesh, bones and all; the members of the clan are disguised to resemble the totem, imitate its sounds and movements as though to stress its identity with them. There is also an awareness of performing an act that is forbidden to each individual, and which can only be justified by the participation of all; and no one may be excluded from the killing and the meal. After the act the murdered animal is mourned and lamented. The lament for the dead is made obligatory by fear of revenge; its chief purpose, as Robertson Smith observes of a similar occasion, is to disclaim responsibility for the killing.[70]

But after this mourning comes the rowdiest feasting, the unfettering of all instincts and the granting of licence for satisfactions of all kinds. Here we do not have the slightest trouble gaining an insight into the nature of the feast.

A feast is a permitted, or rather a compulsory excess, a solemn infringement of a prohibition. Men commit these excesses not because they are feeling cheerful as the result of some regulation imposed upon them; it would be more true to say that excess is part of the nature of the feast; the festive mood is created by the freedom to do something normally forbidden.

But how are we to understand the prelude to this festive joy: mourning over the death of the totem animal? If the clansmen rejoice over the killing of the totem, which is otherwise forbidden, why do they also mourn it?

We have heard that clan members sanctify themselves by consuming the totem, reinforcing their identification with it and with each other. The fact that they have absorbed into themselves the sacred life, whose bearer is the substance of the totem, might explain the festive atmosphere and everything that follows from it.

Psychoanalysis has revealed to us that the totem animal is really the substitute for the father, and this probably accords with the contradiction that it is otherwise forbidden to kill it, and that its killing becomes a festivity, that the animal is killed and yet also mourned. It might be that the ambivalent emotional attitude which is characteristic of the father-complex in our children even today, and which often continues into adult life, also extends to the father-substitute of the totem animal.

But if we bring together the translation of the totem provided by psychoanalysis with the fact of the totem meal and the Darwinian conjecture concerning the primeval state of human society, the possibility arises of a deeper understanding, a prospect of a hypothesis which may appear fantastic, but which offers the advantage of creating an unsuspected unity in a series of phenomena that have hitherto remained separate.

The Darwinian primal horde, of course, has no place for the beginnings of totemism. All we find there is a violent, jealous father who keeps all the females to himself and drives his sons away as they grow up. This primeval state of society has never been observed. The most primitive organization that we encounter, and which persists in certain tribes even today, are bands of men consisting of members who enjoy equal rights and are subject to the restrictions of the totemistic system and inheritance along the matriarchal line. Can the one have emerged from the other, and in what way would that have been possible?

We may be able to provide an answer with reference to the celebration of the totem meal; one day[71] the expelled brothers joined forces, killed and devoured their father and thus put an end to the father's horde. United, they risked and accomplished something that the individual could not have achieved. (It might be that a cultural advance, perhaps the use of a new weapon, had given them a feeling of superiority.) It was thought natural among such cannibalistic savages to eat their victim. The violent primal father had certainly been the feared and envied model for each of the brothers. Now, by eating him, they accomplished their identification with him, and each of them appropriated a piece of his strength. The totem meal, perhaps humanity's first feast, could be seen as the repetition and commemoration of this curious, criminal deed that saw the beginning of so many institutions – social organization, moral restrictions and religion.[72]

To find these consequences credible, leaving their premises aside, we need only assume that the tumultuous band of brothers was governed by the same contradictory emotions towards their father which we can show to be the content of the ambivalence of the father-complex in all present-day children and neurotics. They hated their father, who stood so powerfully in the way of their need for power and their sexual demands, but they also loved and admired him. Once they had removed him, satisfied their hatred and achieved their desire for identification with him, the impulses of affection that they had overcome in the process were bound to emerge.[73] A sense of guilt came into being, here coinciding with the general remorse. The dead man now became stronger than the living man had been; and we can see all of this in human destinies even today. That which he had previously prevented by virtue of his existence they now forbade themselves in the psychical situation so familiar to us from psychoanalytic treatment, 'deferred obedience'. They revoked their deed by declaring the killing of the father-substitute, the totem, to be forbidden, and renounced its fruits by abandoning their claim to the women who had been freed for them. In this way they turned the son's sense of guilt into the two fundamental taboos of totemism, which for that very reason had to coincide with the two repressed desires of the Oedipus complex. Anyone contravening those taboos was guilty of the two single crimes that were of the greatest concern to primitive society.[74]

The two taboos of totemism, which represent the beginning of human morality, are not psychologically equivalent to one another. Only one, the sparing of the totem animal, is wholly based on emotional motives; the father had been removed, and the deed could not be undone. But there was also a powerful practical explanation for the other taboo, the prohibition on incest. Sexual need does not unite men, it divides them. If the brothers had united in order to overcome the father, they were all rivals now with respect to the women. Each of them would have wanted, like the father, to have all the women to himself, and in the battle of all against all the new organization would have collapsed. None of them would have had the overwhelming strength to assume the father's role successfully. Thus the brothers had no choice, if they wished to live together, except – perhaps after a series of crises – to erect the prohibition on incest, with which they all, and all at once, renounced the women they desired, for the sake of whom they had in fact despatched their father. In this way they saved the organization which had made them strong, and which may have been based on homosexual feelings and acts that would probably manifest themselves among them during their exile. Perhaps it was also this situation that formed the seed of what Bachofen identified as the institutions of matriarchy, until it was in turn supplanted by the patriarchal family organization.

On the other hand, the claim of totemism to be seen as an early attempt at a religion rests on the other taboo, the one protecting the life of the totem animal. If the son perceived the animal as the natural and obvious substitute for the father, the treatment of it that they found imposed upon them expressed more than the need to express their remorse. With the father surrogate, they could attempt to appease their searing sense of guilt, and effect a kind of reconciliation with the father. The totemistic system was, so to speak, a contract with the father, in which the latter granted everything that the childish imagination might expect from a father, which is to say protection, care and consideration. In return for this the brothers guaranteed to honour his life, that is, not to repeat the deed they had performed against him, in which the real father had perished. There was also an attempt at self-justification in totemism. 'If our father had treated us as the totem does, we would never have been tempted to kill him.' In this way totemism helped to smooth over the situation, and to make everyone forget the event that had led to its origin.

In the process certain characteristics came into being which would henceforth continue to define the nature of religion from this point onwards. Totemic religion had emerged out of the sons' sense of guilt as an attempt to appease that emotion, and to propitiate the injured father by deferred obedience to him. All later religions can be seen as attempts to solve the same problem, in different ways according to the stage of civilization in which they came into being and on the paths that they chose, but they all have the same goal, and they are all reactions to this same great event which saw the beginning of civilization, and which has not given humanity a moment's peace since then.

Another characteristic that religion has faithfully preserved was already present in totemism at this time. The tension of ambivalence was probably too great to be compensated for by any sort of device, or perhaps it may be that the psychological conditions are not favourable to the resolution of these contradictory emotions. We also observe that the ambivalence attached to the father-complex persists into totemism and into religions in general. The totemic religion not only encompassed expressions of remorse and attempts at propitiation, but also led to the commemoration of the triumph over the father. The satisfaction obtained from that triumph led to the establishment of the commemorative totem meal, at which the restrictions of deferred obedience fall away, and obliged them to repeat the crime of patricide over and over again in the sacrifice of the totem animal, whenever the fruit of that deed, the appropriation of the qualities of the father, threatens to disappear as a result of the changing conditions of life. We will not be surprised to find that a part of the son's rebellion, often in the most curious disguises and inversions, reappears in later religious formations.

So far we have followed, in religion and moral prescription – which in totemism are still not very sharply differentiated – the consequences of the affectionate current towards the father, which has been transformed into remorse; we are not, however, seeking to ignore the fact that the tendencies urging towards patricide have emerged triumphant. From now on and for a long time to come, the social and fraternal emotions upon which the entire revolution was based continued to exert the most profound influence upon the development of society. The brothers expressed these emotions in the sanctification of their common blood, stressing the solidarity of all the lives in the same clan. In thus guaranteeing one another's lives, the brothers were announcing that none of them might be treated by any of the others as their father had been treated by them all together. They were ruling out a repetition of their father's fate. Now the religiously based prohibition on killing the totem was joined by the socially based prohibition on fratricide. After that, it was still a long time before the commandment was stripped of the restriction to the clan members and assumed the simple wording: Thou shalt not murder. First of all, the paternal horde was supplanted by the band of brothers, which ensured its own existence through the blood-bond. Society was now based on shared guilt for the crime that had been committed communally, and religion was based on the sense of guilt and remorse for that crime, and morality in part on the needs of this society, and in part on the penance required by the sense of guilt.

In contrast to more recent views of the totemistic system, and borrowing from the older ones, psychoanalysis thus allows us to argue that there is a most profound connection between totemism and exogamy, and that they originated at the same time.

6

Many powerful motives keep me from attempting to describe the further development of religions from their beginnings in totemism up to the condition in which they occur today. I wish only to pursue two threads where I see them appearing with particular clarity: the motive of the totemic sacrifice and the son's relationship with the father.[75]

Robertson Smith has taught us that the ancient totem meal returns in the primitive form of sacrifice. The meaning of the act is the same: sanctification by participation in the communal meal. The sense of guilt, which can only be appeased by the solidarity of everyone participating, has remained a part of it. A fresh addition is the tribal deity in whose imagined presence the sacrifice takes place, who participates in the meal like a clansman, and with whom the participants identify by consumption of the sacrifice. How does the god come to be a part of this situation, which was originally strange to him?

The answer might be that the idea of God has appeared in the meantime – no one knows where it came from – and has dominated the whole of religious life; and like everything else that wished to survive, the totem meal had been forced to become a part of the new system. But psychological examination of the individual human being teaches with a quite particular emphasis that for each person God is based on their father, that his personal relationship with God depends on his relationship with his bodily father, that it oscillates and changes along with it, and that God is basically nothing but a heightened father. Here again, as in the case of totemism, psychoanalysis advises us to lend credence to those believers who call God the father, just as they called the totem their ancestor. If psychoanalysis is at all worthy of our attention, without prejudice to any other sources and meanings of the idea of God, on which psychoanalysis is unable to shed any light, the paternal aspect of that idea must be a very important one. But if that is the case, the father is represented twice in the situation of primitive sacrifice, once as a god and once as a totemic sacrificial animal, and even allowing for the narrow range of solutions open to psychoanalysis, we must ask whether that is possible and what it might mean.

We know that there are several types of relationship between the god and the sacred animal (the totem or the sacrificial animal): 1) Each god has one animal, often several, sacred to him. 2) In certain particularly sacred, 'mystical' sacrifices, the animal consecrated to the god is the one sacrificed to him.[76] 3) The god was often worshipped in the form of an animal or, to put it another way, animals enjoyed divine worship long after the age of totemism. 4) In myths, the god frequently turned into an animal, often the one that was consecrated to him. This would lead us to assume that the god himself was the totem animal, and had at a later stage of religious feeling developed out of it. But we are released from any further discussion by the consideration that the totem itself is nothing but a father-substitute. Thus the totem may have been the first form of father-substitute, and the god a later one, in which the father regained his human form. Such a new creation from the root of all religious formation, the longing for the father, could become possible if, over the course of the ages, something essential in the relations with the father – and perhaps also with the animal – had altered.

Such changes can be easily guessed at, even if we ignore from the outset a certain psychical alienation from the animal and the disruption of totemism by domestication.[77] Present in the situation created by the elimination of the father was a factor which must have intensified longing for him to an extraordinary degree. Each of the brothers who had joined forces to kill the father had been inspired by the wish to be his equal, and had expressed that wish by incorporating parts of the substitute for him into the totem meal. The wish was destined to remain unfulfilled because of the pressure which the bonds of the fraternal clan exerted on all of its members. Now, no one was able or permitted to attain the father's perfection of power for which they had all been striving. Thus, over the course of a long period of time, the bitterness towards the father which had compelled their act of patricide faded away, the longing for him grew, and an ideal was able to come into being, the content of which was the abundance of power and the freedom from restriction of the primal father whom they had previously fought against, and a readiness to submit to him. The original democratic equality of all individual clansmen could no longer be maintained because cultural changes had intervened; out of this there arose a tendency, borrowing from the veneration of individual human beings who had distinguished themselves over others, to revive the ancient ideal of the father by creating gods. The idea of a human being becoming a god and of a god dying, which strikes us as so infuriatingly unreasonable, was by no means offensive to the classical imagination.[78] But the elevation of the once murdered father to a god from whom the tribe now traced its descent was a much more serious attempt at expiation than had been the contract with the totem.

I cannot say where within this evolution we should place the great mother goddesses who may have preceded the paternal gods.

But it does seem certain that the transformation in relations with the father was not restricted to the religious field, but consistently invaded the other side of human life that was influenced by the elimination of the father: social organization. With the institution of the paternal deities, the fatherless society gradually became patriarchal. The family was a reconstitution of the former primal horde, and also gave fathers back a large share of their former rights. Now there were fathers once again, but the social functions of the band of brothers had not been abandoned, and the actual difference between the new family fathers and the unrestricted primal father of the horde was great enough to ensure the continuation of the religious need, the maintenance of the unappeased longing for the father.

In the scene of sacrifice to the tribal god the father is thus really present twice, as god and as sacrificial totem animal. But in the attempt to understand this situation we shall guard against interpretations which seek to translate it two-dimensionally, as an allegory, ignoring its historical stratifications. The ambivalent attitude towards the father has found three-dimensional expression here, and so has the victory of affectionate emotional impulses of the son over his hostile emotions. Here the scene in which the father is overcome, his greatest humiliation, has become the material for his greatest triumph. The significance that the sacrifice has generally acquired lies in the fact that it offers the father satisfaction for the ignominy meted out to him in the very act that perpetuates the memory of that crime.

Over time the animal lost its sacred status, and the sacrifice lost its connection with the totemic feast; it became a simple offering to the deity, an act of renunciation performed for the god. God himself was now elevated so high above human beings that the only way of communicating with him was via the mediation of the priest. At the same time the social order encountered godlike kings, who introduced the patriarchal system to the state. It must be admitted that the revenge of the father, first deposed and then restored, was a harsh one, and the dominance of authority reached its peak. The subjugated sons used the new relationship to unburden themselves even further of their sense of guilt. The sacrifice in the form that it now assumed was entirely outside their responsibility. It was God himself who had demanded and ordained it. This phase included myths in which the god in person killed the animal that was sacred to him, which was actually the god himself. This was the extreme denial of the great crime which saw the inception of society and the sense of guilt. It expresses satisfaction over the fact that the former father-substitute has been abandoned in favour of the higher idea of the god. The flatly allegorical translation of the scene more or less coincides here with its psychoanalytical interpretation. That is: it is shown that the god overcomes the animal part of its nature.[79]

At the same time we would be mistaken in believing that in these times of renewed paternal authority the hostile impulses belonging to the father-complex had fallen completely silent. It would be more true to say that in the first phases of the rule of the two new father-substitute formations, gods and kings, we recognize the most energetic manifestations of that ambivalence which remains characteristic of religion.

In his great work *The Golden Bough*, Frazer voiced the supposition that the first kings of the Latin tribes were outsiders who played the role of a deity and in this role on a particular festival were solemnly executed. The annual sacrifice (or in its variant form, self-sacrifice) of a god seems to have been an essential feature of the Semitic religions. The ceremonial of human sacrifice in various parts of the inhabited world leaves little doubt that these individuals met their end as representatives of the deity, and the substitution of a lifeless imitation (a doll) for human beings enables us to pursue this sacrificial custom into late times. The theanthropic sacrifice of the god – into which I am unfortunately unable to go as deeply as I did into animal sacrifice – sheds a bright retrospective light on the meaning of the older forms of sacrifice. It reveals, with an honesty that could barely be excelled, that the object of the sacrificial act was always the same, identical with the one which is now worshipped as a god, and which is therefore the father. The question of the relationship between animal and human sacrifice is now easily resolved. The original animal sacrifice was already a substitute for a human sacrifice, for the solemn killing of the father, and when the father-substitute regained its human form, the animal sacrifice was also able to change back into the human sacrifice.

Thus the memory of that first great act of sacrifice had been shown to be indestructible, despite all efforts to forget it, and at the very point where people wanted to be as far as possible from the motives leading to it, its undistorted repetition in the form of the sacrifice of the god had to come to light. I need not dwell here upon the developments of religious thought which made this return possible in the form of rationalizations. Robertson Smith, who is of course a long way from our idea of tracing the sacrifice back to that great event in human prehistory, admits that the ceremonies performed at the feasts with which the ancient Semites celebrated the death of a deity were interpreted as 'commemoration of a mythical tragedy', and that the lament which formed a part of it did not have the character of spontaneous sympathy, but had something compulsory about it, enforced by the fear of divine rage.[80] We believe we may acknowledge that this interpretation was correct, and that the feelings of the celebrants were properly explained by the underlying situation.

Let us now accept as a fact that in the further development of religions the two driving factors, the son's sense of guilt and his filial defiance, never subside. All attempts to resolve the religious problem, all kinds of reconciliation between the two conflicting psychical powers eventually collapse, probably under the combined influence of historical events, cultural changes and internal psychical transformations.

The son's efforts to take the place of the father-god emerge with ever greater clarity. With the introduction of agriculture the importance of the son in the patriarchal family increases. He risks new expressions of his incestuous libido, which find a symbolic satisfaction in the working of Mother Earth. The divine figures of Attis, Adonis, Tammuz and others come into being, and at the same time youthful deities who enjoy the loving favours of maternal deities commit incest with the mother in defiance of the father. But the sense of guilt appeased by these creations was expressed in myths which gave these youthful lovers of the mother goddesses a short life and punishment either through castration or through the anger of the father-god in animal form. Adonis is killed by the boar, the animal sacred to Aphrodite; Attis, the lover of Cybele, dies by castration.[81] The lamentation over the deaths of these gods, and joy at their resurrection, has passed into the ritual of another son-deity who was destined to have lasting success.

When Christianity began to penetrate the ancient world, it encountered competition in the form of the religion of Mithras, and for a while it was unclear which deity would emerge victorious.

But the bright form of the youthful Persian god has remained obscure to our understanding. We may perhaps conclude from the depictions of Mithras' killing of bulls that he represented the son who alone performed the sacrifice of the father, thus releasing the brothers from original sin.

The doctrine of original sin is Orphic in origin; it was preserved in the mysteries, and from there it made its way into the philosophical schools of ancient Greece.[82] Human beings were the descendants of Titans, who had killed and dismembered the young Dionysos-Zagreus; the burden of this crime weighed heavily upon them. According to a fragment from Anaximander, the unity of the world was destroyed by a primal crime, and all that emerged from it must continue to bear the punishment for that crime.[83] If the deed of the Titans, with its characteristics of ganging together, of killing and dismemberment, to some extent recalls the totemic sacrifice described by St Nilus – as, incidentally, do many other myths of antiquity, such as the death of Orpheus himself – what we find disturbing here is the difference that in this case the victim is a young god.

In the Christian myth, man's original sin is without a doubt a sin against God the father. If Christ now releases mankind from the oppression of original sin by sacrificing his own life, he forces us to conclude that the sin was an act of murder. According to the law of talion, deeply rooted in human emotions, murder can only be atoned for by the sacrifice of another life; self-sacrifice refers back to blood-guilt.[84] And if this sacrifice of one's own life effects a reconciliation with God the father, the crime to be atoned for must have been the murder of the father.

Hence, in Christian doctrine, human beings frankly confess to the guilty deed of primeval times, because they have now found the most generous atonement for it in the sacrificial death of the only son. The reconciliation with the father is all the more complete in that, at the same time as this sacrifice there follows the complete renunciation of the women on whose account rebellion against the father had first begun. But now the psychological fate of ambivalence also calls in its dues. In the same deed which offered the father the greatest possible atonement the son also achieved the goal of the wishes he harboured against his father. He himself became a god, alongside and, in fact, in place of his father. The son-religion supplanted the father-religion. As a sign of this substitution the old totem meal was revived in the form of communion, in which the band of brothers enjoyed the flesh and blood of the son, no longer that of the father, sanctified themselves through their consumption and became identified with him. In this way we can trace down the ages the identity of the totem meal with animal sacrifice, theanthropic human sacrifice and the Christian Eucharist, and can recognize in all those solemn rituals the after-effect of that crime which so oppressed humanity, and of which it must therefore have been so proud. But Christian communion is basically a new elimination of the father, a repetition of the deed that calls for atonement. We can see that Frazer is right when he says, 'the Christian communion has absorbed within itself a sacrament which is doubtless far older than Christianity'.[85]

7

An event like the elimination of the primal father by the band of brothers inevitably left ineradicable traces in the history of humanity, and the less the act was remembered the more numerous the substitute formations in which it was expressed.[86] I shall resist the temptation to demonstrate these traces in mythology, where they are not hard to find, and turn towards another field, following a hint from S. Reinach in a richly suggestive essay about the death of Orpheus.[87]

In the history of Greek art there is a situation which shows striking similarities with the scene of the totem meal as recognized by Robertson Smith, and equally profound divergences from it. It is the situation of the most ancient Greek tragedy. A horde of people, all identically named and identically dressed, surrounded a single figure, hanging upon his every word and deed: these were the Chorus and the actor playing the hero, originally the only one. Subsequent developments brought a second and a third actor to represent antagonists and figures split off from the hero, but the character of the hero, as well as his relationship with the Chorus, remained unaltered. The tragic hero had to suffer; even today, this is the essential content of a tragedy. He had assumed the burden of so-called 'tragic guilt', which is not always easily explained; often it is not guilt in the sense in which we understand it in our everyday lives. It generally consisted in the rejection of a divine or human authority, and the Chorus accompanied the hero with its sympathetic feelings, attempted to restrain him, to warn him and to moderate him, and mourned him after he had met with the punishment, which is shown to be deserved, for his bold undertaking.

But why must the hero of the tragedy suffer, and what is the significance of his 'tragic' guilt? I shall curtail discussion with a quick reply. He must suffer because he is the primal father, the hero of that great primal tragedy which is here being repeated in a tendentious way, and the tragic guilt is the one that he alone must shoulder in order to free the Chorus from theirs. The scene on the stage has been produced by deliberate distortion of the historical scene; we might even call it the product of refined hypocrisy. In that ancient reality it was the members of the Chorus who caused the hero's suffering; here, though, they stop at sympathy and regret, and the hero himself is responsible for his own suffering. The crime placed upon him, the arrogance and rejection of a great authority, is the very one which in reality oppresses the members of the Chorus, the horde of brothers. In this way the tragic hero – still against his will – becomes the saviour of the Chorus.

If, to take the specific example of Greek tragedy, the content of the performance consists of the suffering of the divine goat Dionysus and the lament of the goats who were his followers, we will easily understand how it was that the drama, which had become extinct, was rekindled in the Middle Ages with the Passion of Christ.

Thus to conclude this highly condensed investigation, I should like to state that it is in the Oedipus complex that the beginnings of religion, morality, society and art coincide, in complete accord with the finding of psychoanalysis that this complex forms the core of all the neuroses which have so far presented themselves to our understanding. It continues to surprise me that these problems within man's psychical life should find their solution in such a single concrete point as the relationship with the father. Perhaps in this context we might also introduce another psychological problem. We have so often had occasion to demonstrate the emotional ambivalence in the true sense of the term, the coincidence of love and hatred towards the same object, at the root of important cultural formations. We know nothing about the origin of this ambivalence. We might assume that it is a fundamental phenomenon of our emotional life. But one other possibility seems to me to be worthy of note; while it may originally have been alien to emotional life, humanity acquired it from the father-complex,[88] the very point at which psychoanalytical examination of the individual is still, even today, at its strongest.[89]

Before reaching my conclusion, I must observe that the high level of convergence, pointing towards a single comprehensive nexus, which we have achieved in these discussions, cannot blind us to the uncertainties of our assumptions and the difficulties of our results.

First of all, it cannot have escaped anyone that we are constantly positing the assumption of a mass psyche, in which psychical processes occur as they would in the psychical life of an individual. Above all we assume that the sense of guilt about a particular act has

survived over several millennia, and has remained active in generations that could have known nothing of the deed in question. We
allow an emotional process such as might have come into being
among generations of sons who were mistreated by their father to
continue on to new generations that had escaped such treatment by
virtue of the removal of the father. These do seem to be serious considerations, and any other explanation that could avoid such
assumptions would seem to be preferable.

But one further consideration shows that we are not necessarily
alone in bearing responsibility for such audacity. Without assuming
the existence of a mass psyche, a continuity in the emotional life of
mankind which allows us to disregard the interruptions of psychical acts caused by the passing of individuals, social psychology
could not exist at all. If the psychical processes of one generation
did not continue into the next, if each had to form its attitude to life
anew, there would be no progress in this field, and as good as no
development. Two new questions now arise: how confident we can
be about psychical continuity from one generation to the next, and
the ways and means that one generation uses to pass on its psychical conditions to the next. I am not about to claim that these
problems have been adequately resolved, or that the direct communication and tradition which automatically come to mind are up
to the task. Generally speaking, social psychology is not greatly
concerned with the way in which the required continuity in the
psychical life of successive generations is produced. Part of the task
seems to be performed by the inheritance of psychical dispositions,
although these require certain stimuli in the individual life if they
are to come into effect. This may be the meaning of the poet's
words: *Was du ererbt von deinen Vätern hast, erwirb es, um es zu
besitzen* ['What you have inherited from your forefathers, you must
earn it to possess it'].[90] The problem would seem even more difficult if we were able to accept the existence of psychical impulses
which can be suppressed so thoroughly that they leave no trace.
But such impulses do not exist. Even the strongest suppression
must leave room for distorted substitute impulses and reactions
following on from them. But given that that is the case we may

assume that no single generation is capable of concealing significant psychical processes from the next. In fact psychoanalysis has taught us that each human being possesses an apparatus within his unconscious mental activity which allows him to interpret the reactions of others, that is, to undo the distortions that the other person has applied to the expression of his emotions. So by unconsciously understanding all the customs, ceremonies and statutes left behind by the original relationship with the primal father, later generations may also have succeeded in taking over that emotional legacy.

There is one further consideration which might also be raised from the analytical point of view. We have understood the first moral precepts and restrictions of primitive society as the reaction to an act that gave its perpetrators the concept of crime. They regretted that act, and decided that it should not be repeated, and that its performance should bring no gain. This creative sense of guilt has not been extinguished among us even in the present day. We find it active in an asocial form among neurotics, as a way of generating new moral precepts, persistent restrictions, as atonement for those crimes that have already been committed, and as a precaution against those that have yet to occur.[91] But if we ask these neurotics about the deeds that have prompted such reactions, we will be disappointed. We find no actions, only impulses, emotions which call for evil actions but have been restrained from carrying them out. It is only *psychical* realities, not *factual* ones, that underlie the sense of guilt in neurotics. Neurosis is characterized by the fact that neurotics elevate psychical reality above factual reality, and react just as seriously to thoughts as normal people do to realities.

Might a similar state of affairs not have pertained among primitive people? We are justified in ascribing to them, as one of the partial phenomena of their narcissistic organization, an extraordinary over-valuation of their psychical acts.[92] This being the case, mere impulses of hostility towards the father, the existence of the wish-fantasy of killing and devouring him, would have been enough to produce the moral reaction which in turn generated totemism and taboo. This would free us from the need to trace the beginning of our civilization, of which we are so rightly proud, back to a terrible crime which offends all our emotions. The causal link from that beginning to our own present day would not be damaged in the process, because the psychical reality would be significant enough to bear all these consequences. It may be objected that a change in society from the form of the paternal horde to that of a band of brothers actually did take place. This is a powerful argument, but it is not a decisive one. The change might have occurred with less violence, and might still have contained the condition for the emergence of the moral reaction. As long as the pressure of the primal father was felt, hostile feelings towards him were justified, and regret over them had to wait for another time. No more compelling is the second objection, to the effect that everything derived from the ambivalent relationship towards the father, taboo and the rules relating to sacrifice, bears the characteristic of extreme seriousness and the most complete reality. But the ceremonials and inhibitions of obsessive neurotics demonstrate this characteristic as well, and yet they are derived only from psychical reality, from intention rather than action. In our matter-of-fact world we are sometimes disdainful of that which is merely thought and wished; we should take care not to transfer our contempt to the world of primitive man and neurotics, where all the wealth lies within.

Here we find ourselves facing a particularly difficult decision. Let us begin, however, by admitting that the difference which might seem fundamental to others does not, in our judgement, get to the heart of the subject. If, for primitive man, wishes and impulses have the full status of facts, it is up to us to pursue that vision sympathetically rather than correcting it to comply with our own standards. So let us look yet more closely at the model of neurosis itself, which has brought us to this uncertainty. It would not be accurate to say that obsessive neurotics, burdened with an excessive morality, are defending themselves only against the psychical reality of temptations and punishing themselves for impulses that they have only felt. There is also a good deal of historical reality involved; in their childhood these people knew nothing but evil impulses, and where their childish powerlessness allowed them to, they also turned these impulses into actions. Each of these excessively virtuous individuals had a period of wickedness in childhood, a perverse phase that was the precursor to and the precondition for the phase of excessive morality. So the analogy between primitive men and neurotics will be established much more thoroughly if we assume that in the former instance, too, psychical reality, about the form of which we can have no doubt, initially coincided with factual reality, which is to say that primitive men actually did do what all the evidence suggests they intended to do.

Nor can we allow our judgement of primitive people to be too much influenced by the analogy with neurotics. There are also differences to be taken into account. It is certainly the case that the sharp distinctions that we ourselves would make between thought and action are present neither in savages nor in neurotics. But the neurotic is inhibited above all in action. For him, the thought is full substitute for the deed. Primitive man is uninhibited, the thought simply becomes the deed, the deed is, for him, so to speak, more of a substitute for thought, and for that reason, without claiming to bring the discussion to a definitive close, I think we may, in the case under consideration, assume: In the beginning was the deed.[93]

(1912–13)

Notes

1. p. 139.
2. *Revue scientifique*, October 1900, published in the author's four-volume work, *Cultes, Mythes et Religions*, 1909, vol. I, p. 17ff.
3. But perhaps we would first be well advised to present the reader with the difficulties against which observations/findings in this field must do battle: First: the people who collect the observations are not the same as those who process and discuss them, the former being travellers and missionaries, and the latter learned people who may never have seen the objects of their research. – Communication with the savages is not easy. Not all of the observers are familiar with these people's languages, but had to use interpreters, or deal with their interlocutors in the lingua franca of pidgin

English. The savages do not tend to communicate the most intimate details
of their culture, and open up only to those outsiders who have spent many
years in their midst. For the most diverse motives (cf. Frazer, 'The
Beginnings of Religion and Totemism among the Australian Aborigines',
Fortnightly Review, 1905; *Totemism and Exogamy*, I, p. 150) they often
provide false or ambiguous information. – While we are on this subject we
should not forget that primitive peoples are not young peoples, but are
actually just as old as the most civilized, and that we should not expect them
to have preserved their original ideas and institutions for our attention
without any evolution or distortion. Rather it is certain that among primitive people transformations of all kinds have occurred, so that it is never
straightforwardly possible to decide what aspects of their current conditions and beliefs have preserved their original past, like a fossil, and what
corresponds to a distortion and change in it. Hence the abundant disputes
among the authors about which of the peculiarities of a primitive culture
should be grasped as primary, and which as a later, secondary formation.
Consequently the establishment of the original state always remains a matter of construction. – Finally, it is not easy to empathize with primitive
people's way of thinking. We misunderstand them just as easily as we do
children, and are always inclined to interpret their actions and feelings in
terms of our own psychical arrangements.

4. 'Totemism', Edinburgh 1887, published in the first volume of the great
work *Totemism and Exogamy*.
5. Cf. the essay on taboo [Essay II].
6. Like, in our own times, the wolves in the cage on the Capitol in Rome,
or the bears in the dungeon in Berne.
7. Like the 'white lady' in some aristocratic families.
8. Op. cit., p. 45. – See the discussion of the sacrifice below.
9. See the first essay.
10. p. 116.
11. This text is supported by the conclusion concerning totemism that
Frazer draws in his second work on the subject ('The Origin of Totemism',
Fortnightly Review, 1899): 'Thus, Totemism has commonly been treated as
a primitive system both of religion and of society. As a system of religion it
embraces the mystic union of the savage with his totem; as a system of
society it comprises the relations in which men and women of the same
totem stand to each other and to the members of other totemic groups. And
corresponding to these two sides of the system are two rough and ready
tests or canons of Totemism: first, the rule that a man may not kill or eat his
totem animal or plant; and second the rule that he may not marry or cohabit

with a woman of the same totem.' [Reprinted in Frazer, *Totemism and Exogamy*, London, 1910, vol. I, p.101.] Frazer then adds something that leads us directly into the midst of the discussions about totemism: 'Whether the two sides – the religious and the social – have always co-existed or are essentially independent, is a question which has been variously answered.'

12. With regard to one such change of mind, he wrote the following fine sentences: 'That my conclusions on these difficult questions are final, I am not so foolish as to pretend. I have changed my views repeatedly, and I am resolved to change them again with every change of the evidence, for like a chameleon, the candid enquirer should shift his colours with the shifting colours of the ground he treads.' Preface to the first volume of *Totemism and Exogamy*, 1910.

13. 'By the nature of the case, as the origin of totemism lies far beyond our powers of historical examination or of experiment, we must have recourse as regards this matter to conjecture,' A. Lang, *The Secret of the Totem*, p. 27. – 'Nowhere do we see absolutely *primitive* man, and a totemic system in the making', p. 29.

14. Originally, in all probability, only after animals.

15. 'The Worship of Animals and Plants', *Fortnightly Review*, 1869–70. 'Primitive Marriage', 1865; both works published in *Studies in Ancient History*, 1876, 2nd edition 1886.

16. *The Secret of the Totem*, 1905, p. 34.

17. After A. Lang, *Secret of the Totem*, p. 34.

18. Ibid., [A. H. Keane, *Man, Past and Present*, Cambridge 1899.]

19. After A. Lang. [F. Max-Müller, *Contributions to the Science of Mythology*, London 1897.]

20. Pikler and Somló, *Der Ursprung des Totemismus* [The Origin of Totemism], 1900. The authors rightly characterize their attempt at explanation as a 'contribution to a materialist theory of history'.

21. 'The Origin of Animal Worship', *Fortnightly Review*, 1870. *Principles of Sociology*, vol. 1, §§ 169–76.

22. *Kamilaroi und Kurnai* [Kamilaroi and Kurnai], p. 165, 1880 (after A. Lang, *Secret* etc.).

23. Cf. above, the essay on taboo, p. 57ff.

24. Op. cit., [S. Reinach, *Cultes, Mythes et Religions*] vol. I, p. 41.

25. [Presidential] Address to the Anthropological Section, British Association, Belfast, 1902. After Frazer, op. cit., vol. IV, p. 50 and ff.

26. *The Native Tribes of Central Australia* by Baldwin Spencer and F. J. Gillen, London, 1899.

27. 'There is nothing vague or mystical about it, nothing of that metaphysical haze which some writers love to conjure up over the humble beginnings of human speculation, but which is utterly foreign to the simple, sensuous, and concrete modes of thought of the savage.' (*Totemism and Exogamy*, vol. I, p. 117).

28. Op. cit., p. 121ff.

29. *L'année sociologique*, vols. I, V, VIII and elsewhere. See particularly the essay 'Sur le totémisme' ['On totemism'], vol. V, 1902.

30. *Social Origins* and *The Secret of the Totem*.

31. Frazer, *The Golden Bough*, vol. II, p. 332.

32. 'It is unlikely that a community of savages should deliberately parcel out the realm of nature into provinces, assign each province to a particular band of magicians, and bid all the bands to work their magic and weave their spells for the common good.' *Totemism and Exogamy*, vol. IV, p. 57.

33. *Totemism and Exogamy*, vol. II, p. 89, and IV, p. 59.

34. Ibid., vol. IV, p. 63.

35. 'That belief is a philosophy far from primitive.' A. Lang, *Secret of the Totem*, p. 192.

36. Frazer, *Totemism and Exogamy*, vol. IV, p. 45 and ff.

37. Ibid, p. 48ff.

38. Wundt, *Elemente der Völkerpsychologie* [Elements of Folk Psychology].

39. *L'année sociologique*, 1898–1905.

40. See the criticism of Durkheim's views in Frazer, *Totemism and Exogamy*, vol. IV, p. 101.

41. *Secret* etc., p. 125.

42. For example Frazer, loc. cit., IV, p. 75: 'The totem clan is a totally different social organism from the exogamous class, and we have good grounds for thinking that it is far older.'

43. *Primitive Marriage*, 1865.

44. Frazer, op. cit., vol. IV, pp. 71–92.

45. Cf. the first essay.

46. [L. H.]Morgan, *Ancient Society*, 1877. – Frazer, *Totemism and Exogamy*, IV, p. 105ff.

47. Frazer, op. cit., p. 106.

48. *Origin and Development of the Moral Ideas*, vol. II, *Marriage*, 1906, [p. 368]. Note also the author's self-defence against objections that had been raised against him.

49. Cf. [E.] Durkheim, 'La prohibition de l'inceste' ['The Prohibition on incest']. *L'année sociologique*, I, 1898.

50. Charles Darwin says of savages: 'They are not likely to reflect on distant evils to their progeny.'

51. Cf. the first essay [Essay I].

52. 'Thus the ultimate origin of exogamy and with it the law of incest – since exogamy was devised to prevent incest – remains a problem nearly as dark as ever.' *Totemism and Exogamy*, I, p. 165.

53. *Descent of Man*, vol. II, Ch. 20, pp. 362ff.

54. *Primal Law*, London 1903 (with A. Lang, *Social Origins*).

55. *Secret of the Totem*, pp. 114, 143.

56. 'If it be granted that exogamy existed in practice, on the lines of Mr Darwin's theory, before the totem beliefs lent to the practice a *sacred* sanction, our task is relatively easy. The first practical rule would be that of the jealous Sire, "No males to touch the females in my camp", with expulsion of adolescent sons. *In efflux of time that rule, become habitual*, would be, "No marriage within the local group". Next, let the local groups receive names, such as Emus, Crows, Opossums, Snipes, and the rule becomes, "No marriage within the local group of animal name; no Snipe to marry a Snipe". But, if the primal groups were not exogamous, they would become so, as soon as totemic myths and tabus were developed out of the animal, vegetable, and other names of small local groups.' *Secret of the Totem*, p. 143. (The emphasis in the middle of this passage is mine.) In his last statement on the subject (Folklore, December 1911), Lang incidentally remarks that he has abandoned the derivation of exogamy from the 'general totemic' taboo.

57. M. Wulff, 'Beiträge zur infantilen Sexualität' ['Contributions to infantile sexuality'], *Zentralblatt für Psychoanalyse*, 1912, II, No. 1, p. 15ff.

58. Op. cit. (*Gesammelte Werke*, vol. VII).

59. The giraffe fantasy.

60. S. Ferenczi, 'Ein kleiner Hahnemann' ['A little chanticleer']. *Intern. Zeitschrift für ärztliche Psychoanalyse*, 1913, I, No. 3.

61. On the substitution of blinding – as also contained in the Oedipus myth – for castration, cf. the papers by Reitler, Ferenczi, Rank and Eder in *Internationale Zeitschrift für ärztliche Psychoanalyse*, 1913, I, No. 2.

62. Which, according to Frazer, contains the essence of totemism: 'Totemism is an identification of a man with his totem.' *Totemism and Exogamy*, IV, p. 5.

63. It is to Otto Rank that I owe the communication of a case of dog-phobia in an intelligent young man, whose explanation about how he began to suffer from it sounds remarkably similar to the totem theory of the Arunta mentioned above (pp. 119–20). He said he had learned from his father that his mother had once been startled by a dog when she was pregnant with him.

64. W. Robertson Smith, *The Religion of the Semites*, second edition, London 1894.

65. 'The inference is that the domestication to which totemism inevitably leads (when there are any animals capable of domestication) is fatal to totemism.' [F. B.] Jevons, *An Introduction to the History of Religion*, 1911, fifth edition, p. 120.

66. [W. Robertson Smith,] op. cit., p. 313.

67. *The Golden Bough*. Part V, *Spirits of the Corn and of the Wild*; 1912, in the sections: 'Eating the God' and 'Killing the Divine Animal'.

68. Frazer, *Totemism and Exogamy*, vol. II, p. 590.

69. The objections raised by various authors (Marillier, Hubert and Mauss, among others) against this theory of sacrifice have not significantly detracted from the impression of the teachings of Robertson Smith.

70. *Religion of the Semites*, 2nd edition, 1894, p. 412.

71. Lest the reader receive a mistaken impression of this account, I should ask that the closing sentences of the subsequent section be taken as a corrective.

72. Atkinson also sees the seemingly monstrous hypothesis that the tyrannical father was overcome and killed by the combined forces of the expelled sons as a direct consequence of the conditions of the Darwinian primal horde. 'A youthful band of brothers living together in forced celibacy, or at most in polyandrous relation with some single female captive. A horde as yet weak in their impubescence they are, but they would, when strength was gained with time, inevitably wrench by combined attacks, renewed again and again, both wife and life from the paternal tyrant' (*Primal Law*, pp. 220–21). Atkinson, who incidentally spent his life in New Caledonia and had unusual opportunities to study the natives, also refers to the fact that the conditions of the primal horde imagined by Darwin are easily observed in wild herds of cattle and horses, and regularly lead to the killing of the father animal. He then suggests that after the removal of the father the horde collapses amidst the bitter fighting of the victorious sons amongst each other. A new organization of society would never come about in this way: 'An ever recurring violent succession to the solitary paternal tyrant by sons whose parricidal hands were so soon again clenched in fratricidal strife' (p. 228). Atkinson, who did not have the suggestions of psychoanalysis at his command, and who was unfamiliar with the studies of Robertson Smith, finds a less violent transition from the primal horde to the next social stage, in which large numbers of men live together in peaceful community. He holds maternal love responsible for the fact that at first only the youngest, later also other sons remain in the horde, for which reason these tolerated individuals acknowledged the father's privilege in the form of the restraint that they show towards their mother and sisters.

This is the most remarkable theory put forward by Atkinson; it coincides with the present theory in its *essential* points, but its divergence from it implies the abandonment of a great deal else.

I may present the vagueness, the temporal abbreviation and the compression of his material as an abstention required by the nature of the subject. It would be just as foolish to strive for precision where this material is concerned as it would be unfair to demand certainties.

73. This new emotional attitude must also be supported by the fact that the deed could not bring complete satisfaction to its perpetrators. In a certain respect it had remained in vain. After all, none of the sons was able to accomplish his original wish to assume the place of the father. But failure is, as we know, far more liable to produce a moral reaction than satisfaction.

74. 'Murder and incest, or offences of a like kind against the sacred laws of blood, are in primitive society the only crimes of which the community as such takes cognizance . . .' *Religion of the Semites*, p. 419.

75. Cf. the work of C. G. Jung, 'Wandlungen und Symbole der Libido' ['Transformations and Symbols of the Libido'], which is dominated by views that differ to some extent from my own. *Jahrbuch für psychoanalytische Forschungen*, IV, 1912.

76. Robertson Smith, *Religion of the Semites*.

77. See above, p. 137

78. 'To us moderns, for whom the breach which divides the human and the divine has deepened into an impassible gulf, such mimicry may appear impious, but it was otherwise with the ancients. To their thinking gods and men were akin, for many families traced their descent from a divinity, and the deification of a man probably seemed as little extraordinary to them as the canonization of a saint seems to a modern Catholic.' Frazer, *Golden Bough*, Part I, *The Magic Art and the Evolution of Kings*, vol. II. p. 177f.

79. It is generally known that the overcoming of one generation of gods by another in mythology means the historical process of the replacement of one religious system by a new one, whether as the result of conquest by a foreign people or along the channel of psychological development. In the latter case the myth comes close to the 'functional phenomena' in H. Silberer's sense. The idea that the god who kills the animal is a symbol of the libido, as C. G. Jung (op. cit.) suggests, assumes a concept of the libido other than the one used hitherto, and appears to me to be generally questionable.

80. *Religion of the Semites*, pp. 412–13. 'The mourning is not a spontaneous expression of sympathy with the divine tragedy, but obligatory and enforced by fear of supernatural anger. And a chief object of the mourners is to *disclaim responsibility for the god's death* – a point which has already come before us in connection with theanthropic sacrifices, such as the "ox-murder at Athens".'

81. The fear of castration plays an extraordinarily large role in the disturbance of the relationship with the father in present-day young neurotics. From the fine observations of Ferenczi we have seen that the boy recognizes his totem in the animal that snaps at his little member. When our children learn of ritual circumcision, they equate this with castration. The social-psychological parallel to this attitude in children has to my knowledge not yet been carried out. Circumcision, as carried out in primeval times and so frequent among primitive people, is performed at the moment of initiation into manhood, where it must find its significance, and has only as a secondary development been brought back to an earlier age. It is of great interest to find that among primitive peoples circumcision is combined with the cutting off of hair and the knocking out of teeth, or is replaced by these, and that in their anxiety our children, who can know nothing of this state of affairs, treat these two operations as really being equivalents of castration.

82. Reinach, *Cultes, Mythes et Religions*, II, p. 75ff.

83. '*Une sorte de péché proethnique*', ibid. p. 76.

84. The suicidal impulses among our present-day neurotics regularly prove to be self-punishments for death-wishes directed at other people.

85. 'Eating the God', [Frazer, *Golden Bough*, Part V, *Spirits of the Corn and of the Wild*, vol. 2] p. 51. No one familiar with the literature on the subject will assume that tracing Christian communion back to the totem meal is an idea of the author of this essay.

86. Ariel in *The Tempest* [Act I, scene 2]:

> Full fathom five thy father lies:
> Of his bones are coral made;
> Those are pearls that were his eyes:
> Nothing of him that doth fade,
> But doth suffer a sea-change
> Into something rich and strange.

87. *La Mort d'Orphée* in the book often quoted here: *Cultes, Mythes et Religions*, vol. II, p. 100ff.

88. Or parent complex.

89. Being accustomed to misunderstandings, I believe it may be worth stressing explicitly that the derivations presented here do not ignore the complex nature of the phenomena to be explained, and that they claim only to add a new element to the origins of religion, morality and society whether known or still unknown – an element that emerges from consideration of the implications of psychoanalysis. I shall have to leave it up to others to synthesize the explanation into a whole. It is, however, in the nature of this new contribution that it could not help playing the central role in such a synthesis, even though the overcoming of large affective resistances might be required before it was granted such significance.

90. Goethe, *Faust*, Part I, 1. 682–3.

91. Cf. the second essay in this series, on the subject of taboo [Essay II].

92. See the essay on animism, magic and the omnipotence of thoughts [i.e. essay III].

93. [*'Im Anfang war die Tat.'* Goethe, *Faust*, Part I, 1. 1237.]

Timely Reflections on War and Death

I

The Disillusion of War

Caught up in the vortex of this bellicose age, and given only one-sided information, with no detachment from the great changes that have already taken place or are about to do so, and with no sense of the future that is forming, we begin to have doubts about the meaning of the impressions crowding in on us, we begin to doubt the value of our own judgements. It seems to us that no event has ever destroyed so much of the precious common property of humanity, so many of the clearest minds have been made confused, the high has been brought so thoroughly low. Even science has lost its passionate impartiality; its most determined servants are trying to strip it of its weapons, as a way of contributing to the battle with the enemy. The anthropologist is obliged to declare the enemy to be inferior and degenerate, the psychiatrist must announce his diagnosis of the disturbance of intellect or psyche. But our perception of the evil of our own time is probably immoderate, and we are not entitled to compare it with the evil of other ages that we have not lived through ourselves.

The individual who is not a combatant, and has thus become a tiny cog within the vast war machine, feels confused in his bearings and inhibited in his activities. In my opinion he will welcome any hint, however small, that might make it easier for him at least to locate his bearings within himself. Among the factors responsible for the psychical distress of those who have remained at home, I should like to stress two, and deal with them in this paper: the disillusion that this war has provoked, and the altered attitude towards death which – like all other wars – it forces upon us.

When I speak of disillusion, everyone will immediately know

what I am referring to. One does not need to be a sentimentalist. One may recognize the biological and psychological necessity of suffering for the economy of human life and still condemn the means and ends of war, and long for an end to all wars. Certainly, we have said that wars would not end while different nations lived under such different conditions, while they had such different conceptions of the value of individual life, and while the animosities dividing them represented such strong psychical drive-forces. So we were prepared to expect wars between primitive and civilized peoples, between the races of humanity who are divided by the colour of their skin, for some considerable time to come; or wars with and between those nations of Europe which were not highly developed or which had reverted to a less civilized state. But we dared to hope otherwise. Of the great world-dominating nations of the white race, to which the leadership of the human race has fallen, and which we knew to have the interests of the world at heart, whose creations include technical advances in the control of nature as well as artistic and scientific cultural values, we had expected that they would be capable of bringing disagreements and conflicts of interest to a different kind of resolution. Within all of these nations high moral standards had been set for the individual, and it was according to those that he was expected to order the conduct of his life if he wished to participate in the civilized community. These regulations, often disproportionately severe, demanded a great deal of him – a high degree of self-restraint, extensive renunciation of the satisfaction of his instincts. Above all he was forbidden to exploit the extraordinary advantages that can be gained by the use of lies and treachery in competition with his neighbour. The civilized state held these moral standards to be the basis of its existence, and came down harshly on anyone who dared to tamper with them, often declaring it improper even to subject them to critical examination. It was therefore assumed that the individual himself would wish to respect them, and would not consider undertaking anything against them, because in doing so he would have contradicted the foundation of his own existence. Finally, no doubt, it could be observed that there were, embedded within these civilized nations, certain remnants of other peoples which were generally disliked, and which were therefore only allowed reluctantly, and not fully, to participate in the communal work of civilization, for which they had shown themselves suitable enough. But one might have been forgiven for thinking that the great nations themselves had acquired so great an understanding of what they had in common, and such a degree of tolerance for their differences, that 'foreigner' and 'enemy' could no longer be allowed to melt into a single concept as they had done in classical antiquity.

Relying on this unity within the civilized nations, countless people have swapped their residence in their homeland for life abroad, and made their lives reliant on the systems of communication that exist between the friendly countries. But anyone who was not by force of circumstance confined to a single place was able to assemble, from all the merits and charms of the civilized countries, a new, bigger fatherland in which he was able to move, uninhibited and free of suspicion. In this way he enjoyed both the blue sea and the grey, the beauty of the snowy mountains and the great meadow plains, the enchantment of the northern forests and the magnificence of the southern vegetation, the mood of the landscapes on which great historical memories repose, and the silence of nature in its virgin state. This new fatherland was also a museum for him, filled with all the treasures that artists had created and left behind for civilized humanity over the course of many centuries. As he wandered from one room of this museum to another, he was able to observe, with impartial gratitude, how many different types of perfection the mixing of blood, history and the unique features of mother earth had produced among his other compatriots. Here cool, inflexible energy had developed, there the graceful art of beautifying life, elsewhere a sense of order and law or some other of those properties that have made mankind the lords of the earth.

Let us also recall that every citizen of the civilized world had created his own particular 'Parnassus' and 'School of Athens'. From among the great thinkers, poets and artists of all nations he had selected those to whom he thought he owed all that was accessible to him of the enjoyment and understanding of life, and venerated them alongside the immortal ancients and the familiar masters of his own tongue. None of these great men had seemed foreign to him because they had spoken in a different language, neither the unparalleled explorer of human passions nor the intoxicated worshipper of beauty, nor the fiercely threatening prophet, nor the keen-witted satirist, and he never reproached himself with having become disloyal to his own nation and his beloved mother tongue.

Voices sometimes disturbed the enjoyment of the community of civilization, warning that old traditional differences made wars even between the members of that community unavoidable. We did not want to believe that it would happen, but how did we imagine such a war, if things were to come to that? As an opportunity to demonstrate the advance in the sense of community among people since the time when the Greek Amphictyonic Council had ruled that no city belonging to the league might be destroyed, nor its olive trees felled nor its water supply cut off; as a chivalrous combat whose sole purpose was to establish the superiority of one side, avoiding where possible any serious suffering that could contribute nothing to the resolution of the conflict, and granting full immunity to the wounded who were forced to withdraw from the contest, and to the doctors and nurses who devoted themselves to their recovery. Of course all due consideration would be given to the non-combatant part of the population, the women who stayed far from the business of war, and to the children on both sides who, once they were grown, would become one another's friends and helpers. And all the international undertakings and institutions in which the civilized community of peace-times had been embodied would be preserved.

Such a war would always have held enough that was terrible and difficult to bear, but it would not have interrupted the development of ethical relations between the collective individuals of humanity, the nations and states.

Then the war we did not want to believe in broke out, and it brought – disillusion. Not only is it bloodier and more destructive than any previous war, because of the massively advanced weapons of attack and defence, but it is at least as cruel, bitter and merciless as any previous war. It ignores all the restrictions to which one signs up in times of peace, which is known as 'international law', it does not acknowledge the rights of the wounded and the physician, the distinction between the peaceful and the combatant sections of the population, or private property rights. In blind fury it demolishes everything that stands in its way, as though there would be no future and no peace among men once it had passed. It severs all common bonds among the warring nations and threatens to leave behind a bitterness that will make it impossible for them to renew those bonds for a long time to come.

Moreover it has brought to light a barely comprehensible phenomenon, that the civilized nations know and understand each other so little that one can turn against the other with hatred and revulsion. Indeed, that one of the great civilized nations can become so universally disliked that others will venture to exclude it as 'barbaric' from the civilized community, even though it has demonstrated its right to be considered a member by making the greatest contributions to that community for a very long time. We continue to hope that an impartial history will prove that this nation, the one in whose language we are writing, for whose victory our loved ones are fighting, has been the one that has sinned least against the laws of civilized human behaviour. But who, at such a time, will dare to set himself up as a judge in his own cause?

Peoples are more or less represented by the states that they form; and those states in turn are represented by the governments that rule them. In this war the individual member of a people is able to convince himself with horror of what he sometimes found himself thinking even in peace-time, that the state has forbidden the individual to do wrong, not because it wishes to abolish wrongdoing but because it wishes to monopolize it, like salt and tobacco. The belligerent state permits itself any injustice, any violence that would disgrace the individual. It does not restrict itself to the accepted ruses, but also perpetrates deliberate lies and deliberate treachery against the enemy, and to a degree that seems to exceed what was customary in earlier wars. The state demands extremes of obedience and sacrifice in its citizens while at the same time treating them like children, with an excess of secrecy, and censorship of information and expression of opinion, that renders the spirits of those who are thus intellectually oppressed defenceless against any unfavourable situation or any grim rumour. It liberates itself from all guarantees and treaties that bound it to other states, it brazenly confesses to its greed and its striving for power, which the individual is then expected to approve for patriotism's sake.

It should not be objected that the state cannot manage without wrongdoing because that would place it at a disadvantage. Adherence to moral standards, the renunciation of the brutal deployment of power is generally very disadvantageous, even to the individual, and only rarely does the state show itself capable of compensating the individual for the sacrifice that it has demanded of him. Neither should we be surprised that the loosening of all moral ties between the collective individuals of humanity has been manifested in repercussions upon the morality of those individuals, because our conscience is not the inflexible judge that ethicists claim it to be, it is by origin 'social anxiety' and nothing else. Where the community ceases to accuse, the suppression of evil desires is also abolished, and people commit deeds of cruelty, cunning, treachery and barbarism the possibility of which one would have considered irreconcilable with their level of civilization.

So well may the civilized cosmopolitan whom I introduced above stand helplessly in this world that has now grown strange to him, his great fatherland collapsed, the common possessions ruined, his fellow citizens divided and degraded!

We might permit ourselves some critical remarks about his disillusion. Strictly speaking it is not justified, because it consists in the destruction of an illusion. Illusions are recommended to us by the fact that they spare feelings of displeasure and allow us to enjoy satisfactions in their place. We must then accept it without complaint if at some point they collide with a piece of reality upon which they shatter.

Two aspects of this war have left us disillusioned: the lack of morality shown outwardly by the states which present themselves to their own citizens as the guardians of moral standards, and brutality in the behaviour of individuals whom, as participants in the highest human civilization, one would not have thought capable of such things.

Let us begin with the second point, and attempt to sum up in a single sentence the view that we wish to criticize. How do we actually picture the process through which an individual person attains a higher stage of morality? The first answer will probably be: he is good and noble from birth, from the very first. No further heed will be paid to that answer here. A second one will consider the proposition that a process of development must be involved, and will probably assume that in the course of this development man's tendencies to evil are eradicated and replaced, under the influence of upbringing and cultural environment, by tendencies to good. In that case, though, it is surprising that evil should once again come so powerfully to the fore in someone who has been brought up in that manner.

But contained within this answer is also the thesis that we wish to contradict. There is in fact no 'eradication' of evil. Rather, psychological – more strictly speaking psychoanalytic – investigation shows that man's deepest essence lies in drive-impulses that are elemental in nature and identical in all people, and are aimed at the satisfaction of certain primal needs. These drive-impulses are, in themselves, neither good nor evil. We classify them and their manifestations in this way, according to their relationship with the needs and requirements of the human community. It should be admitted that all those impulses abhorred as evil – let us take selfishness and cruelty as their representatives – are among these primitive ones.

These primitive impulses undergo a lengthy process of development before they are permitted in adults. They are inhibited, directed towards other goals and spheres, and when merged with others they change their objects, partially turning back upon the individual. Reactive formations against certain drives assume the deceptive form of a transformation in their content, as though selfishness had turned into altruism, and cruelty into pity. These reactive formations benefit from the fact that some drive-impulses appear, almost from the beginning, in pairs of opposites, a very curious relationship unknown to lay people, which has been given the name of 'emotional ambivalence'. Easiest to observe and to understand is the fact that strong love and strong hatred can so frequently coexist in a single person. To this, psychoanalysis adds the fact that in many cases these two opposite emotional impulses have the same people as their object.

It is only once all such 'drive vicissitudes' have been overcome that we see the emergence of what is called a person's character, and what can, as is well known, be only very inadequately classified as 'good' or 'bad'. The individual is seldom inherently good or bad, being usually 'good' in one area, 'bad' in another, or 'good' in some external circumstances and decidedly 'bad' in others. What is interesting is the discovery that the pre-existence of strong 'bad' impulses in childhood can often be seen as the actual pre-condition for a distinct inclination towards 'good' in the adult. Those most intensely egoistic in childhood can become the most helpful and self-sacrificing citizens; most sentimentalists, humanitarians and protectors of animals have developed out of little sadists and animal-tormentors.

The transformation of 'bad' drives is the work of two factors working concurrently, one internal and one external. The internal factor consists in influence upon the bad – we might say, egoistic – drives of eroticism, man's need of love in the broadest sense. Through the admixture of the *erotic* components the egoistic drives are transformed into *social* drives. We learn to value being loved as an advantage that allows us to renounce other advantages. The external factor is the compulsion of upbringing, which represents the demands of the cultural environment and is then continued by the direct influence of the cultural milieu. Civilization has been won by the renunciation of drive-satisfaction, and requires each new arrival to make the same renunciation of his drives. During the in-dividual life external compulsions are constantly transformed into internal compulsions. Cultural influences lead to an increasing transformation, by the admixture of erotic elements, of egoistic tendencies into altruistic and social tendencies. Finally, we may assume that every internal compulsion which makes itself felt in the development of the individual was originally – in *the history of mankind*, that is – only an external compulsion. People who are born today bring with them as an inherited organization a certain inclination (predisposition) to transform egoistic drives into social ones, and this predisposition is easily stimulated to perform the transformation. Another part of this drive-transformation must be achieved in life itself. So the individual human being is not only influenced by his present cultural milieu, but is also subject to the influence of the cultural history of his forefathers.

If we call a person's capacity to transform the egoistic drive under the influence of eroticism his *susceptibility to civilization*, we may state that it consists of two parts, one of which is innate and one acquired in life, and that the relationship between these two parts and their relationship with the untransformed drives is highly variable.

In general we are inclined to set too much store by the innate part, and furthermore we run the risk of over-estimating the overall susceptibility to civilization in its relationship with the drives, which have remained primitive, that is, we are led to judge people as being 'better' than they really are. There is also another factor that dims our judgement and falsifies the result in their favour.

Other people's drive-impulses are naturally withheld from our perception. We deduce them from their actions and their behaviour, which we trace back to *motives* from their drives. Such a deduction is inevitably mistaken in a number of cases. The same, culturally 'favourable' actions can sometimes derive from 'noble' motives, and sometimes not. Ethical theorists call only those actions 'good' which are the expression of a good drive-impulse, and they refuse to acknowledge others. But society, which is practical in its goals, is not entirely concerned with this distinction; it is content for a person to direct his behaviour and his actions according to the rules of civilization, and does not pose too many questions about his motives.

We have heard that the *external compulsion* exerted upon the individual by upbringing and environment effects a further transformation of his drives towards good, a turn from egoism to altruism. But this is not the inevitable or regular effect of the external compulsion. Upbringing and environment do not only offer benefits in terms of love, but also offer other kinds of incentive, in the form of rewards and punishments. As a result they may have the effect that the person subject to their influence decides upon good actions in the cultural sense without any ennoblement of his drives, without any transformation of egoistic into social inclinations. The consequence will be broadly the same; only under certain conditions will it be apparent that one person always does good because the inclinations of his drives oblige him to, while another will only be good in so far as cultural behaviour brings gain to his selfish aims. But superficial acquaintance with the individual will not enable us to distinguish between the two cases, and our optimism will certainly seduce us into grossly over-estimating the number of individuals who have been altered by civilization.

Civilized society, then, which demands good conduct and is not concerned with its instinctual foundation, has won for civil obedience a large number of people who are not following their nature in behaving in this way. Encouraged by this success, it has allowed itself to be induced to raise moral standards as high as possible, and thus forced its participants even further away from their instinctive predisposition. They are now subjected to an advanced suppression of drives whose tension is made apparent in the most curious reactive and compensatory manifestations. In the field of sexuality, where such suppression is most difficult to impose, it thus leads to the reactive formations of different kinds of neurosis. Elsewhere, the pressure of civilization may have no pathological consequences, but it is manifested in distortions of character and in the constant readiness of the inhibited drives to break through to be satisfied at any passing opportunity. Anyone who is thus required constantly to react in terms of rules which are not the expression of his instinctive inclinations, will be living, psychologically speaking, beyond his means, and may objectively be described as a hypocrite, regardless of whether or not he has become clearly aware of the discrepancy. It cannot be denied that our contemporary culture encourages the formation of this kind of hypocrisy to an extraordinary extent. We might go so far as to claim that it is actually constructed upon such hypocrisy, and would be forced to deal with profound changes if people began to live in a psychologically truthful way. So there are disproportionately more individuals hypocritically simulating civilization than there are truly civilized people, indeed we might discuss the view that a certain degree of hypocritical pretence is indispensable for the maintenance of civilization, because the susceptibility to civilization of people living today might not be adequate to the task. On the other hand, the maintenance of civilization, even on so questionable a foundation, offers the prospect, with each new generation, of paving the way for a further-reaching transformation of the drives, which will be the bearer of a better civilization.

We may draw one consolation from our reflections so far: that our injury and painful disillusion at the uncivilized behaviour of our fellow citizens of the world in this war were unjustified. They were based upon an illusion to which we had yielded. Those citizens, in fact, have not fallen as far as we feared, because they had not risen nearly so far as we imagined. The fact that the collective individuals of humanity, the peoples and states, abandoned their moral restrictions towards one another, prompted the individual citizens to withdraw for a time from the pressure of civilization and grant temporary satisfaction to the drives that they had been reining in. It seems likely that this did not cause a breach in their relative morality within their nations.

But we can deepen our understanding of the change that the war can be seen to have wrought on our former compatriots, while at the same time receiving a warning not to do them an injustice. There is, in fact, a curious feature in the life of the psyche which is not present in any other evolutionary process. When a village grows into a town, or a child into a man, village and child are swallowed up in the town and the man. Only memory can etch the old features into the new picture; in fact the old materials or forms are removed and replaced by new ones. Mental development takes place differently. One cannot describe this incomparable state of affairs except by saying that each earlier stage of evolution remains preserved alongside the later one that it has become; succession helps to shape a coexistence, although the same materials are used throughout the whole sequence of modifications. The earlier mental state may not have been expressed for years, but it continues to exist to such an extent that one day it can once more become the mode of expression – indeed the only one – of the forces at work in the mind, as though all later developments had been annulled and undone. There is a limit to the directions that this extraordinary plasticity of mental developments can take; it can be described as a particular capacity for involution – regression – since in some cases a later and superior stage of development, once abandoned, may not be reached again. But the primitive states can always be re-established; the primitive mind is, in the fullest sense, imperishable.

The so-called mental illnesses must give the layman the impression that intellectual and psychical life have been destroyed. In fact the destruction only applies to later acquisitions and evolutionary phases. The essence of mental illness consists in a return to earlier stages of affective and functioning life. An excellent example of the plasticity of mental life is provided by the sleeping state which we strive for each night. Since we have learned to understand even mad and confused dreams, we know that every time we go to sleep we cast aside our hard-earned morality, acquired as though it were a piece of clothing, to put it back on again in the morning. This baring of ourselves is, of course, not dangerous, because we pose no threat, being paralysed by the sleeping state and condemned to inactivity. Only dreams can tell us anything about the regression of our emotional life to one of the earliest stages of development. Thus, for example, it is noteworthy that all our dreams are governed by purely selfish motives. An English friend put forward this thesis to a scientific gathering in America, whereupon a lady in the audience observed that while this might be true of people from Austria, she was able to say on behalf of herself and her friends that they felt altruistic even in their dreams. My friend, although himself a member of the English race, felt obliged firmly to contradict the lady on the basis of his own experiences in the analysis of dreams: even noble American women were, in their dreams, just as egoistic as Austrians.

So even the transformation of drives upon which our suscepti-

bility to civilization is based can be set back – lastingly or temporarily – by the effects of life. Without a doubt the influences of war are
among the forces that can produce such involution, and for that
reason we do not need to deny that susceptibility to all those who
are at present behaving in an uncivilized fashion, and we may expect
that the ennoblement of their drives will be re-established in more
peaceful times.

But there is another symptom at work among our fellow world-
citizens that has perhaps shocked and surprised us no less than their
fall, so painful to us, from their ethical heights. What I am referring
to is the lack of understanding that is apparent among the best
minds, their obduracy, their lack of openness to the most forceful
arguments, their uncritical willingness to believe the most flawed
assertions. This certainly produces a sad picture, and I am particularly anxious to stress that I am not a blind partisan who finds all the
intellectual shortcomings on one side alone. But this phenomenon
is even more easily explained and far less questionable than the one
considered above. Philosophers and students of human nature
taught us long ago that we are mistaken in considering our intelligence as an autonomous power, ignoring its dependence upon our
emotional lives. They say that our intellect can only function reliably
if it is removed from the influence of strong emotional impulses; in
the opposite case, it simply acts as an instrument in the hands of a
will, and provides the result that the will imposed upon it. So logical
arguments are powerless in the face of affective interests, and this
is why arguing on the basis of reasons which are, in Falstaff's phrase,
'as plenty as blackberries', is so pointless. The experience of psychoanalysis may even have reinforced this assertion. Every day it is able
to show that the keenest-minded people will suddenly behave without insight, like idiots, once the required insight encounters an
emotional resistance in them, but also reacquire all their understanding once the resistance has been overcome. The logical blind-
ness into which this war has often plunged the best of our fellow
citizens is therefore a secondary phenomenon, a consequence of
affective excitement, and is, one hopes, destined to disappear along
with it.

Having thus regained our understanding of our estranged fellow citizens, it will be that much easier for us to bear the disillusion that the collective individuals of humanity, the nations, have caused us, since we may now make only much more modest claims upon them. They may be replicating the evolution of individuals, and today still appear at a very primitive stage in terms of organization and the formation of higher entities. In accordance with this, the educative factor of the external compulsion to morality, which we found to be so effective in the individual, is barely demonstrable in them. Admittedly, we had hoped that the great community of interests generated by commerce and production would yield the beginning of such a compulsion, but it appears that nations are at present pursuing their passions much more closely than their interests. At most they use their interests to *rationalize* their passions; they bring their interests to the fore in order to justify the satisfaction of their passions. Certainly, a mystery remains about why individual peoples actually hate, despise and loathe one another, even in peace-times, with each nation set against every other. I cannot say why it should be. In this case, it is just as though, once we take a large number, even millions of people, all the moral acquisitions of individuals are obliterated, and only the most primitive, the oldest and most brutal psychical attitudes remain. It may be that only later stages of evolution will be able to do anything about this regrettable state of affairs. But a little more truthfulness and honesty on all sides, in relations between people and between the people and those who govern them, could also pave the way for this transformation.

II

Our Attitude towards Death

The second factor to which I trace back our current state of estrangement from our world, which was once so fine and so congenial, is the disturbance it has wrought in the attitude that we had hitherto maintained towards death.

That attitude was not an honest one. Outwardly, we were of course prepared to support the view that death is the inevitable outcome of all life, that each of us owes nature a death and must be prepared to settle the debt, in short, that death is natural, undeniable and inevitable. In reality, however, we tend to behave as though things were otherwise. We have shown the unmistakable tendency to push death aside, to eliminate it from life. We have tried to keep it deadly silent; after all, we have the saying in German: to think of something as if it were death.[1] Meaning our own death, of course. Our own death is indeed unimaginable, and however often we try to imagine it, we realize that we are actually still present as onlookers. Thus, the psychoanalytic school could venture to say: fundamentally no one believes in his own death or, which comes to the same thing: in the unconscious each of us is convinced of his immortality.

Where the death of someone else is concerned, civilized man is careful not to speak of this possibility in the hearing of the person who may be about to die. Only children disregard this restriction; they shamelessly threaten one another with the possibility of death, and even go so far as to say to their loved ones things like, 'Dear Mama, when you have sadly passed away, I'm going to do such-and-such a job'. The civilized adult will also be unable to think about another's death without seeming harsh or wicked to himself; unless he deals with death professionally, as a doctor or a lawyer or something of the kind. Least of all will he allow himself to think about another person's death if that event is connected with a gain in his own freedom, property or position. Of course these tender feelings of ours cannot prevent deaths from occurring; when they have done so we are always profoundly moved, and it is as though our expectations have been severely shaken. We regularly stress the arbitrary nature of death, accident, illness, infection, old age, thus revealing our attempt to reduce death from an inevitability to chance. An accumulation of simultaneous deaths strikes us as something utterly terrible. To the dead person himself we bring a most particular attitude, almost one of admiration for someone who has accomplished something very difficult. We suspend criticism of him, overlook his misdeeds, declare that '*de mortuis nil nisi bonum*' [do not speak ill of the dead], and consider it justifiable to praise everything most favourable about him in the funeral oration and on his gravestone. Concern for the deceased, which is no longer of any use to him, is more important to us than the truth, and to most of us it is surely also more important than concern for the living.

This cultural and conventional attitude towards death is now complemented by our complete collapse when death comes to someone close to us, a parent or spouse, a sibling, child or dear friend. We bury our hopes, our demands, our pleasures with that person, we are inconsolable and refuse to replace them. We then behave as a kind of Asra,[2] who *die too when those whom they love die*.

But this attitude to death has a powerful effect upon our life. Life becomes impoverished, it loses its interest when the highest stake in the game of life, life itself, cannot be risked. It becomes as stale, as lacking in content as, for example, an American flirtation in which it is clear from the start that nothing is going to happen, unlike a continental affair, in which both parties must always bear the grievous consequences in mind. Our emotional bonds, the unbearable intensity of our grief, make us disinclined to seek out dangers for ourselves and our loved ones. We do not dare to consider a number of enterprises which are dangerous, but actually indispensable, such as learning to fly, expeditions to far-off countries, experiments with explosive substances. We are paralysed by the thought of who would replace the mother's son, the wife's husband, the children's father, if an accident were to occur. The inclination to exclude death from our reckoning of life leads to many other renunciations and exclusions. And yet the motto of the Hanseatic League was: *Navigare necesse est, vivere non necesse!* Sailing is necessary, living is not.

So we have no option but to find compensations in the world of fiction, in literature, in the theatre for that which we have lost in life. There we still find people who know how to die, indeed, who are capable of killing others. That, too, is the only place where we see the fulfilment of the condition under which we might reconcile ourselves with death if we were able to preserve a life intact behind all of life's vicissitudes. For it is too sad that things can happen in life as they do in a game of chess, where a false move can force us to resign the game, but with the difference that there is no possibility of a return match. In the sphere of fiction we find the plurality of lives that we need. We die in our identification with one hero, but survive him and are ready to die a second time, equally unharmed, with another.

It is clear that war is bound to sweep away this conventional attitude towards death. Death can now no longer be denied; we are obliged to believe in it. People are really dying, not individually now, but in large numbers, often tens of thousands in a single day. And it is no longer a matter of chance. To be sure, it still appears arbitrary whether a bullet hits one man or another. But a second bullet may easily hit the second man: accumulation abolishes chance. Life has certainly become interesting once again, it has regained its essence.

Here one would have to undertake a division into two groups, separating those who give up their own lives in battle from the others who remain at home and must only wait to lose one of their dear ones to death through injury, illness or infection. It would certainly be very interesting to study the changes in the psychology of the combatants, but I know too little about it. We shall have to keep to the second group, to which we ourselves belong. I said above that I think that the confusion and paralysis of our abilities from which we are suffering are also to a great degree determined by the fact that we are unable to maintain our earlier attitude to death, and have not yet found another one. Perhaps it will help us if we direct our psychological investigation towards two other attitudes, one which we may attribute to primitive, prehistoric man, and that other which is preserved in each one of us but hides, invisible to our consciousness, within the deeper strata of our psychical life.

Of course we only know prehistoric man's attitude towards death from inferences and deductions, but I think that these methods have given us fairly trustworthy information.

Primeval man had a most remarkable attitude towards death, and a highly contradictory one. On the one hand he took death seriously, acknowledged it as the abolition of life and used it in that sense, but at the same time he denied death and reduced it to nothing. This contradiction was made possible by the fact that he adopted radically different attitudes towards the death of the other, the stranger, the enemy, and to his own. The death of another was fine by him, he saw it as the destruction of something hated, and he had no compunction about causing it. He was certainly a very passionate being, crueller and more malicious than other animals. He enjoyed murder, and took it for granted. We need not attribute to him the instinct that is supposed to keep other animals from killing and devouring other members of the same species.

Hence the primeval history of humanity is also filled with murder. Even today, what our children learn as global history in school is essentially a sequence of genocides. The dark sense of guilt that has hung over humanity since primitive times, which in some religions has condensed into the hypothesis of an *original sin*, is probably the manifestation of a blood-guilt with which primitive man had burdened himself. In my book *Totem and Taboo* (1913), following the suggestions of W. Robertson Smith, J. J. Atkinson and Charles Darwin, I have tried to guess the nature of that ancient guilt, and believe that we can infer it from contemporary Christian teaching. If God's son had to sacrifice his life to free humanity from original sin, then according to the law of talion, the recompense of like by like, that sin must have been a killing, a murder. That alone could require as its expiation the sacrifice of a life. And if original sin was an offence against God the father, then humanity's oldest crime must have been a patricide, the killing of the primal father of the primitive human horde, whose memory-image was later transfigured into a deity.[3]

Primeval man's death was just as unimaginable and unreal to him as our own death is to each of us today. But for him there was one case in which the two opposed attitudes towards death collided and came into conflict with one another, and this case became very significant and rich in long-lasting consequences. It occurred when primitive man saw someone close to him die, his wife, his child, his friend, whom he would certainly have loved just as we do our own, for love cannot be much younger than the lust to kill. Then he was brought up against the fact that one could also die oneself, and his whole being raged against admitting this. Each of these loved ones was a part of his own beloved self. On the other hand, such a death was also fine by him, because in each of the loved ones there was also something of the stranger. The law of emotional ambivalence, which still governs our emotional relationships with the people we love, would certainly have applied even more generally in primeval times. Thus these beloved dead had also been strangers and enemies who had provoked some degree of hostile emotion in him.[4]

Philosophers have claimed that it was the intellectual mystery presented to primeval man by the image of death that forced him to reflect, and became the source of all speculation. I believe that the philosophers are being too – let us say – philosophical here, they are not taking the primarily effective motives properly into account. I should like for that reason to limit and correct the claim I made above: primeval man will have triumphed over the corpse of the murdered enemy, without finding cause to rack his brains over the mystery of life and death. It was not the intellectual mystery, or each individual death, but the emotional conflict about the death of someone who was both beloved and at the same time strange and hated, that provoked man's first research. From this emotional conflict, what is born first is psychology. Man could no longer keep death at a distance, since he had tasted of it in his pain over the deceased, but he did not wish to accept it, since he was unable to imagine himself being dead. So he settled for a series of compromises: he admitted his own death, but disputed its significance as the annihilation of life, although he had no motive for denying that significance where the death of his enemy was concerned. It was by the corpse of the beloved person that he invented spirits, and it was his sense of guilt over the satisfaction that was mixed with his grief that meant that the first spirits he created were fearful, evil demons. The physical changes of death suggested to him the division of the individual into a body and a soul – originally several souls; in this way his train of thought ran in parallel with the process of decomposition brought about by death. The constant memory of the dead person became the foundation of the hypothesis of other forms of life, and first gave him the idea of life continuing after apparent death.

At first these later existences were only supplements to the one ended by death, shadowy, lacking in content and held in low esteem until later times; they still bore the character of meagre information. We recall the reply that the soul of Achilles gives to Odysseus:

> 'No winning words about death to *me*, shining Odysseus!
> by god, I'd rather slave on earth for another man –
> some dirt-poor tenant farmer who scrapes to keep alive –
> than rule down here over all the breathless dead.'

(*Odyssey* XI, v, 484–91)[5]

Or in the powerful, bitterly parodic version of Heinrich Heine:

> *Der kleinste lebendige Philister*
> *Zu Stuckert am Neckar, viel glücklicher ist er*
> *Als ich, der Pelide, der tote Held,*
> *Der Schattenfürst in der Unterwelt.*[6]

[The smallest living Philistine in Stuckart on the Neckar is far happier than I, the son of Peleus, the dead hero, the prince of shades in the underworld]

Only later did the religions come to represent this afterlife as being more desirable and truly valid, and to reduce the life ended by death to a mere preparation. After that it was only consistent for life to be extended into former lives, and for people to come up with the ideas of metempsychosis and reincarnation, all with the intention of robbing death of its significance as the abolition of life. The denial of death, which we have described as a conventional and cultural attitude, began as early as this.

What came into being by the side of the loved one's corpse was not only the theory of souls, belief in immortality and a powerful root for the human sense of guilt, but also the first ethical commandments. The first and most significant prohibition of the awakening conscience was: *Thou shalt not kill*. It had been won as a reaction against the satisfaction of the hatred hidden behind grief for the beloved dead, and was gradually extended to unloved strangers and finally even to the enemy.

Civilized man no longer has a sense of this. If the furious struggle of this war is ever resolved, each of the victorious combatants will return cheerfully home to his wife and children, unchecked and undisturbed by thoughts of the enemies whom he has killed either in close combat or with long-distance weapons. It is remarkable that the primitive peoples who still live on this earth, and who are certainly closer to primeval man than ourselves, behave differently in this respect – or did so until they experienced the influence of our culture. The savage – Australian, Bushman, Tierra del Fuegan – is by no means a remorseless murderer; when he returns victorious from an expedition, he may not enter his village or touch his wife before he has expiated the murders committed in wars through often long and tedious acts of penance. Of course the obvious explanation lies in his superstition; the savage still fears the revenge of the spirits of the slain. But the spirits of the slain foe are nothing but the expression of his bad conscience over his blood-guilt; behind this superstition there lurks a piece of ethical sensitivity which civilized people like ourselves have lost.[6]

Pious souls, who believe our nature to be remote from any contact with anything evil or base, will not fail to draw consoling conclusions, from the early appearance and the urgency of the prohibition on murder, about the strength of the ethical impulses that must be implanted in us. Unfortunately this argument proves the contrary even more. Such a strong prohibition can only be directed against an equally strong impulse. What no man's soul desires calls for no prohibition,[7] it automatically excludes itself. The very emphasis on the commandment: Thou shalt not kill, makes us certain that we are descended from an endless series of generations of murderers who had the lust to kill, as we perhaps do ourselves, in their blood. The ethical strivings of humanity, the strength and significance of which should not be played down, are an acquisition of human history; in unfortunately very variable amounts they then became the inherited possession of contemporary mankind.

Let us now leave primeval man and turn to the unconscious in our own psychical life. Here we depend wholly on the investigative method of psychoanalysis, the only one that probes to such depths. We ask: how does our unconscious respond to the problem of the dead. The answer must be: almost exactly as primeval man did. In this, as in many other respects, prehistoric man lives on unchanged in our unconscious. So our unconscious does not believe in its own death, it acts as though it were immortal. What we call our 'unconscious', the deepest strata of our psyche, consisting of drive-impulses, knows nothing negative, no denial – in it, opposites coincide – and for that reason too it does not know its own death, to which we can only give a negative content. So there is nothing instinctive within us that responds to a belief in death. This might even be the mystery of heroism. The rational explanation of heroism is based on the judgement that one's own life cannot be as precious as certain abstract and universal possessions. But more frequent, in my opinion, is that instinctive and impulsive heroism that ignores such motivation and simply defies dangers in the spirit of Steinklopferhanns in the play by Anzengruber: '*Es kann dir nix g'scheh'n*' ['Nothing can happen to you']. Or else that motivation serves to sweep aside hesitations which might hold up the heroic reaction corresponding to the unconscious. The fear of death, which dominates us more often than we ourselves know, is on the other hand something secondary, and usually emerges from the sense of guilt.

On the other hand, we acknowledge death for foreigners and enemies, and consign them to it just as readily and unhesitatingly as primeval man did. Here, of course, a difference becomes apparent, which will turn out to be crucial where real life is concerned. Our unconscious does not perform the killing, it merely imagines and desires it. But it would be wrong so completely to underestimate this *psychical* reality in comparison with *factual* reality. It is significant and consequential enough. Every hour of every day, in our unconscious impulses, we remove everyone who gets in our way, everyone who has insulted and harmed us. The cry of 'the devil take him' that crosses our lips so often in joking annoyance, and which actually means 'death take him', is in our unconscious a serious, powerful desire for death. Indeed, our unconscious even murders for trivial reasons; like the old Athenian code of Draco it knows no other punishment for crime than death and, with a certain consistency, for any damage to our all-powerful and autocratic ego, is basically a crime of *lèse-majesté*.

So, to judge by our unconscious wishful impulses, we ourselves are also, like primeval men, a gang of murderers. It is lucky that all these wishes do not have the power that people still attributed to them in primeval times; in the crossfire of the reciprocal maledictions humanity would have been destroyed long ago, the best and wisest of the men along with the loveliest and fairest of the women.

Psychoanalysis generally meets with no credence for such assertions as these among laypeople. They reject them as slanders refuted by conscious experience, and skilfully ignore the little suggestions by which even the unconscious is liable to betray itself to conscious-ness. So it is appropriate to point out that many thinkers who could not have been influenced by psychoanalysis have accused our unspoken thoughts of being willing to ignore the prohibition on murder and remove what stands in our way. For this I shall choose a single famous example in the place of many others.

In *Le Père Goriot,* Balzac refers to a passage in the works of Jean-Jacques Rousseau in which that author asks the reader what he would do if – without leaving Paris and of course without being discovered – he could, with a mere act of will, kill an old mandarin in Peking whose demise would inevitably bring him great profit. One can guess that he does not consider the life of the dignitary to be very safe. 'Tuer son mandarin' [killing one's mandarin] then became proverbial for this secret willingness, present even among our contemporaries.

There are also a large number of cynical jokes and anecdotes that provide a similar kind of evidence, such as the words attributed to the husband: if one of us two dies, I'm moving to Paris. Such cynical jokes would not be possible if their purpose were not to communicate an unacknowledged truth that could not be admitted if it were uttered seriously and undisguised. In jest, as everyone knows, one may even tell the truth.

As for primeval man, so for our unconscious, one case arises in which the two opposing attitudes to death, the one that acknowledges it as the annihilation of life, and the other that denies it as unreal, collide and come into conflict. And this case is, as it was in primeval times, the death or the threatened death of our loved ones, a parent or spouse, a sibling, child or dear friend. These dear ones are on the one hand an inner possession of ours, components of our own ego, but on the other hand they are also to some extent strangers, even enemies. A very few situations aside, there adheres to the most tender and profound of our loving relationships a little piece of hostility which can stimulate the unconscious desire for death. But this conflict of ambivalence does not produce, as it once did, the doctrine of the soul and ethics, but neurosis, which also allows us profound insights into the normal life of the psyche. How often have doctors working with psychoanalysis dealt with the symptom of over-sensitive concern with the well-being of relations or with completely unfounded self-reproaches after the death of a loved one. The study of these cases has left no doubt about the extent and significance of unconscious death-wishes.

The layman feels an extraordinary horror at the possibility of this emotion, and takes this revulsion as a legitimate reason for disbelief in the claims of psychoanalysis. Wrongly, in my opinion. No disparagement of our own love is intended, and none is present. It is of course as remote from our intelligence as it is from our emotions to couple love and hate in such a way, but while nature works with this pair of opposites, it manages always to keep love awake and fresh, to guard it against the hatred that lurks behind it. We might say that we owe the finest aspects of our love to the *reaction* against the hostile impulse that we sense within our breast.

To summarize: our unconscious is just as deaf to the idea of our death, just as filled with blood-lust against strangers, just as ambivalent towards loved ones as man was in primeval times. But how far we have moved from that primal state in our conventional and cultural attitude towards death!

It is easy to see how war intervenes in this separation. It strips away our later stratifications of culture and brings the primeval man in us back to the surface. It forces us once again to be heroes who cannot believe in their own death; it describes foreigners to us as enemies whose death we should cause or desire; it advises us to disregard the death of our loved ones. But war cannot be done away with; as long as the conditions of life of the various nations are so different and the conflicts between them so violent, wars will be inevitable. Here the question arises: should we not be the ones to give in and adapt to war? Should we not admit that we have once again been living psychologically beyond our means with our civilized attitude to death, and turn around and admit the truth? Would it not be better to give death the place in reality and in our thoughts that is its due, and bring out our unconscious attitude to death, which we have hitherto so carefully suppressed, a little more? It does not seem to be an advance to a higher level, and in many respects it is more of a backward step, a regression, but it has the advantage of paying more due to truthfulness and making life bearable to us again. Bearing life is, after all, the first duty of all living beings. The illusion loses its value if it hinders us in that.

We remember the old proverb: *Si vis pacem, para bellum*. If you wish to preserve peace, arm for war.

This might be the time to alter it to read as follows: *Si vis vitam, para mortem*. If you wish to endure life, prepare yourself for death.

(1915)

Notes

1. [To consider something unlikely.]

2. [A tribe of Arabs in a poem, 'Der Asra', by Heinrich Heine, who 'die when they love'.]

3. See: 'The Recurrence of Totemism in Childhood', the last essay in *Totem and Taboo*.

4. See 'Taboo and the Ambivalence of the Emotions', the second essay in *Totem and Taboo*.

5. [Quoted in the translation by Robert Fagles, 1996.]

6. See *Totem and Taboo* [Essay IV].

7. Cf. Frazer's brilliant argument, quoted in *Totem and Taboo*.

Transience

Some time ago I took a walk through a blossoming summer land-scape in the company of a silent friend and a young and already well-known poet. The poet admired the beauty of the nature around us, but it did not delight him. He was disturbed by the idea that all this beauty was bound to fade, that it would vanish through the winter, like all human beauty and everything beautiful and noble that people have created and could create. All the things he would otherwise have loved and admired seemed to him to be devalued by the fate of transience for which they were destined.

We know that such absorption in the susceptibility to decay of all that is beautiful and perfect can produce two different impulses in the mind. One of these leads to the painful world-weariness of the young poet, the other to revolt against the asserted fact. No, it cannot be that all these wonders of nature and art, of our emotion-al world and the world outside, should dissolve into nothing. It would be too senseless and too wicked to believe it. Such beauty must be able to go on existing in some way, far from all destructive influences.

But this demand for eternity is too clearly a consequence of our wishes to be able to lay claim to reality. That which is distressing may none the less be true. I could resolve neither to contest uni-versal transience nor to force an exception for things beautiful and perfect. But I disputed the pessimistic poet's view that the tran-sience of the beautiful meant a loss of value.

On the contrary, its value is heightened! The value of transience is one of scarcity over time. The limitation of the possibility of enjoyment makes it even more precious. It was incomprehensible,

I declared, that the thought of the transience of loveliness should cloud our delight in it. As to the beauty of nature, it returns the following year after the ravages of winter, and that return may be seen as eternal in terms of the length of our lives. We see the beauty of the human form and face vanishing for ever as our own lives pass, but their evanescence only lends them additional charms. If there is a flower that blossoms for only a single night, its blossom seems no less glorious to us for that. Neither could I see how the beauty and perfection of a work of art or an intellectual accomplishment should be devalued by their limitation within time. If there should come a time when the paintings and statues that we admire today have fallen into ruin, or a race of human beings should appear who no longer understand the works of our poets and philosophers, or even a geological era in which everything that lives upon the earth has passed away, the value of all of these beautiful and perfect things is defined only by its significance for our own emotional lives, it need not live beyond them, and is for that reason independent of absolute duration.

I thought these considerations to be incontestable, but noticed that I had made no impression upon the poet and my friend. From this failure I concluded that there must be a strong affective element disturbing their judgement, and believe I found it later on. It must have been the psychical revolt against grief that devalued the pleasure of beautiful things for them. The idea that all this beauty was transient gave the two sensitive characters a foretaste of grief over its destruction, and as the psyche shrinks instinctively from everything painful, they felt their enjoyment of beauty to be spoiled by the idea of its transience.

Mourning over the loss of something that we have loved or admired seems so natural to the layman that he takes it quite for granted. But for the psychologist, mourning is a great mystery, one of those phenomena that one does not explain oneself, but to which other obscurities may be traced back. We believe that we possess a certain capacity to love, called the libido, which is at the earliest stages of our development applied to our own ego. Later, though still from very early on, it turns away from the ego and towards the objects which are thus to an extent absorbed into our ego. If those objects are destroyed or if we lose them, our capacity for love (the libido) becomes free once more. It can take other objects as a substitute, or return temporarily to the ego. But we are at a loss to understand why this removal of the libido from its objects should be such a painful process, and we have at present no hypothesis to explain the fact. We see only that the libido clings to its objects and does not wish to abandon those which are lost even when a substitute is ready and available. That, then, is mourning.

My conversation with the poet took place in the summer before the war. A year later war broke out and robbed the world of its beauties. It destroyed not only the beauty of the landscapes through which it passed, and the artworks that it encountered on its way, it also shattered our pride at the accomplishments of our civilization, our respect for so many thinkers and artists, our hopes of finally overcoming the differences among peoples and races. It sullied the sublime impartiality of our science, brought our instincts to the surface, unleashed within us the evil spirits that we thought had been tamed by centuries of education on the part of our most noble men. It made our fatherland small again, and made the rest of the world remote once more. In this way it robbed us of so much that we had loved, and showed us the fragility of much that we had considered stable.

It should come as no surprise that our libido, so impoverished in objects, has clung all the more intensely to that which remains to us, and that the love of the fatherland, the affection for our neighbours and pride in what we have in common have been suddenly reinforced. But have those other qualities, now lost, really been devalued to us because they have proved to be so frail and unresisting? To many of us it appears that way, but again, I think, wrongly. I believe that those who think this way, and who seem prepared for lasting renunciation because that which is precious has not been proved to be enduring, are only in a state of mourning over their loss. We know that mourning, however painful it may be, comes to an end of its own accord. Once it has renounced everything that is lost, it has also consumed itself, and then our libido becomes free once again, so that, as long as we are still young and active, it is able to replace the lost objects with objects that are, where possible, equally precious, or with still more precious new ones. It is to be hoped that things will be no different where the losses of this war are concerned. Once mourning is overcome, it will be apparent that the high esteem in which we hold our cultural goods has not suffered from our experience of their fragility. We will once again build up everything that the war has destroyed, perhaps on firmer foundations and more lastingly than before.

(1916)

Mourning and Melancholia

Dreams having served us as the normal model for narcissistic mental disorders, we shall now attempt to cast some light on the nature of melancholia by comparing it to the normal affect of mourning. This time, though, we must begin our account with an admission which should warn us against overestimating our conclusions. Melancholia, the definition of which fluctuates even in descriptive psychiatry, appears in various different clinical forms; these do not seem amenable to being grouped together into a single entity, and some of them suggest somatic rather than psychogenetic diseases. Apart from those impressions that are available to any observer, our material is restricted to a small number of cases whose psychogenetic nature was beyond a doubt. We shall therefore relinquish all claim to the universal validity of our results, and console ourselves by reflecting that with the means of investigation presently at our disposal we could hardly find something that was not typical, if not of a whole class of illnesses, then at least of a smaller group.

The correlation between melancholia and mourning seems justified by the overall picture of the two conditions.[1] Further, the causes of both in terms of environmental influences are, where we can identify them at all, also the same. Mourning is commonly the reaction to the loss of a beloved person or an abstraction taking the place of the person, such as fatherland, freedom, an ideal and so on. In some people, whom we for this reason suspect of having a pathological disposition, melancholia appears in place of mourning. It is also most remarkable that it never occurs to us to consider mourning as a pathological condition and present it to the doctor for treatment, despite the fact that it produces severe deviations from normal behaviour. We rely on it being overcome after a certain period of time, and consider interfering with it to be pointless, or even damaging.

Melancholia is mentally characterized by a profoundly painful depression, a loss of interest in the outside world, the loss of the ability to love, the inhibition of any kind of performance and a reduction in the sense of self, expressed in self-recrimination and self-directed insults, intensifying into the delusory expectation of punishment. We have a better understanding of this when we bear in mind that mourning displays the same traits, apart from one: the disorder of self-esteem is absent. In all other respects, however, it is the same. Serious mourning, the reaction to the loss of a loved one, contains the same painful mood, the loss of interest in the outside world – except as it recalls the deceased – the loss of ability to choose any new love-object – which would mean replacing the mourned one – turning away from any task that is not related to the memory of the deceased. We can easily understand that this inhibition and restriction of the ego is a manifestation of exclusive devotion to mourning, leaving nothing over for other interests and intentions. The only reason, in fact, why this behaviour does not strike us as pathological is that we are so easily able to explain it.

We also endorse the comparison that identifies the mood of mourning as a 'painful' one. Its justification will probably be clear to us when we are capable of providing an economical characterization of pain.

So what is the work that mourning performs? I do not think I am stretching a point if I present it in the following manner: reality-testing has revealed that the beloved object no longer exists, and demands that the libido as a whole sever its bonds with that object. An understandable tendency arises to counter this – it may be generally observed that people are reluctant to abandon a libido position, even if a substitute is already beckoning. This tendency can become so intense that it leads to a person turning away from reality and holding on to the object through a hallucinatory wish-psychosis (see the essay ['Metapsychological Complement to Dream Theory']).[2] Normally, respect for reality carries the day. But its task cannot be accomplished immediately. It is now carried out piecemeal at great expenditure of time and investment of energy, and the lost object persists in the psyche. Each individual memory and expectation in which the libido was connected to the object is adjusted and hyper-invested, leading to its detachment from the libido. Why this compromise enforcement of the reality command-ment, which is carried out piece by piece, should be so extraordi-narily painful is not at all easy to explain in economic terms. It is curious that this pain-unpleasure strikes us as natural. In fact, the ego is left free and uninhibited once again after the mourning-work is completed.

Let us now apply to melancholia what we have learned from mourning. In a large number of cases it is clear that it too may be a reaction to the loss of a beloved object; when other causes are present, it may be possible to recognize that the loss is more notion-al in nature. The object may not really have died, for example, but may instead have been lost as a love-object (as, for example, in the case of an abandoned bride). In yet other cases we think that we should cling to our assumption of such a loss, but it is difficult to see what has been lost, so we may rather assume that the patient can-not consciously grasp what he has lost. Indeed, this might also be the case when the loss that is the cause of the melancholia is known to the subject, when he knows *who* it is, but not *what* it is about that person that he has lost. So the obvious thing is for us somehow to relate melancholia to the loss of an object that is withdrawn from consciousness, unlike mourning, in which no aspect of the loss is unconscious.

In the case of mourning, we found that inhibition and apathy were fully explained by the absorption of the ego in the mourning-work. The unknown loss in the case of melancholia will also lead to similar internal work, and will consequently be responsible for the inhibition of melancholia. But melancholic inhibition seems puzzling to us because we are unable to see what it is that so completely absorbs the patient. There is one other aspect of melan-cholia that is absent from mourning, an extraordinary reduction in self-esteem, a great impoverishment of the ego. In mourning, the world has become poor and empty, in melancholia it is the ego that has become so. The patient describes his ego to us as being worthless, incapable of functioning and morally reprehensible, he is filled with self-reproach, he levels insults against himself and expects ostracism and punishment. He abases himself before everyone else, he feels sorry for those close to him for being connected to such an unworthy person. He does not sense that a change has taken place in him, but extends his self-criticism to cover the past; he asserts that he has never been any better. The image of this – predominantly moral – sense of inferiority is complemented by sleeplessness, rejection of food, and an overcoming of the drive – most curious from the psychological point of view – which compels everything that lives to cling to life.

It would be fruitless both from the scientific and the therapeutic point of view to contradict the patient who levels such reproaches against his ego in this way. In all likelihood he must in some way be right, and must be describing a state of affairs as it appears to him. Indeed, we must immediately confirm some of his information straight away. He really is as apathetic, as incapable of love and achievement as he says he is. But that, as we know, is secondary, it is the consequence of the internal work, unknown to us and comparable to mourning, that is devouring his ego. He also seems to us to be right in some of his other self-reproaches, and only to be grasping the truth more keenly than others who are not melancholic. If, intensifying his self-criticism, he describes himself as a petty, egoistic, insincere and dependent person, who has only ever striven to conceal the weaknesses of his nature, he may as far as we know have come quite close to self-knowledge, and we can only wonder why one must become ill in order to have access to such truth. For there can be no doubt that anyone who has reached such an assessment of himself, and expresses it to others – an assessment like that which Prince Hamlet has ready for himself and everyone else[3] – is sick, whether he is telling the truth or treating himself more or less unjustly. And it is not difficult to observe that there is, in our judgement, no correspondence between the extent of self-abasement and its justification in reality. A hitherto well-behaved, efficient and dutiful woman will not speak of herself more favourably in melancholia than a woman who is really negligent of her household; in fact the former is more likely to fall ill with melancholia than the latter, a person about whom we ourselves would be unable to find anything good to say. Finally, we must be struck by the fact that the melancholic does not behave just as someone contrite with remorse and self-reproach would normally do. The shame before others that characterizes the latter state is missing, or at least not conspicuously present. In the melancholic one might almost stress the opposite trait of an insistent talkative-ness, taking satisfaction from self-exposure.

It is not, then, crucially important whether the melancholic is being accurate in his painful self-disparagement when this criticism coincides with the judgement of others. It is more a question of him providing an accurate description of his psychological situation. He has lost his self-esteem, and must have good reason for doing so. Then we find ourselves facing a contradiction which presents us with a mystery that is difficult to solve. Following the analogy with mourning, we were obliged to conclude that he has suffered a loss of object; his statements suggest a loss of his ego.

Before we address ourselves to this contradiction, let us linger for a while over the insight that the emotion of the melancholic gives us into the constitution of the human ego. In him, we see how one part of the ego presents itself to the other, critically assesses it and, so to speak, takes it as its object. Our suspicion that the critical agency which has split off from the ego in this case might also be able to demonstrate its autonomy under other circumstances is confirmed by all further observations. We will actually find a reason for separating this agency from the rest of the ego. What we are seeing here is the agency that is commonly called conscience; we will count it among the great institutions of the ego, along with censorship of consciousness and reality-testing, and somewhere we will find the proofs that it can become ill on its own account. The clinical picture of melancholia stresses moral disapproval of the patient's own ego over other manifestations: the subject will far more rarely judge himself in terms of physical affliction, ugliness, weakness and social inferiority; only impoverishment assumes a privileged position among the patient's anxieties or assertions.

One observation, and one that is not even difficult to make, leads to an explanation of the contradiction set out above. If we listen patiently to the many and various self-reproaches of the melancholic, we will be unable to avoid a sense that the most intense among them often have little to do with the patient himself, but may with slight modifications be adapted to another person whom the patient loves, has loved or is supposed to love. Each time we look into the facts, the patient confirms this supposition. This means that we have in our hands the key to the clinical picture, recognizing self-reproaches as accusations against a love-object which have taken this route and transferred themselves to the patient's own ego.

The woman who loudly pities her husband for being bound to such a useless woman is actually seeking to accuse her husband of uselessness, in whatever sense the term may be used. We should not be too surprised that some authentic self-reproaches are scattered among those applied to the speaker; they may come to the fore because they help to conceal the others and to impede knowledge of the actual facts, since they emerge from the pros and cons of the conflict of love that has led to the loss of love. Now the behaviour of the patients also becomes much more comprehensible. Their laments [*Klagen*] are accusations [*Anklagen*], in the old sense of the German word; they are not ashamed, they do not conceal themselves, because everything disparaging that they express about themselves is basically being said about someone else; and they are a long way away from communicating to those around them the humility and submissiveness that would befit such unworthy people; rather they are aggravating to a very high degree, they always seem as though they have been slighted, and as though a great wrong has been done to them. All of this is possible only because their reactions, as seen in their behaviour, still emanate from the mental constellation of rejection, which has, as the result of a certain process, been transferred to melancholic remorse.

There is then no difficulty in reconstructing this process. An object-choice had occurred, a bond had been formed between the libido and a particular person; through the influence of a real slight or disappointment on the part of the beloved person, that object-relation had been subjected to a shock. The result of this was not the normal one of the withdrawal of the libido from this object and its displacement on to a new one, but another, which seems to require a number of different conditions in order to come into being. Investment in objects proved not to be very resistant, and was suspended. The free libido was not, however, displaced on to another object, but instead drawn back into the ego. But it did not find any application there, serving instead to produce an identification of the ego with the abandoned object. In this way the shadow of the object fell upon the ego, which could now be condemned by a particular agency as an object, as the abandoned object. Thus the loss of object had been transformed into a loss of ego, and the conflict between the ego and the beloved person into a dichotomy between ego-criticism and the ego as modified by identification.

Some things may immediately be guessed about the preconditions and results of such a process. On the one hand a strong fixation on the love object must be present, but on the other hand, and in contradiction to that fixation, there must be minimal resistance in the form of object-investment. This contradiction seems to require the object-choice, in accordance with a telling observation by Otto Rank, to have occurred on a narcissistic foundation, so that the object-investment, if it encounters difficulties, is able to regress to narcissism. The narcissistic identification with the object then becomes the substitute for the love-investment, with the result that the love relationship, despite the conflict with the loved one, must not be abandoned. This substitution of identification for object-love is a significant mechanism for the narcissistic illnesses. K. Landauer recently uncovered it in the treatment of a case of schizophrenia.[4] It naturally corresponds to the regression of a type of object-choice to original narcissism. Elsewhere we have explained that identification is the preliminary stage of object-choice, and the first way, ambivalent in its manifestation, in which the ego selects an object. It may assimilate this object, and, in accordance with the oral or cannibalistic phase of libido development, may do so by eating it. Abraham is probably right in tracing the rejection of nourishment, which is apparent in severe forms of the melancholic state, back to this connection.

The conclusion which the theory calls for, and which would transfer the predisposition to melancholic illness, or a part of it, to the predominance of the narcissistic type of object-choice, has unfortunately not been confirmed by investigation. In the introductory sentences of this paper I have confessed that the empirical material on which this study is based is inadequate for our claims. Were we able to assume an agreement between observation and our deductions, we should not hesitate in seeing the oral phase of the libido, which still belongs to narcissism, as one of the characteristics of melancholia. Identifications with the object are by no means rare, even in transference neuroses, and are indeed a well-known mechanism of symptom-formation, particularly in hysteria. But we may see the difference between narcissistic and hysterical identification as lying in the fact that in the former the object-investment is relinquished, while in the latter it continues to exist and manifests an effect that is usually restricted to certain individual actions and innervations. Even in the case of transference neuroses, identification is the manifestation of something held in common that may signify love. Narcissistic identification is the older of the two, and grants us access to an understanding of the less well-studied hysterical form.

So melancholia derives some of its characteristics from mourning, and the rest from the process of regression from the narcissistic object-choice to narcissism. On the one hand it is, like mourning, a reaction to the real loss of the love-object, but it also has a condition which either is absent from normal mourning or, where it is present, transforms it into pathological mourning. The loss of the love-object is an excellent opportunity for the ambivalence of love relationships to come to the fore. Consequently, where the predisposition to obsessive neurosis is present, the conflict of ambivalence gives mourning a pathological shape and forces it to manifest itself in the form of self-reproaches for having been oneself responsible for the loss of the love-object, of having wanted that loss. In such obsessive neurotic depressions after the death of loved ones we are shown what the conflict of ambivalence can achieve on its own when the regressive pull of the libido is not involved. For the most part, the causes of melancholia go beyond the clear case of loss through death, and include all the situations of insult, slight, setback and disappointment through which an opposition of love and hate can be introduced to the relationship, or an ambivalence already present can be intensified. This conflict of ambivalence, now more real, now more constitutive in origin, should not be neglected among the preconditions of melancholia. If the love of the object, which cannot be abandoned while the object itself is abandoned, has fled into narcissistic identification, hatred goes to work on this substitute object, insulting it, humiliating it, making it suffer and deriving a sadistic satisfaction from that suffering. The indubitably pleasurable self-torment of melancholia, like the corresponding phenomenon of obsessive neurosis, signifies the satisfaction of tendencies of sadism and hatred,[5] which are applied to an object and are thus turned back against the patient's own person. In both of these illnesses, patients manage to avenge themselves on the original objects along the detour of self-punishment, and to torment their loved ones by means of being ill, having taken to illness in order to avoid showing their hostility directly. The person who provoked in the patient the emotional disturbance from which his form of illness took its orientation will generally be found in the patient's immediate milieu. Thus the melancholic's love-investment in his object has undergone a second fate; in part it has regressed to identification, but it has also been moved back, under the influence of the conflict of ambivalence, to the sadistic stage to which it is closer.

It is this sadism that solves the mystery of the inclination to suicide which makes melancholia both so interesting and so dangerous. We have acknowledged this great self-love of the ego as the primal state from which the life of the drives emanates, and we see in the anxiety that appears when our lives are endangered the liberation of so much narcissistic libido that we cannot grasp how the ego could ever consent to self-destruction. Certainly, we have known for a long time that no neurotic nurtures suicidal intentions who does not turn them back from an impulse to murder others, but we have achieved no understanding of the play of forces that could turn such an intention into action. Now the analysis of melancholia teaches us that the ego can only kill itself when it is able to treat itself as an object because of the return of object-investment, if it is able to direct the hostility that applies to the object back against itself and represents the original reaction of the ego against objects in the outside world. (See 'Drives and Their Fates'.) Thus in the regression of the narcissistic object-choice the object may have been abolished, but it has proved more potent than the ego itself. In the two contrasting situations of extreme passion and suicide the ego, although in entirely different ways, is overwhelmed by the object.

Hence, as regards the one particularly striking characteristic of melancholia, the emergence of the fear of impoverishment, it seems natural to trace it back to anal eroticism, torn from its context and regressively transformed.

Melancholia confronts us with other questions which to some extent it fails to answer. The fact that it passes after a certain amount of time, without leaving any broad or demonstrable changes, is a characteristic that it shares with mourning. It was there that we observed that time is required for the detailed implementation of the reality-testing command, after which the ego's libido is freed from the lost object. We may consider the ego busy with an analogous task during melancholia; in neither case do we have an economic understanding of its origin. The sleeplessness of melancholia testifies to the inflexibility of the condition, the impossibility of implementing the general drawing-in of investments required for sleep. The complex of melancholia behaves like an open wound, drawing investment energies to itself from all sides (energies which we have, in the case of transference neuroses, called 'counter-investments'), and draining the ego to the point of complete impoverishment; it can easily prove to be resistant to the ego's desire to sleep.

One element which is probably somatic, and which cannot be explained psychogenetically, becomes apparent in the regular alleviation of the condition that occurs in the evening. These considerations raise the question of whether the loss of the ego, regardless of the object (purely narcissistic injury to the ego) is enough to produce the image of melancholia, and whether an impoverishment of the ego-libido by the consumption of toxins can produce certain forms of the illness.

The most curious property of melancholia, and the one most in need of explanation, lies in its tendency to turn into the symptomatically opposite state of mania. As we know, this is not the fate of all cases of melancholia. Some cases develop in periodic relapses, the intervals between which reveal either no hint of mania at all, or only a very slight degree of it. Others demonstrate the regular alternation of melancholic and manic phases that has found expression in the formulation of cyclical insanity. One would be tempted to exclude these cases as being psychogenetic, had psychoanalytic treatment not brought about a therapeutic solution in several cases of this kind. So it is not only permissible, but actually imperative, to extend an analytic explanation of melancholia to mania as well.

I cannot promise that this attempt will be entirely satisfactory. In fact it does not go far beyond the possibility of an initial orientation. We have two clues at our disposal here, the first a psychoanalytical impression, the second what we might call a universal economic experience. The impression already expressed by a number of psychoanalytical researchers suggests that mania is not different in content from melancholia, that both illnesses battle with the same 'complex' to which the ego probably succumbs in melancholia, while in mania it has overcome it or pushed it aside. The other clue comes from the experience that in all states of joy, jubilation and triumph shown by the normal model of mania, the same economic conditions are apparent. As the result of a particular influence, a large expenditure of psychical energy, maintained over a long period or frequently recurring, finally becomes superfluous, and thus becomes available for many different applications and possibilities of discharge. Thus, for example: if a poor devil is suddenly relieved of his chronic concern about his daily bread by winning a large amount of money, if a long and strenuous struggle is finally crowned by success, if a person suddenly becomes capable of abandoning some pressing compulsion, a false position that he has had to maintain for a long time, and so on. All such situations are marked by a lightened mood, the signs of discharge of joyful emotion, and the intensified readiness for all kinds of actions, just like mania, and in complete contrast to the depression and inhibition of melancholia. One might dare to say that mania is in fact just such a triumph, except that what it has overcome, the source of its triumph, is hidden from the ego. Alcoholic intoxication, which belongs in the same series of states – albeit a more cheerful one – can be explained in much the same way; here there is probably a suggestion, accomplished by toxins, of the expenditure of repression. Lay opinion likes to assume that one is so keen on movement and activity in such a manic state because one is in 'such a cheerful mood'. Of course we will have to unmake this false connection. The economic state within the mental life which we mentioned above has been fulfilled, and that is why we are on the one hand so cheerful, and on the other so uninhibited in our actions.

If we combine these two suggestions, what we find is this: in mania, the ego must have overcome the loss of the object (or mourning over the loss, or perhaps the object itself), and now the total amount of counter-investment that the painful suffering of melancholia had drawn and bound to itself from the ego has become available. The manic person also unmistakably demonstrates his liberation from the object from which he had been suffering by pouncing on his new object-investments like a ravenous man.

This explanation may sound plausible, but first of all it is too vague, and secondly it throws up more new questions and doubts than we can answer. We do not wish to avoid discussing it, even though we cannot expect to find our way to clarity as a result.

In the first place, normal mourning also overcomes the loss of the object while at the same time absorbing all the energies of the ego during the period of its existence. Why, then, once it has run its course, is there not so much as a hint of the economic condition required for a phase of triumph? I cannot give a simple answer to this objection. It also draws our attention to the fact that we cannot even identify the economic means through which mourning accomplishes its task. However, a conjecture might come to our assistance here. To each individual memory and situation of expectation that shows the libido to be connected to the lost object, reality delivers its verdict that the object no longer exists, and the ego, presented with the question, so to speak, of whether it wishes to share this fate, is persuaded by the sum of narcissistic satisfactions that it derives from being alive to loosen its bonds with the object that has been destroyed. We might perhaps imagine that this process of dissolution takes place so slowly and gradually that by the time it is over the expenditure of energy required for its accomplishment has been dispersed.[6]

It is tempting to try to proceed from conjecture about the work of mourning to an account of the work of melancholia. Here, at the outset, we encounter an uncertainty. Hitherto, we have hardly considered melancholia from the topographical point of view, and neither have we asked in and between which psychical systems the work of melancholia occurs. What part of the psychical processes of the disorder is still taking place in relation to the abandoned unconscious object-investments, and what part in relation to their substitute through identification, in the ego?

The quick and easy answer to this is that the 'unconscious (thing-)representation of the object by the libido is abandoned'. But in fact this representation consists of countless individual impressions (or their unconscious traces), and this withdrawal of the libido cannot be a matter of a moment, but must certainly, as in mourning, be a long drawn-out and gradual process. It is not easy to tell whether it begins simultaneously in many different places, or whether it contains some kind of sequence; in analytic treatment one can often observe that now this, now that memory is activated, and that the identical-sounding laments, tiresome in their monotony, have a different unconscious explanation each time. If the object does not have such a great significance for the ego, one that is intensified by thousands of connections, its loss is not apt to lead to mourning or melancholia. The characteristic of detaching the libido piecemeal can thus be attributed equally to melancholia and mourning; it is probably based on the same economic relations and serves the same tendencies in both.

But melancholia, as we have heard, contains more than normal mourning does. In melancholia, the relationship with the object is not a simple one, it is complicated by the conflict of ambivalence. That ambivalence is either constitutional, that is, it is attached to every love relationship of this particular ego, or else it emerges straight out of experiences that imply the threat of the loss of the object. In its causes, then, melancholia can go far beyond mourning, which is as a rule unleashed only by real loss, the death of the object. Thus in melancholia a series of individual battles for the object begins, in which love and hatred struggle with one another, one to free the libido from the object, the other to maintain the existing libido position against the onslaught. These individual battles cannot be transferred to a system other than the unconscious, the realm of memory traces of things (as against verbal investments). It is in this very place that attempts at solution are played out in mourning, but here they face no obstacle, since these processes continue on their normal way to consciousness through the preconscious. This path is closed to the work of melancholia, perhaps because of the large number of causes or because of the fact that they are all working together. Constitutional ambivalence essentially belongs to the repressed, and the traumatic experiences with the object may have activated other repressed material. Thus everything about these battles of ambivalence remains withdrawn from consciousness until the characteristic outcome of melancholia has been reached. As we know, this consists in the threatened libido-investment finally leaving the object, only to return to the place in the ego from which it had emerged. So it is by taking flight into the ego that love escapes abolition. After this regression of the libido, the process can become conscious, and represents itself to consciousness as a conflict between one part of the ego and the critical agency.

So what consciousness learns about in the work of melancholia is not the essential part of it, nor is it the part to which we may attribute an influence to the solution of suffering. We see the ego debasing itself and raging against itself, and have as little understanding as the patient about where that can lead and how it can change. We can more readily attribute such an accomplishment to the unconscious part of the work, because it is not difficult to discover a significant analogy between the work of melancholia and that of mourning. Just as mourning impels the ego to renounce the object by declaring its death, and offers the ego the reward of staying alive, each individual battle of ambivalence loosens the fixation of the libido upon the object by devaluing, disparaging and, so to speak, even killing it. There is a possibility of the process in the unconscious coming to an end, either once the fury has played itself out or after the object has been abandoned as worthless. We cannot tell which of these two possibilities brings melancholia to an end, either in all cases or in most, and what influence this termination has upon the further development of the case. The ego may enjoy the satisfaction of acknowledging itself to be the better of the two, and superior to the object.

Even if we accept this view of the work of melancholia, there is still one point upon which we were seeking enlightenment that it does not help to explain. We expected that an explanation of the economic condition for the emergence of mania with the passing of melancholia might be found in the ambivalence that dominates the disorder; this might find support in analogies drawn from various other areas. But there is one fact before which that expectation must bow. Of the three preconditions for melancholia: the loss of the object, ambivalence and the regression of the libido into the ego, we find the first two once more in the obsessive reproaches that we encounter after someone has died. There, it is beyond a doubt ambivalence that represents the main driving force of the conflict, and observation shows that once it has passed, nothing of the triumph of a manic constitution remains. This leads us to the third element as the sole factor responsible. The accumulation of investment, which is freed once the work of melancholia is concluded, and which makes mania possible, must be linked to the regression of the libido to narcissism. The conflict within the ego which melancholia exchanges for the battle over the object must behave like a painful wound requiring an extraordinarily high counter-investment. But here, once again, it makes sense for us to come to a halt and put off any further explanation of mania until we have gained an insight into the economic nature first of physical pain and then of the mental pain analogous to it. We know already that the interdependence of the complex problems of the psyche requires us to break off each investigation before it is completed – until the results of some other investigation can come to its aid.[7]

(1917)

Notes

1. Abraham, to whom we owe the most significant of the few analytic studies of the subject at hand, also took this as his starting-point (*Zentralblatt für Psychoanalyse*, II, 6, 1912).

2. ['Metapsychologische Ergänzung der Traumlehre' (1917), which preceded 'Mourning and Melancholia' in the volume *Das Ich und das Es* (*The Ego and the Id*).]

3. 'Use every man after his desert, and who shall 'scape whipping?' *Hamlet*, II, 2.

4. [K. Landauer, 'Spontanheilung einer Kata tonie'] *Intern. Zeitschr. für ärztl. Psychoanalyse*, II, 1914.

5. On the difference between them, see the paper on 'Drives and Their Fates'.

6. Hitherto, little attention has been paid to the economic viewpoint in psychoanalytical works. As an exception to this we might mention the essay by V. Tausk, 'Entwertung des Verdrängungsmotivs durch Rekompense' ['Devaluation of the motive of repression through recompense'] (*Intern. Zeitschr. für ärztl. Psychoanalyse*, I, 1913).

7. [*Addition 1925:*] See further discussion of the problem of mania in *Mass Psychology and Analysis of the 'I'* (*Ges. Werke.*, vol. XIII).

Why War?

Dear Professor Einstein,

When I heard that you planned to invite me to take part in an exchange of ideas on a subject in which you take a great interest, and which you deem worthy of the interest of others, I readily agreed. I expected you to choose a problem at the limits of our current knowledge, to which each of us, the physicist and the psychologist, could forge his own particular path, so that, coming from different directions, those paths would meet on the same ground. You then surprised me by asking what one could do in order to fend off the fate of war from humanity. I was initially startled, having a sense of my – I almost said our – incompetence, because this struck me as a practical task, one that normally falls to statesmen. Then, however, I understood that you were not raising the question as a scientific researcher and physicist, but as a humanitarian, who had heeded the suggestions of the League of Nations, just as the polar explorer Fridtjof Nansen had taken it upon himself to bring help to the starving and to the homeless victims of the World War. I also reflected that I was not being expected to make practical suggestions, but only to suggest how the problem of the prevention of war presented itself to psychological consideration.

But once again, in your letter you yourself had said most of what needed to be said on the subject. You had, so to speak, taken the wind out of my sails, but I am happy to drift in your wake and content myself with confirming all your arguments while expanding upon them at greater length to the best of my knowledge – or the best of my surmise.

You begin with the relationship between law and power. That is certainly the correct starting point for our inquiry. Might I substitute for the word 'power' the harsher, harder word 'violence'? Today, we see law and violence as opposites. It is easy to demonstrate that the one has developed out of the other, and if we return to the very beginnings and check how it was that this first occurred, the solution of the problem presents itself to us without any difficulties. Do forgive me, though, if I give an account of things that are generally known and acknowledged as though they were new; the context requires it of me.

So conflicts of interest between human beings are in principle resolved by the use of violence. That is how things are throughout the whole of the animal kingdom, from which man should not exclude himself; for man, however, these conflicts of interest are joined by conflicts of opinion which extend to the highest peaks of abstraction and seem to require another technique for their resolution. But that is a later complication. At the very beginning, in a small horde of people, greater muscle-power decided to whom something should belong, or whose will should be enforced; the victor is the one with the better weapons, or the one who uses them more skilfully. With the introduction of weapons, intellectual superiority is already beginning to assume the place of raw muscle-power; the final purpose of the struggle remains the same, one side is to be obliged, by the damage inflicted upon it and by the paralysis of its forces, to abandon its claim or its resistance. This is accomplished most thoroughly when the adversary is permanently removed by the use of violence, which is to say: killed. There are two advantages to this, first that he is unable to resume his hostility, and second that his fate deters others from following his example. In addition, the killing of the enemy satisfies a compulsive tendency that we will have cause to mention below. The intention to kill can be resisted by the consideration that the enemy might be employed to perform useful services if kept alive and in fear. In that case, then, force contents itself with subjecting rather than killing him. This is the beginning of the practice of sparing the enemy, but from now on the victor must reckon with a lurking desire for revenge on the part of the loser, and relinquishes a part of his own security.

That, then, is the original state, the dominance of greater might, of raw or intellectually supported force. We know that this regime changed over the course of its development, and a path led from force to law – but which path? There is only one, in my opinion. It led via the fact that the greater strength of the one could find competition in the unity of several weak partners. '*L'union fait la force*' [unity is strength]. Force is broken by unity, the power of these unified forces now represents law in contrast to the force of the individual. We can see that law is the power of a community. It is still force, ready to be applied against any individual who resists it, it works with the same means, pursues the same ends; the only real difference lies in the fact that it is no longer the force of an individual which is being applied, but that of the community. But in order that this transition from force to the new law may take place, there is one psychological condition that must be fulfilled. The unification of the many must be stable and lasting. If it were generated solely in order to fight against the single superior army, and collapsed once that army had been overwhelmed, nothing would have been achieved. The next army which considered itself stronger would in turn strive for a dominance of force, and the game would be repeated *ad infinitum*. The community must be permanently maintained, it must organize itself, create rules preventing feared rebellions, assign institutions to watch over the observance of the rules – laws – and ensure the imposition of legitimate acts of violence. In the acknowledgement of such a community of interest, emotional bonds are formed among the members of a united group of people, feelings of community that will represent their actual strength.

This, I think, gives us all the essentials: the overcoming of violence by the transfer of power to a greater entity, held together by the emotional bonds of its members. All else is merely an enactment and repetition. Relations remain simple as long as the community consists only of a number of equally strong individuals. The laws of this association then determine the degree of personal freedom to use strength in a violent way, which the individual must relinquish if people are to live together in safety. But such a state of peace is conceivable only in theory, and the situation is complicated by the fact

On Murder, Mourning and Melancholia

that the community incorporates unequally powerful elements from the outset – men and women, parents and children – and soon, as a result of war and subjection, victors and losers who then become masters and slaves. Community law then becomes the manifestation of the unequal power relations in their midst, the laws are made by and for the ruling bodies, and few rights are granted to those who have been subjected. From that point onward the community contains two sources of legal disturbance, but also of further legal development. First of all, the attempts of some masters to rise above the restrictions which apply to one and all, and to fall back from legitimate domination to domination by violence, and secondly the constant efforts of the oppressed to achieve greater power for themselves, and to see these changes acknowledged by law, and to strive from a situation of unequal rights to equal rights for all. This last current will become particularly significant if shifts in power relations actually occur within the community, something that can happen as the result of many different historical factors. The law can then gradually adapt to the new power relations or else, as more often happens, the ruling class will be unwilling to accept the change, and there is rebellion, civil war and thus the temporary suspension of law, and new trials of violence, after the outcome of which a new legal order is enforced. There is yet another source of legal change which manifests itself only in a peaceful way, and that is the cultural transformation of the members of the community, but that belongs in a context which can only be taken into account later on.

So we can see that even within a community the resolution of conflicts of interest by violence has not been avoided. But the needs and communalities that derive from living together in the same territory favour a swift end to such struggles, and the likelihood of peaceful solutions under these conditions constantly increases. But a glance at the history of mankind shows us an endless series of conflicts between one community and one or more others, between larger and smaller entities, city states, regions, peoples, empires, which are almost always resolved by the trial of strength that is war. Such wars end either in plunder or in the complete subjection and conquest of one of the parties. Wars of conquest cannot all be judged in the same way. Some, like those of the Mongols and the Turks, have brought nothing but disaster, while others, on the contrary, have contributed to the transformation of violence into law, by producing larger units within which the possibility of the use of violence had been abolished, and in which conflicts were resolved by a new legal order. Thus the conquests of the Romans gave the Mediterranean countries the precious *pax romana*. The desire for expansion on the part of the French kings created a flourishing France that was united in peace. Paradoxical as it may sound, we must admit that war is a means not unsuited to the production of the longed-for 'eternal' peace which, because it is capable of creating those great entities within which a strong central force renders further wars impossible. But it is not yet capable of producing that peace, because the results of conquest are not in general long-lasting; the newly created entities fall apart again, generally because of the lack of cohesiveness among the parts which have been united with one another by violence. And furthermore, conquest has hitherto been able to forge only partial unifications, however sizeable these may be, the conflicts of which have cried out for violent resolution. Thus the sole consequence of all these belligerent efforts has been that humanity has swapped numerous, endless minor wars for wars on the larger scale, rare but all the more destructive.

Applying this to the present day, we come to the same conclusion that you yourself have reached on a shorter path. Wars will only be prevented with any certainty if humanity unites to bring into effect a central authority which will have jurisdiction in all conflicts of interest. This clearly combines two requirements, that such a supreme agency be created, and that it should be granted the power it requires. One of these on its own would not be enough. Now the League of Nations is conceived as just such an agency, but in it the second condition is not fulfilled; the League of Nations has no power of its own, and can only achieve power if the members of the new association, the individual states, are ready to resign their power to it. But at present there seems little prospect of that. The institution of the League of Nations would, however, be incomprehensible, if we did not know that this was an experiment that has not often been risked in the history of humanity, and perhaps never to the present extent. It is an attempt to achieve the authority – that is, the coercive influence – that is otherwise based on the possession of power, by appealing to certain idealistic attitudes of mind. We have heard that there are two things which keep a community together: the compelling force of violence and the emotional bonds – technically called 'identifications' – of its members. If one factor is absent, the community may perhaps be maintained by the other. Of course such ideas only have any significance when they give expression to the important affinities of the members, and one might in that case wonder how strong they are. History teaches us that they have actually had an effect. The pan-Hellenic idea, for example, the awareness of being superior to the surrounding barbarians, which found such powerful expression in the Amphictyonic Council, the oracles and the games, was strong enough to moderate the customary practices of warfare among Greeks, but of course it was not capable of preventing belligerent conflicts between the different factions among the Greek people, or even, indeed, of keeping a city or an association of cities from allying themselves with the Persian enemy in order to defeat a rival. Neither did the Christian sense of community, powerful enough during the Renaissance, prevent Christian towns and cities from recruiting the aid of the Sultan in their wars against each other. Neither is there any idea in our own times which we might expect to supply such a unifying authority. Indeed it is all too clear that the national ideals which dominate nations today are impelling them in the opposite direction. There are some who predict that it is only the universal penetration of Bolshevik thought that will be able to bring wars to an end, and suggest that this might only be accomplished after terrible civil wars. Thus it would seem that the attempt to replace actual violence with the power of ideas is still condemned to failure today. We shall be making a miscalculation if we do not bear in mind the fact that law was originally brute force, and cannot, even today, do without the support of violence.

I can now set about glossing another of your propositions. You are surprised that it is so easy to rouse people to enthusiasm about war, and suspect that there is something at work in them, a drive to hate and to destroy, which meets such incitement halfway. Once again I can only wholeheartedly agree with you. We believe in the existence of such a drive, and have been trying over the past few years to study its manifestations. May I take this opportunity to present to you a piece of the drive theory which we have reached in the field of psychoanalysis after a great deal of fumbling and indecision?

According to our hypothesis, man's drives are of two kinds only, those which seek to preserve and unite – we call them erotic, exactly in the sense in which Plato uses the word Eros in his *Symposium*, or sexual, with a deliberate over-extension of the popular conception of sexuality – and others which seek to destroy and kill; we sum these up as the drive to aggression or the drive to destruction. You will see that this is actually only the theoretical transfiguration of the universally familiar opposition of love and hate, which may have some primal relationship with the polarity of attraction and repulsion that has a part to play in your discipline. Now let us not be too hasty in assessing these drives as representing good and evil. Each one of these drives is just as essential as the other, and the manifestations of life arise out of the concurrent and mutually opposing effects of each. Now it would appear that a drive of one kind can barely be effective in isolation, it is always connected, or as we would say, alloyed with a certain contribution from the other side, which modifies its goal or, under certain circumstances, makes its accomplishment possible. Thus, for example, the drive to self-preservation is certainly erotic in nature, but this drive more than most requires access to aggression if it is to impose its aims. Similarly, the drive to love, directed towards objects, requires a supplement from the drive to possess if it is to apprehend its object. It is the difficulty in isolating the manifestations of the two kinds of drive that has kept us from knowing them for so long.

If you will follow me for a little way, you will hear that human actions reveal a complication of another kind. The action is very seldom the work of a single drive-impulse, which must essentially be already assembled from the erotic and the destructive drives. Generally speaking, several motives constructed in similar fashion must coincide to make the action possible. One of your scientific

227

colleagues has already observed this, one Prof. G. Ch. Lichtenberg, who taught physics in Göttingen in the days of our classical thinkers; but he may have been more significant as a psychologist than as a physicist. He invented the Compass of Motives, writing: 'The motives that lead us to do anything could be organized like the thirty-two winds, and their names formed in a similar way, for example bread-bread-fame, or fame-fame-bread.' So if people are being roused to war, a whole number of motives must reply in agreement, both noble and vulgar, and others which are kept silent. This is not the place to reveal them all. The pleasure taken in aggression and destruction is certainly among them; countless cruelties in history and everyday life bear out its strength and existence. The combination of these destructive tendencies with others, erotic and idealistic, naturally makes it easier for them to be satisfied. Sometimes, hearing of the horrors of history, we have a sense that idealistic motives had served only as pretexts for the destructive cravings, and at other times, for example in the cruelties of the Holy Inquisition, we think that the idealistic motives had pushed to the front of consciousness while the destructive ones had given them unconscious reinforcement.

I am concerned not to abuse your interest, which is concerned with the prevention of war rather than our theories. But I should like for a moment to stay with our drive to destruction, whose randomness certainly does not keep pace with its significance. With some expenditure of speculation, in fact, we have reached the view that this drive works within every living creature, and then endeavours to bring it to destruction, and to bring life back to a state of inanimate material. In all seriousness it merited the name of a death-drive, while the erotic drives represent the drives to life. The death-drive becomes the drive to destruction, when it is applied externally, against objects, with the help of certain organs. The organism preserves its own life, so to speak, by destroying that which is strange to it. But a certain part of the death-drive remains active within the living creature, and we have attempted to derive a whole number of normal and pathological phenomena from this internalization of the drive to destruction. We have even committed the heresy of explaining the origin of our conscience with reference to the involution of aggression. You will notice that it is hardly a trivial matter if this process is carried too far, in fact it is actually unhealthy. But if these same forces turn to destruction in the outside world the organism is relieved, and the effect must be beneficial. This would serve as the biological excuse for all the ugly and dangerous strivings which we fight against. It must be admitted that they are closer to nature than our resistance to them, for which we have not yet found an explanation either. You may have the impression that our theories are a kind of mythology, and not even a pleasant one in this case. But does not every science rest on such a kind of mythology? Is contemporary physics any different in that respect?

For our immediate purposes we may say, on the basis of what we have said above, that there is no point in wishing to wipe away mankind's aggressive tendencies. In fortunate parts of the earth, where nature provides for all man's needs, there are supposed to be tribes whose lives are passed in gentleness, and among whom compulsion and aggression are unknown. I can hardly believe this, and should like to learn more about these happy folk. The Bolsheviks, too, hope that they can make human aggression disappear, that they can deliver satisfaction of material needs and in other respects produce equality among the members of the community. I consider this to be an illusion. For the moment they keep themselves very carefully armed, and bind their devotees together not least through their common hatred of all outsiders. Incidentally, as you yourself observe, it is not a matter of fully removing the human inclination to aggression; one can attempt to divert it in such a way that it need not find expression in war.

From our mythological drive-theory we can easily derive a formula for the indirect ways of combating war. If willingness to engage in war is a product of the drive to destruction, the obvious thing is to appeal to the antagonist of this drive, Eros. Everything that creates emotional bonds among human beings must work against war. These relationships can be of two kinds: first of all, relationships like those towards a love-object, albeit without sexual goals. Psychoanalysis need not be ashamed if it speaks of love here, because religion says the same thing: love your neighbour as yourself. That is easier said than done. The other kind of emotional bond is the one that comes through identification. Everything that produces significant affinities between human beings produces such shared emotions, such identifications. A significant part of the structure of human society is based on them.

In a complaint that you made about the misuse of authority I hear a second suggestion, indicating a way to combat the inclination to war. It is a part of the innate and ineradicable inequality of men that they divide into leaders and followers. The latter are the vast majority, they require an authority to make their decisions for them, and generally submit to that authority without question. This suggests that greater effort should be made to achieve than has been hitherto, in order to achieve an upper stratum of independent-minded people, resistant to intimidation and unstinting in their pursuit of truth, who could assume the role of guiding the dependent masses. It goes without saying that the encroachments of the forces of the state, and the church's encroachments upon freedom of thought are not favourable to the elevation of such a class. The ideal condition, of course, would be a community of people who have subjected their drives to the dictatorship of reason. Nothing else could prompt such a complete and robust unification of humanity, even if there were no emotional bonds between them. But in all likelihood that is a utopian hope. Certainly, the other paths towards the indirect prevention of war are more viable, but they do not promise swift success. An image comes disagreeably to mind, of mills that grind so slowly that people might starve before they had their flour.

You will see that not much is achieved by calling in the unworldly theoretician to solve practical problems. It would be better to strive in each individual case to meet the danger with the means that happen to be at hand. But I should like to address one more question which you do not raise in your essay, and which is of particular interest to me. Why are we so enraged about war, you and I and so many others, why do we not accept it as another of humanity's hardships?

After all, it seems natural and biologically well-founded, and in practical terms barely avoidable. Do not be angry with my question. For the purposes of an investigation one may perhaps adopt the mask of superior detachment to which one cannot really lay claim. The answer will be because every human being has a right to his own life, because war destroys hope-filled human lives and brings the individual human being into humiliating situations, forcing him to murder others against his will, destroys precious material values, the product of human toil, and much else besides. There is also the fact that war in its present form no longer provides an opportunity to fulfil the old heroic ideal, and that a future war, because of such great advances in the means of destruction, would mean the extermination of one or perhaps both adversaries. That is all true, and seems so indisputable that one is only amazed that warfare has not been rejected by general agreement of humanity. Certainly, we may discuss these points one by one. It is questionable whether the community should not also have a right to dispose of individual human lives. Not all kinds of war can be equally condemned; as long as there are empires and nations willing to engage in the reckless destruction of others, then those others must be armed for war. But we shall pass over all that quickly, these are not the subjects that you challenged me to discuss. I have something else in mind: I believe that the major reason why we are furious about war is that there is no way around it. We are pacifists because for organic reasons we must be. That makes it easy for us to justify our attitude through arguments.

That is probably incomprehensible without further explanation. What I have in mind is the following: since time immemorial, mankind has been moving through the process of cultural evolution. (I know that there are those who prefer the term civilization.) It is to this process that we owe the best that we have become, and a great deal of that which causes us suffering. Its causes and origins are obscure, its outcome uncertain, and some of its features may be easily discerned. Perhaps it will lead to the extinction of the human species, because it compromises the sexual function in more than one respect, and even today uncivilized races and backward strata of the population are multiplying more rapidly than those with a high level of culture. Perhaps this process is comparable to the domestication of certain species of animal; without a doubt it involves physical changes; we have not yet familiarized ourselves with the idea that cultural evolution is such an organic process. The psychical changes that go hand in hand with the cultural process are striking and unambiguous. They consist in a progressive displacement of the drive-goals and a restriction of the drive-impulses. Sensations that were pleasurable to our forefathers have become indifferent to us, or even insufferable; if our ethical and aesthetic ideals have changed, there are organic reasons for that. Among the psychological features of civilization, two seem to be the most important: the strengthening of the intellect, which is beginning to dominate the instinctive life, the life of the drives, and the internalization of the tendency towards aggression, with all its consequences, whether they be favourable or dangerous. The mental attitudes that the process of civilization imposes upon us are most harshly contradicted by war, which is why we must rage against it, we can simply bear it no longer, it is not merely an intellectual and emotional rejection, among us pacifists it is a constitutional intolerance, an idiosyncrasy magnified, so to speak, to a very high degree. And indeed the aesthetic humiliations of war have not much less to do with our rejection of it than do its cruelties.

How long must we wait before the others become pacifists as well? We cannot say, but perhaps it is not a utopian hope that the influence of these two factors, the cultural attitude and the justified fear of the effects of a future war, will put an end to warfare within the foreseeable future, along which paths or deviations we cannot guess. Meanwhile we may say to ourselves: everything that promotes the development of civilization also works against war.

I give you my most cordial greetings, and ask your forgiveness if my reflections have disappointed you.

Yours

Sigmund Freud

(1933)

Letter to Romain Rolland

(A Disturbance of Memory on the Acropolis)

My dear friend!

Urgently pressed to contribute a written text to the celebration of your seventieth birthday, I have tried for a long time to find something that would be in some sense worthy of you, something that could express my admiration for your love of truth, your openness, your humanitarianism and your generosity. Or something that would attest to my gratitude to a writer who has given me so much pleasure and delight. I tried in vain; I am a decade older than you, and my work is over. What I finally have to offer you is the gift of an impoverished man who 'has seen better days'.

You are aware that my academic work set itself the goal of illuminating unusual, abnormal and pathological phenomena in the life of the mind, that is, of tracing them back to the psychical forces at work behind them, and revealing the mechanisms in operation. I first attempted this upon my own person, then on others too, and finally, in a bold assault, upon the human race as a whole. One such phenomenon, which I myself experienced a generation ago, in 1904, and had never understood, has come to my mind repeatedly over the past few years; initially I did not know why. I finally resolved to analyse the little experience, and below I shall tell you the result of this study. In doing so, of course, I must ask you to devote greater attention to details from my personal life than they would otherwise deserve.

A *disturbance of memory on the Acropolis*

In those days, every year in late August or early September, I used to set off with my younger brother on a holiday that lasted several weeks and took us to Rome, some region of Italy or the Mediterranean coast. My brother is ten years younger than I am, and thus the same age as you – a coincidence that strikes me only now. That year my brother explained that his business dealings meant a long absence was impossible, and that he could stay away for a week at most, so our trip would have to be curtailed. Therefore we decided to travel via Trieste to the island of Corfu and to spend our brief holiday there. In Trieste my brother visited a business colleague, and I went with him. The man kindly inquired about our further plans, and, hearing that we were planning on going to Corfu, he urgently advised us against it. 'What are you going to do there at this time of year? It's so hot that you won't be able to do anything at all. You'd be better off going to Athens. The Lloyds steamer sets off this afternoon, it will give you three days to see the city, and pick you up on the way back. That will be more worthwhile and more pleasant for you.'

When we had left the Triestine gentleman, we were both strangely downcast. We discussed the plan that had been suggested to us, found it utterly pointless, seeing nothing but obstacles to its implementation, and also assumed that we would not be allowed into Greece without passports. During the hours before the opening of the Lloyds office, we drifted morosely and irresolutely around the city. But when the time came, we went to the counter and bought tickets to Athens, as though it were quite natural, without worrying about the supposed difficulties, and indeed without even discussing with each other the reasons for our decision. This behaviour was indeed very peculiar. We later acknowledged that we had immediately and readily accepted the suggestion to travel to Athens rather than Corfu. Why then had we spoiled the time leading up to the opening of the counter by being depressed, pretending that we could see only hindrances and difficulties?

Then, when I stood on the Acropolis on the afternoon after our arrival, and my eye took in the landscape, the curious thought suddenly came to me: *So this all really does exist, just as we learned in school!* To describe the situation more precisely, the person delivering the comment was distinguished, much more sharply than would usually have been noticeable, from another who perceived it, and both were amazed, although not by the same thing. One of these persons behaved as though, under the impression of an irrefutable observation, he was obliged to believe in something the reality of which had until then seemed uncertain to him. To exaggerate slightly: it was as though someone walking along Loch Ness were suddenly to see the body of the famous monster washed ashore, and found himself forced to admit: so the sea serpent that we didn't believe in really does exist. But the other person was rightly surprised, because he had not known that the real existence of Athens, the Acropolis and this landscape had ever been a matter of doubt. That person had rather been prepared for an expression of ecstasy and delight.

One might now be inclined to say that the disconcerting thought that came to me on the Acropolis merely emphasized the fact that it is one thing to see something with one's own eyes and quite another only to hear or to read about it. But that would be a strange way of dressing up an uninteresting commonplace. Or else I might go so far as to claim that as a schoolboy I had believed I was convinced of the historical reality of the city of Athens and its history, but had learned from the idea that came to me on the Acropolis that I had not in fact believed in it in my unconscious; only now had I acquired a conviction that 'extended into the unconscious'. Such an explanation sounds very profound, but it is easier to postulate than it is to prove, and will be highly contestable from a theoretical point of view. No, I think that the two phenomena, our depressed state in Trieste and the thought on the Acropolis, are closely linked. The former is the more easily understandable, and may help us to explain the latter.

Furthermore, the experience in Trieste is, it should be noted, nothing but an expression of disbelief. 'We are to see Athens? But that's out of the question, it will be too difficult.' In that case the accompanying depression corresponds to regret that the trip will never happen. It would have been too lovely! And now we understand what we are dealing with. It is one of those instances of 'too good to be true' that we know so well. An example of the kind of disbelief that so frequently occurs when we are surprised by a piece of good news, that we have won the lottery or a prize, or when a girl learns that the man she has loved in secret has presented himself to her parents as a suitor, and so on.

Once we have established that a phenomenon exists, the next question, of course, is to inquire into its cause. This disbelief is clearly an attempt to reject a piece of reality, but there is something strange about it. We would not be at all surprised if such an attempt were directed against a piece of reality that threatened to bring displeasure; our psychical mechanism, we might say, works along those lines. But why such disbelief about something which, on the contrary, promises to deliver a high degree of pleasure? Truly paradoxical behaviour! But I recall that I have in the past dealt with the similar case of those individuals who, as I put it, 'are wrecked by success'. Under normal circumstances one succumbs to failure, the non-fulfilment of a need or desire of great importance to one's life; with these people, however, it is the other way around; they fall ill, they are wrecked by the fulfilment of an overwhelmingly strong desire. But the contradiction between the two situations is not as great as it might at first appear. In the paradoxical case an internal frustration has simply assumed the place of the external one. The subject does not allow himself to be happy; the internal frustration orders him to cling to the external one. But why? Because, the answer runs in many cases, we cannot expect fate to supply anything so good. Hence, once again, 'too good to be true', the expression of a pessimism which many of us seem to harbour within ourselves to a large degree. In some other cases, as for example among those wrecked by success, we encounter a feeling of guilt or inferiority that may be translated as follows: I am not worthy of such good fortune, I do not deserve it. But these two motivations are essentially the same, the one being merely a projection of the other. For, as has been known for some time, the fate that we expect to treat us so badly is a materialization of our conscience, of the severe Super-ego within us, in which the punitive agency of our childhood finds residual expression.

This, I believe, explains our behaviour in Trieste. We could not believe that we were destined for the joy of seeing Athens. The fact that the piece of reality that we wished to reject was at first only a possibility determined the strange qualities of our initial reaction. Then, when we stood on the Acropolis, that possibility had become reality, and the same reaction now found an altered but far clearer expression. In undistorted form, that should have been: 'I would really not have believed that I should ever be granted the chance to see Athens with my own eyes, as is now indubitably the case!' When I recall the passionate yearning to travel and see the world that dominated me during my grammar-school years and beyond, and how long it was before that yearning was fulfilled, I am no longer surprised by its after-effect on the Acropolis; I was forty-eight at the time. I did not ask my younger brother whether he felt anything similar. A certain reticence surrounded the whole experience, and had already prevented us from exchanging our thoughts in Trieste.

But if I have correctly guessed the meaning of the thought that came to me on the Acropolis, and it did indeed express my delighted amazement at now being in that place, the further question arises of why that meaning had, in that thought, been subjected to such a distorted and distorting disguise.

The essential content of the thought has been preserved even in its distortion: it is disbelief. 'According to the evidence of my senses, I am now standing on the Acropolis, but I can't believe it.' But the expression of that disbelief, that doubt about a piece of reality, was doubly displaced, first by being shifted back into the past and secondly by being transferred away from my relation to the Acropolis to the Acropolis's very existence. Thus something came into being which amounted to the assertion that I had in the past doubted the real existence of the Acropolis, although my memory rejected this as incorrect and, indeed, impossible.

The two distortions involve two quite separate problems. We can attempt to penetrate more deeply into the process of transposition. Without for the moment elaborating upon how I reached this idea, I wish to start from the hypothesis that the original factor must have been a feeling at the time that there was something dubious and unreal about the situation. That situation included myself, the Acropolis and my perception of it. I could not account for that doubt, indeed I could not cast doubt upon my sensory impressions of the Acropolis. But I recalled that I did in the past doubt something to do with this locality, and it was here that I found the means required to shift the doubt into the past. But in the process the content of the doubt was lost. I could not just remember doubting, in my early years, whether I myself would ever see the Acropolis, but asserted that at the time I disbelieved in the reality of the Acropolis. It is precisely this result of the distortion that leads me conclude that the actual situation on the Acropolis contained an element of doubt about reality. I am still a long way from explaining the process, so I shall briefly conclude by saying that the entire psychical situation, apparently confused and difficult to describe, is precisely resolved by the hypothesis that I had – or could have had – the momentary feeling on the Acropolis: '*What I am seeing there is not real.*' This is called a 'feeling of estrangement'. I attempted to ward it off, and succeeded in doing so at the expense of making a false statement about the past.

These estrangements are very curious phenomena that are still very little understood. They are described as 'sensations', but they are clearly complicated processes bound up with particular contents and linked with decisions made concerning those contents. While they occur very frequently in certain mental illnesses, they are also not unknown to normal people, just as healthy individuals have occasional hallucinations. But they are certainly failed actions, and like dreams – which, despite their regular occurrence in healthy people, we see as models of mental disturbance – they are abnormal in their structures. These phenomena can be observed in two different forms; the subject feels that a piece of reality or a piece of his own self has become strange. In the latter case we speak of 'depersonalization'; estrangement and depersonalization are very closely connected. There are other phenomena in which we can recognize what we might call their positive counterparts, so-called *'fausse reconnaissance'* [false recognition], *'déjà vu'*, *'déjà raconté'* [already recounted], illusions in which we seek to assume something as belonging to our own selves, just as, in the case of estrangement, we attempt to exclude something from ourselves. A naively mystical, unpsychological attempt at explanation seeks to exploit the phenomena of *déjà vu* as proof of former existences of our psychical self. The path from depersonalization leads to the extremely curious condition of *'double conscience'* [double consciousness], more correctly called 'split personality'. This is all still so obscure, so little mastered by science that I must refrain from talking to you about it any further.

It will be enough for my purposes if I return to two universal characteristics of the phenomena of estrangement. First, they all serve the purposes of defence, they seek to keep something away from the ego, to deny it. Now the ego is approached on two sides by fresh elements that can prompt defensive measures, from the real external world and from the internal world of the thoughts and impulses appearing within the ego. It may be that this alternative coincides with the difference between actual estrangements and depersonalizations. There are an extraordinarily large number of methods, mechanisms, we might say, employed by the ego as it accomplishes its defensive tasks. Very close to myself, a work is now underway which will deal with the study of these defensive methods; my daughter, the child analyst, is writing a book on the subject. Our deeper understanding of psychopathology had its source in the most primitive and thorough of these methods, 'repression'. Between repression and the 'normal' way of defending ourselves against things that are painful and unbearable, through recognition, consideration, judgement and appropriate action, there lies a whole series of modes of behaviour on the part of the ego that are more or less clearly pathological in character. May I stop for a moment to discuss a marginal case of such defence? You are familiar with the famous lament of the Spanish Moors, '*Ay de mi Alhama*' ['Alas for my Alhama'], which relates how King Boabdil receives the news of the fall of his city of Alhama. He senses that this loss means the end of his rule. But he is not willing to accept it, and decides to treat the news as though it had not come. The verse runs:

> *Cartas le fueron venidas.*
> *de que Alhama era ganada.*
> *Las cartas echó en el fuego*
> *y al mensajero mataba.*

[Letters reached him saying that Alhama was taken. The letters he threw in the fire, and killed the messenger.]

It is easy to guess that this behaviour on the part of the king is in part determined by the need to fight against his feeling of powerlessness. By burning the letters and having the messenger killed, he is still trying to demonstrate his absolute power.

The second general characteristic of estrangements, their dependence upon the past, upon the hoard of memories within the ego and earlier painful experiences that may in the meantime have succumbed to repression, is not accepted without dispute. My experience on the Acropolis, which ends in a disturbance of memory, a falsification of the past, helps us to demonstrate that influence. It is not true to say that I doubted the real existence of Athens during my time as a grammar-school boy. I only doubted that I would ever be able to see Athens. It struck me as utterly beyond the realms of possibility that I would travel such a long way, that I would 'come so far'. That had to do with the strictures and poverty of our living conditions in my youth. The longing to travel was certainly also an expression of the wish to escape that pressure, like the urge that compels so many adolescents to run away from home. I had realized long ago that much of the pleasure in travel consists in the fulfilment of those early desires, and is thus rooted in dissatisfaction with home and family. The first time one sees the sea, crosses the ocean, experiences cities and countries as realities which were for so long remote, inaccessible objects of desire, one feels like a hero who has accomplished incredible feats. Back then, on the Acropolis, I could have asked my brother, 'Do you remember how, in our youth, we made the same journey day after day, from —— Street to school, and then how we went every Sunday to the Prater or on one of those outings to the countryside with which we were already so familiar, and now here we are in Athens standing on the Acropolis! We really have come a long way!' And if one may compare something so small with something larger, did Napoleon I not turn to one of his brothers during his coronation as Emperor in Notre Dame – it was probably the eldest, Joseph – and observe, 'What would *Monsieur notre père* say if he could see us now?'

But here we reach the solution of the little problem of why the pleasure of our trip to Athens was disturbed while we were still in Trieste. There must be a feeling of guilt associated with the satisfaction of having come such a long way; there is something involved in it that is wrong, something that has for a long time been forbidden. It has to do with criticism of our father in childhood, with the undervaluation that had replaced that overvaluation of his character which had prevailed in early childhood. It seems as though the essential aspect of success lies in getting further than one's father, as though wishing to outdo one's father were forbidden.

To this generally valid motive we should add one element particular to our own case: the very subject of Athens and the Acropolis contains a reference to the superiority of sons. Our father had been a businessman, he had no grammar-school education, Athens would not have meant much to him. What disturbed our enjoyment of the trip to Athens, then, was an impulse of *piety*. And now you will no longer be surprised that the memory of the experience on the Acropolis has haunted me so often now that I myself am old and in need of forbearance, and can no longer travel.

Yours very sincerely

Sigmund Freud

January 1936

READ MORE IN PENGUIN

In every corner of the world, on every subject under the sun, Penguin represents quality and variety – the very best in publishing today.

For complete information about books available from Penguin – including Puffins, Penguin Classics and Arkana – and how to order them, write to us at the appropriate address below. Please note that for copyright reasons the selection of books varies from country to country.

In the United Kingdom: Please write to *Dept. EP, Penguin Books Ltd, Bath Road, Harmondsworth, West Drayton, Middlesex UB7 0DA*

In the United States: Please write to *Consumer Services, Penguin Putnam Inc., 405 Murray Hill Parkway, East Rutherford, New Jersey 07073-2136.* VISA and MasterCard holders call 1-800-631-8571 to order Penguin titles

In Canada: Please write to *Penguin Books Canada Ltd, 10 Alcorn Avenue, Suite 300, Toronto, Ontario M4V 3B2*

In Australia: Please write to *Penguin Books Australia Ltd, 487 Maroondah Highway, Ringwood, Victoria 3134*

In New Zealand: Please write to *Penguin Books (NZ) Ltd, Private Bag 102902, North Shore Mail Centre, Auckland 10*

In India: Please write to *Penguin Books India Pvt Ltd, 11 Community Centre, Panchsheel Park, New Delhi 110017*

In the Netherlands: Please write to *Penguin Books Netherlands bv, Postbus 3507, NL-1001 AH Amsterdam*

In Germany: Please write to *Penguin Books Deutschland GmbH, Metzlerstrasse 26, 60594 Frankfurt am Main*

In Spain: Please write to *Penguin Books S. A., Bravo Murillo 19, 1°B, 28015 Madrid*

In Italy: Please write to *Penguin Italia s.r.l., Via Vittorio Emanuele 45/a, 20094 Corsico, Milano*

In France: Please write to *Penguin France, 12, Rue Prosper Ferradou, 31700 Blagnac*

In Japan: Please write to *Penguin Books Japan Ltd, Iidabashi KM-Bldg, 2-23-9 Koraku, Bunkyo-Ku, Tokyo 112-0004*

In South Africa: Please write to *Penguin Books South Africa (Pty) Ltd, P.O. Box 751093, Gardenview, 2047 Johannesburg*

PENGUIN MODERN CLASSICS

CIVILIZATION AND ITS DISCONTENTS
SIGMUND FREUD

Civilization and its Discontents/'Civilized' Sexual Morality and Modern Nervous Illness

Translated by David McLintock

With an Introduction by Leo Bersani

'Narratives that have the colour and force of fiction' John Updike

In his final years, Freud devoted most of his energies to a series of highly ambitious works on the broadest issues of religion and society.

As early as 1908, he produced a powerful paper on the repressive hypocrisy of 'civilized sexual morality', and its role in 'modern nervous illness'. Deepening this analysis in *Civilization and its Discontents*, he argues that 'civilized' values – and the impossible ideals of Christianity – inevitably distort our natural aggression and impose a terrible burden of guilt. It is also here that Freud developed his last great theoretical innovation: the strange and haunting notion of an innate death drive, locked in a constant struggle with the forces of Eros.

General Editor: Adam Phillips

PENGUIN MODERN CLASSICS

MASS PSYCHOLOGY AND OTHER WRITINGS
SIGMUND FREUD

Compulsive Actions and Religious Exercises / Mass Psychology and Analysis of the 'I' / A Religious Experience / The Future of an Illusion / Moses the Man and Monotheistic Religion / A Comment on Anti-Semitism

Translated by J. A. Underwood

With an Introduction by Jacqueline Rose

'Freud was an explorer of the mind ... an overturner and a re-mapper of accepted or settled geographies and genealogies' Edward Said

These works reveal Freud at his most iconoclastic, asking challenging questions about the powerful attraction of group identity and how this has the power to bind us and drive us to hatred.

In *Mass Psychology* he explores the psyche as a social force, with a compelling analysis of how institutions such as the Church and army can generate unquestioning loyalty to a leader and provoke us to commit atrocities – Freud's findings would prove all too prophetic in the years that followed. Works such as 'Moses the Man', written at the time of Freud's flight from Nazism in 1938, warn of the dangers of nationalism. Writings like 'The Future of an Illusion' examine religion and ritual in an unrelenting critique of religious faith.

General Editor: Adam Phillips

PENGUIN MODERN CLASSICS

BEYOND THE PLEASURE PRINCIPLE AND OTHER WRITINGS
SIGMUND FREUD

On the Introduction of Narcissism / Remembering, Repeating and Working Through / Beyond the Pleasure Principle / The Ego and the Id/Inhibition, Symptom and Fear

Translated by John Reddick

With an Introduction by Mark Edmundson

'Freud's great legacy ... brilliantly exposes the state of the psyche' Mark Edmundson

In Freud's view we are driven by the desire for pleasure, as well as by the desire to avoid pain. But the pursuit of pleasure has never been a simple thing. Pleasure can be a form of fear, a form of memory and a way of avoiding reality. Above all, as these essays show with remarkable eloquence, pleasure is a way in which we repeat ourselves.

The essays collected in this volume explore, in Freud's uniquely subtle and accessible style, the puzzles of pleasure and morality – the enigmas of human development.

General Editor: Adam Phillips

PENGUIN MODERN CLASSICS

STUDIES IN HYSTERIA
SIGMUND FREUD AND JOSEPH BREUER

Civilization and its Discontents / Civilized Sexual Morality and Modern Nervous Illness

Translated by Nicola Luckhurst

With an Introduction by Rachel Bowlby

'The effect that psychoanalysis has had upon the life of the West is incalculable'
Lionel Trilling

The tormenting of the body by the troubled mind – hysteria – is among the most pervasive of human disorders, yet at the same time it is the most elusive. Freud's recognition that hysteria stemmed from traumas in the patient's past transformed the way we think about sexuality.

Studies in Hysteria is one of the founding texts of psychoanalysis, revolutionizing our understanding of love, desire and the human psyche. As full of compassionate human interest as of scientific insight, these case histories are also remarkable, revelatory works of literature.

General Editor: Adam Phillips

PENGUIN MODERN CLASSICS

THE UNCONSCIOUS
SIGMUND FREUD

Formulations on the Two Principles of Psychic Functioning / Drives and their
Fates / Repression / The Unconscious / Negation / Fetishism / The Splitting of the
Ego in Defence Processes

Translated by Graham Frankland

With an Introduction by James Conant

One of Freud's central achievements was to demonstrate how unacceptable
thoughts and feelings are repressed into the unconscious, from where they
continue to exert a decisive influence over our lives.

This volume contains a key statement about evidence for the unconscious, and
how it works, as well as major essays on all the fundamentals of mental
functioning. Freud explores how we are torn between the pleasure principle and
the reality principle, how we often find ways both to express and to deny what we
most fear, and why certain men need fetishes for their sexual satisfaction. His
study of our most basic drives, and how they are transformed, brilliantly
illuminates the nature of sadism, masochism, exhibitionism and voyeurism.

General Editor: Adam Phillips

PENGUIN MODERN CLASSICS

THE PENGUIN FREUD READER
SIGMUND FREUD

Edited by Adam Phillips

'Freudian psychoanalysis changed the self-image of the western mind' Roy Porter

This major new collection brings together the key writings from every stage of Freud's career to offer the perfect introduction to his life and work. Here are the essential ideas of psychoanalytic theory, including Freud's explanations of such concepts as the Id, Ego and Super-Ego, the Death Instinct and Pleasure Principle, along with classic case studies like that of the Wolf Man.

Adam Phillips's marvellous selection provides an ideal overview of Freud's thought in all its extraordinary ambition and variety. Psychoanalysis may be known as the 'talking cure', yet it is also and profoundly a way of reading. Here we can see Freud's writings as readings and listenings, deciphering the secrets of the mind, finding words for desires that have never found expression. Much more than this, however, *The Penguin Freud Reader* presents a compelling reading of life as we experience it today, and a way in to the work of one of the most haunting writers of the modern age.